Some Other Country

SOME OTHER COUNTRY

New Zealand's Best Short Stories

NEW EDITION

Chosen by
Marion McLeod
and Bill Manhire

First published in New Zealand 1984 by
Unwin Paperbacks with the
Port Nicholson Press
Private Bag, Wellington, New Zealand
Reprinted 1985, 1986, 1988, 1990

New edition published in 1992 by
Bridget Williams Books Ltd
P.O. Box 9839, Wellington, New Zealand

ISBN 0 908912 28 5

Cover photography by Bruce Foster
Produced in Malaysia by SRM Production Sdn Bhd

Contents

Introduction

In Dan Davin's story, 'The Quiet One', the narrator, Ned, thinks
to himself that there might be 'some other country' where
'people would see what I really was instead of what I'd always
been'. This yearning for an ideal self which might also prove to be a
real one is familiar enough, and not wholly confined to adolescents;
it also hints at the mood of much New Zealand writing. New
Zealanders are used to thinking of themselves as inhabitants of a
'new' country. Still close to a more or less utopian vision of how
things might turn out, we are nevertheless aware of what things
have actually come to, intimate at once with aspiration and with
failure. So it is hardly surprising that so much New Zealand
literature is governed by rites of passage and myths of loss, nor that
the two are often felt to be the same thing. The first section of
Katherine Mansfield's 'At the Bay' is a quiet, innocently cadenced
account of creation – dawn, a coastline, a shepherd and his flock. It
makes an appropriate place to start.

It was plain, too, once we had made our selection, that the stories
we had chosen reflected a cultural diversity – a number of other
countries – which had grown up and persisted despite all the
pressures towards uniformity of 'official' New Zealand. The range
of regional locations, rural and urban, is striking, and it is a range
which embraces not only a richly rendered Maori world but also a
number of distinct groups within Pakeha society generally. Equally
interesting is the fact that the world which New Zealanders
acknowledge beyond their own shores has become far more
various. The change can be charted in the difference between two
stories. James Courage's 'After the Earthquake' (published in 1948)
records in a rural setting a kind of passage from an English 'Home'
to a New Zealand home. Ian Wedde's 'Paradise' (published in 1975)
is set on the suburban fringes of a large city and has for its chief
character a postman who thinks about Hong Kong or Antarctica as
he delivers letters from Samoa – another home from which New
Zealanders have journeyed.

Some Other Country also implies, we hope, an alternative to more
conventional views of New Zealand. The New Zealand to be
found in these pages is not the place depicted in glossy picture
books or economic profiles. But it is a real place, composed of that
blend of accuracy and vision which only the imagination,
committed to language and experience, can supply. The stories in

Some Other Country do more than disclose an identity, they also enrich it – and enrichment of identity, as Janet Frame has written, is 'something which "scenery" . . . will never give us, nor quantities of sheep, nor famed research in grasses. . .'.

The variety in this book is reassuring, given the predominant tradition of social realism; the tones of voice are many, often low-keyed and mildly puzzled, but sometimes immodest and exuberant. Such variety is not only notable in a society which sometimes seems to lack it, it is also a tribute to the vigorous life the short story form has had in New Zealand – for the form itself readily accommodates 'the lonely voice', tending, in the words of one commentator, to 'filter down experience to the prime elements of defeat and alienation'. Certainly defeat and alienation recur often enough in these pages, but there is no absence of humanity – and occasionally there are glimpses of something better. O. E. Middleton's story, called 'The Loners', ends with the word *family*; and while there are many deaths in these stories, some of those deaths – as in 'A Game of Cards' or 'The Silk' – are as fulfilling as the experience of birth described in Patricia Grace's 'Between Earth and Sky'.

We made our selection with none of the foregoing thoughts in mind. Our final choice was governed by the simple decision to print the best stories we could find. We observed the following guidelines. We decided that no writer would be represented by more than one story (a severe constraint in the case of writers like Mansfield, Sargeson, Duggan and Frame) and we found ourselves opting for stories with a New Zealand setting. We decided to be as generous as possible with recent fiction, and to include nothing before Mansfield. Half of the stories, as it happens, were published in the last fifteen years. We did not set out to be adventurous or provocative in our selection, although we hope we have not been entirely predictable.

Some readers will want to seek out further works by these writers. With this in mind we have included brief notes on contributors. There is also a glossary of Maori words and phrases. The stories themselves are printed in order of the dates of first publication.

Marion McLeod
Bill Manhire

AT THE BAY

Katherine Mansfield

(I)

Very early morning. The sun was not yet risen, and the whole of Crescent Bay was hidden under a white sea-mist. The big bush-covered hills at the back were smothered. You could not see where they ended and the paddocks and bungalows began. The sandy road was gone and the paddocks and bungalows the other side of it; there were no white dunes covered with reddish grass beyond them; there was nothing to mark which was beach and where was the sea. A heavy dew had fallen. The grass was blue. Big drops hung on the bushes and just did not fall; the silvery, fluffy toi-toi was limp on its long stalks, and all the marigolds and the pinks in the bungalow gardens were bowed to the earth with wetness. Drenched were the cold fuchsias, round pearls of dew lay on the flat nasturtium leaves. It looked as though the sea had beaten up softly in the darkness, as though one immense wave had come rippling, rippling – how far? Perhaps if you had waked up in the middle of the night you might have seen a big fish flicking in at the window and gone again. . . .

Ah-Aah! sounded the sleepy sea. And from the bush there came the sound of little streams flowing, quickly, lightly, slipping between the smooth stones, gushing into ferny basins and out again; and there was the splashing of big drops on large leaves, and something else – what was it? – a faint stirring and shaking, the snapping of a twig and then such silence that it seemed someone was listening.

Round the corner of Crescent Bay, between the piled-up masses of broken rock, a flock of sheep came pattering. They were huddled together, a small, tossing, woolly mass, and their thin, stick-like legs trotted along quickly as if the cold and the quiet had frightened them. Behind them an old sheep-dog, his soaking paws covered with sand, ran along with his nose to the ground, but carelessly, as if thinking of something else. And then in the rocky gateway the shepherd himself appeared. He was a lean, upright old man, in a frieze coat that was covered with a web of tiny drops, velvet trousers tied under the knee, and a wideawake with a folded blue handkerchief round the brim. One hand was crammed into his belt, the other grasped a beautifully smooth

1

yellow stick. And as he walked, taking his time, he kept up a very soft light whistling, an airy, far-away fluting that sounded mournful and tender. The old dog cut an ancient caper or two and then drew up sharp, ashamed of his levity, and walked a few dignified paces by his master's side. The sheep ran forward in little pattering rushes; they began to bleat, and ghostly flocks and herds answered them from under the sea. 'Baa! Baaa!' For a time they seemed to be always on the same piece of ground. There ahead was stretched the sandy road with shallow puddles; the same soaking bushes showed on either side the same shadowy palings. Then something immense came into view; an enormous shock-haired giant with his arms stretched out. It was the big gum tree outside Mrs Stubbs's shop, and as they passed by there was a strong whiff of eucalyptus. And now big spots of light gleamed in the mist. The shepherd stopped whistling; he rubbed his red nose and wet beard on his wet sleeve and, screwing up his eyes, glanced in the direction of the sea. The sun was rising. It was marvellous how quickly the mist thinned, sped away, dissolved from the shallow plain, rolled up from the bush and was gone as if in a hurry to escape; big twists and curls jostled and shouldered each other as the silvery beams broadened. The far-away sky – a bright, pure blue – was reflected in the puddles, and the drops, swimming along the telegraph poles, flashed into points of light. Now the leaping, glittering sea was so bright it made one's eyes ache to look at it. The shepherd drew a pipe, the bowl as small as an acorn, out of his breast-pocket, fumbled for a chunk of speckled tobacco, pared off a few shavings and stuffed the bowl. He was a grave, fine-looking old man. As he lit up and the blue smoke wreathed his head, the dog, watching, looked proud of him.

'Baa! Baaa!' The sheep spread out into a fan. They were just clear of the summer colony before the first sleeper turned over and lifted a drowsy head; their cry sounded in the dreams of little children . . . who lifted their arms to drag down, to cuddle the darling little woolly lambs of sleep. Then the first inhabitant appeared; it was the Burnells' cat Florrie, sitting on the gatepost, far too early as usual, looking for their milk-girl. When she saw the old sheep-dog she sprang up quickly, arched her back, drew in her tabby head, and seemed to give a little fastidious shiver. 'Ugh! What a coarse, revolting creature!' said Florrie. But the old sheep-dog, not looking up, waggled past, flinging out his legs from side to side. Only one of his ears twitched to prove that he saw, and thought her a silly young female.

The breeze of morning lifted in the bush and the smell of leaves and wet black earth mingled with the sharp smell of the sea.

Myriads of birds were singing. A goldfinch flew over the shepherd's head and, perching on the tiptop of a spray, it turned to the sun, ruffling its small breast feathers. And now they had passed the fisherman's hut, passed the charred-looking little whare where Leila the milk-girl lived with her old Gran. The sheep strayed over a yellow swamp and Wag, the sheep-dog, padded after, rounded them up and headed them for the steeper, narrower rocky pass that led out of Crescent Bay and towards Daylight Cove. 'Baa! Baaa!' Faint the cry came as they rocked along the fast-drying road. The shepherd put away his pipe, dropping it into his breast-pocket so that the little bowl hung over. And straightway the soft airy whistling began again. Wag ran out along a ledge of rock after something that smelled, and ran back again disgusted. Then pushing, nudging, hurrying, the sheep rounded the bend and the shepherd followed after out of sight.

(II)

A few moments later the back door of one of the bungalows opened, and a figure in a broad-striped bathing-suit flung down the paddock, cleared the stile, rushed through the tussock grass into the hollow, staggered up the sandy hillock, and raced for dear life over the big porous stones, over the cold, wet pebbles, on to the hard sand that gleamed like oil. Splish-Splosh! Splish-Splosh! The water bubbled round his legs as Stanley Burnell waded out exulting. First man in as usual! He'd beaten them all again. And he swooped down to souse his head and neck.

'Hail, brother! All hail, Thou Mighty One!' A velvety bass voice came booming over the water.

Great Scott! Damnation take it! Stanley lifted up to see a dark head bobbing far out and an arm lifted. It was Jonathan Trout — there before him! 'Glorious morning!' sang the voice.

'Yes, very fine!' said Stanley briefly. Why the dickens didn't the fellow stick to his part of the sea? Why should he come barging over to this exact spot? Stanley gave a kick, a lunge and struck out, swimming overarm. But Jonathan was a match for him. Up he came, his black hair sleek on his forehead, his short beard sleek.

'I had an extraordinary dream last night!' he shouted.

What was the matter with the man? This mania for conversation irritated Stanley beyond words. And it was always the same — always some piffle about a dream he'd had, or some cranky idea he'd got hold of, or some rot he'd been reading. Stanley turned over on his back and kicked with his legs till he was a living water-spout. But even then . . . 'I dreamed I was hanging over a terrifically high cliff, shouting to someone below.' You would be!

3

thought Stanley. He could stick no more of it. He stopped splashing. 'Look here, Trout,' he said, 'I'm in rather a hurry this morning.'

'You're WHAT?' Jonathan was so surprised – or pretended to be – that he sank under the water, then reappeared again blowing.

'All I mean is,' said Stanley, 'I've no time to – to – to fool about. I want to get this over. I'm in a hurry. I've work to do this morning – see?'

Jonathan was gone before Stanley had finished. 'Pass, friend!' said the bass voice gently, and he slid away through the water with scarcely a ripple. . . . But curse the fellow! He'd ruined Stanley's bathe. What an unpractical idiot the man was! Stanley struck out to sea again, and then as quickly swam in again, and away he rushed up the beach. He felt cheated.

Jonathan stayed a little longer in the water. He floated, gently moving his hands like fins, and letting the sea rock his long, skinny body. It was curious, but in spite of everything he was fond of Stanley Burnell. True, he had a fiendish desire to tease him sometimes, to poke fun at him, but at bottom he was sorry for the fellow. There was something pathetic in his determination to make a job of everything. You couldn't help feeling he'd be caught out one day, and then what an almighty cropper he'd come! At that moment an immense wave lifted Jonathan, rode past him, and broke along the beach with a joyful sound. What a beauty! And now there came another. That was the way to live – carelessly, recklessly, spending oneself. He got on to his feet and began to wade towards the shore, pressing his toes into the firm, wrinkled sand. To take things easy, not to fight against the ebb and flow of life, but to give way to it – that was what was needed. It was this tension that was all wrong. To live – to live! And the perfect morning, so fresh and fair, basking in the light, as though laughing at its own beauty, seemed to whisper, 'Why not?'

But now he was out of the water Jonathan turned blue with cold. He ached all over; it was as though someone was wringing the blood out of him. And stalking up the beach, shivering, all his muscles tight, he too felt his bathe was spoilt. He'd stayed in too long.

(III)

Beryl was alone in the living-room when Stanley appeared, wearing a blue serge suit, a stiff collar and a spotted tie. He looked almost uncannily clean and brushed; he was going to town for the day. Dropping into his chair, he pulled out his watch and put it beside his plate.

'I've just got twenty-five minutes,' he said. 'You might go and see if the porridge is ready, Beryl?'

'Mother's just gone for it,' said Beryl. She sat down at the table and poured out his tea.

'Thanks!' Stanley took a sip. 'Hallo!' he said in an astonished voice, 'you've forgotten the sugar.'

'Oh, sorry!' But even then Beryl didn't help him; she pushed the basin across. What did this mean? As Stanley helped himself his blue eyes widened; they seemed to quiver. He shot a quick glance at his sister-in-law and leaned back.

'Nothing wrong, is there?' he asked carelessly, fingering his collar.

Beryl's head was bent; she turned her plate in her fingers.

'Nothing,' said her light voice. Then she too looked up, and smiled at Stanley. 'Why should there be?'

'O-oh! No reason at all as far as I know. I thought you seemed rather – '

At that moment the door opened and the three little girls appeared, each carrying a porridge plate. They were dressed alike in blue jerseys and knickers; their brown legs were bare, and each had her hair plaited and pinned up in what was called a horse's tail. Behind them came Mrs Fairfield with the tray.

'Carefully, children', she warned. But they were taking the very greatest care. They loved being allowed to carry things. 'Have you said good-morning to your father?'

'Yes, grandma.' They settled themselves on the bench opposite Stanley and Beryl.

'Good morning, Stanley!' Old Mrs Fairfield gave him his plate.

'Morning, mother! How's the boy?'

'Splendid! He only woke up once last night. What a perfect morning!' The old woman paused, her hand on the loaf of bread, to gaze out of the open door into the garden. The sea sounded. Through the wide-open window streamed the sun on to the yellow varnished walls and bare floor. Everything on the table flashed and glittered. In the middle there was an old salad bowl filled with yellow and red nasturtiums. She smiled, and a look of deep content shone in her eyes.

'You might *cut* me a slice of that bread, mother,' said Stanley. 'I've only twelve and a half minutes before the coach passes. Has anyone given my shoes to the servant girl?'

'Yes, they're ready for you.' Mrs Fairfield was quite unruffled.

'Oh, Kezia! Why are you such a messy child!' cried Beryl despairingly.

'Me, Aunt Beryl?' Kezia stared at her. What had she done now?

5

She had only dug a river down the middle of her porridge, filled it, and was eating the banks away. But she did that every single morning, and no one had said a word up till now.

'Why can't you eat your food properly like Isabel and Lottie?' How unfair grown-ups are!

'But Lottie always makes a floating island, don't you, Lottie?'

'I don't,' said Isabel smartly. 'I just sprinkle mine with sugar and put on the milk and finish it. Only babies play with their food.'

Stanley pushed back his chair and got up.

'Would you get me those shoes, mother? And, Beryl, if you've finished, I wish you'd cut down to the gate and stop the coach. Run in to your mother, Isabel, and ask her where my bowler hat's been put. Wait a minute – have you children been playing with my stick?'

'No, father!'

'But I put it here,' Stanley began to bluster. 'I remember distinctly putting it in this corner. Now, who's had it? There's no time to lose. Look sharp! The stick's got to be found.'

Even Alice, the servant girl, was drawn into the chase. 'You haven't been using it to poke the kitchen fire with by any chance?'

Stanley dashed into the bedroom where Linda was lying. 'Most extraordinary thing. I can't keep a single possession to myself. They've made away with my stick, now!'

'Stick, dear? What stick?' Linda's vagueness on these occasions could not be real, Stanley decided. Would nobody sympathise with him?

'Coach! Coach, Stanley!' Beryl's voice cried from the gate.

Stanley waved his arm to Linda. 'No time to say good-bye!' he cried. And he meant that as a punishment to her.

He snatched his bowler hat, dashed out of the house, and swung down the garden path. Yes, the coach was there waiting, and Beryl, leaning over the open gate, was laughing up at somebody or other just as if nothing had happened. The heartlessness of women! The way they took it for granted it was your job to slave away for them while they didn't even take the trouble to see that your walking-stick wasn't lost. Kelly trailed his whip across the horses.

'Good-bye, Stanley,' called Beryl, sweetly and gaily. It was easy enough to say good-bye! And there she stood, idle, shading her eyes with her hand. The worst of it was Stanley had to shout good-bye too, for the sake of appearances. Then he saw her turn, give a little skip and run back to the house. She was glad to be rid of him!

Yes, she was thankful. Into the living-room she ran and called 'He's gone!' Linda cried from her room: 'Beryl! Has Stanley gone?'

Old Mrs Fairfield appeared, carrying the boy in his little flannel coatee.

'Gone?'

'Gone!'

Oh, the relief, the difference it made to have the man out of the house. Their very voices were changed as they called to one another; they sounded warm and loving and as if they shared a secret. Beryl went over to the table. 'Have another cup of tea, mother. It's still hot.' She wanted, somehow, to celebrate the fact that they could do what they liked now. There was no man to disturb them; the whole perfect day was theirs.

'No, thank you, child,' said old Mrs Fairfield, but the way at that moment she tossed the boy up and said 'a-goos-a-goos-a-ga!' to him meant that she felt the same. The little girls ran into the paddock like chickens let out of a coop.

Even Alice, the servant girl, washing up the dishes in the kitchen, caught the infection and used the precious tank water in a perfectly reckless fashion.

'Oh, these men!' said she, and she plunged the teapot into the bowl and held it under the water even after it had stopped bubbling, as if it too was a man and drowning was too good for them.

(IV)

'Wait for me, Isa-bel! Kezia, wait for me!'

There was poor little Lottie, left behind again, because she found it so fearfully hard to get over the stile by herself. When she stood on the first step her knees began to wobble; she grasped the post. Then you had to put one leg over. But which leg? She never could decide. And when she did finally put one leg over with a sort of stamp of despair – then the feeling was awful. She was half in the paddock still and half in the tussock grass. She clutched the post desperately and lifted up her voice. 'Wait for me!'

'No, don't you wait for her, Kezia!' said Isabel. 'She's such a little silly. She's always making a fuss. Come on!' And she tugged Kezia's jersey. 'You can use my bucket if you come with me,' she said kindly. 'It's bigger than yours.' But Kezia couldn't leave Lottie all by herself. She ran back to her. By this time Lottie was very red in the face and breathing heavily.

'Here, put your other foot over,' said Kezia.

'Where?'

Lottie looked down at Kezia as if from a mountain height.

'Here where my hand is.' Kezia patted the place.

'Oh, *there* do you mean?' Lottie gave a deep sigh and put the second foot over.

7

'Now – sort of turn round and sit down and slide,' said Kezia.

'But there's nothing to sit down *on*, Kezia,' said Lottie.

She managed it at last, and once it was over she shook herself and began to beam.

'I'm getting better at climbing over stiles, aren't I, Kezia?'

Lottie's was a very hopeful nature.

The pink and the blue sunbonnet followed Isabel's bright red sunbonnet up that sliding, slipping hill. At the top they paused to decide where to go and to have a good stare at who was there already. Seen from behind, standing against the skyline, gesticulating largely with their spades, they looked like minute puzzled explorers.

The whole family of Samuel Josephs was there already with their lady-help, who sat on a camp-stool and kept order with a whistle that she wore tied round her neck, and a small cane with which she directed operations. The Samuel Josephs never played by themselves or managed their own game. If they did, it ended in the boys pouring water down the girls' necks or the girls trying to put little black crabs into the boys' pockets. So Mrs S. J. and the poor lady-help drew up what she called a 'brogramme' every morning to keep them 'abused and out of bischief'. It was all competitions or races or round games. Everything began with a piercing blast of the lady-help's whistle and ended with another. There were even prizes – large, rather dirty paper parcels which the lady-help with a sour little smile drew out of a bulging string kit. The Samuel Josephs fought fearfully for the prizes and cheated and pinched one another's arms – they were all expert pinchers. The only time the Burnell children ever played with them Kezia had got a prize, and when she undid three bits of paper she found a very small rusty button-hook. She couldn't understand why they made such a fuss. . . .

But they never played with the Samuel Josephs now or even went to their parties. The Samuel Josephs were always giving children's parties at the Bay and there was always the same food. A big washhand basin of very brown fruit salad, buns cut into four and a washhand jug full of something the lady-help called 'Limmonadear'. And you went away in the evening with half the frill torn off your frock or something spilled all down the front of your openwork pinafore, leaving the Samuel Josephs leaping like savages on their lawn. No! They were too awful.

On the other side of the beach, close down to the water, two little boys, their knickers rolled up, twinkled like spiders. One was digging, the other pattered in and out of the water, filling a small bucket. They were the Trout boys, Pip and Rags. But Pip was so busy digging and Rags was so busy helping that they didn't see their little cousins until they were quite close.

'Look!' said Pip. 'Look what I've discovered.' And he showed them an old, wet, squashed-looking boot. The three little girls stared.

'Whatever are you going to do with it?' asked Kezia.

'Keep it, of course!' Pip was very scornful. 'It's a find – see?'

Yes, Kezia saw that. All the same . . .

'There's lots of things buried in the sand,' explained Pip. 'They get chucked up from wrecks. Treasure. Why – you might find – '

'But why does Rags have to keep on pouring water in?' asked Lottie.

'Oh, that's to moisten it,' said Pip, 'to make the work a bit easier. Keep it up, Rags.'

And good little Rags ran up and down, pouring in the water that turned brown like cocoa.

'Here, shall I show you what I found yesterday?' said Pip mysteriously, and he stuck his spade into the sand. 'Promise not to tell.'

They promised.

'Say, cross my heart straight dinkum.'

The little girls said it.

Pip took something out of his pocket, rubbed it a long time on the front of his jersey, then breathed on it and rubbed it again.

'Now turn round!' he ordered.

They turned round.

'All look the same way! Keep still! Now!'

And his hand opened; he held up to the light something that flashed, that winked, that was a most lovely green.

'It's a nemeral,' said Pip solemnly.

'Is it really, Pip?' Even Isabel was impressed.

The lovely green thing seemed to dance in Pip's fingers. Aunt Beryl had a nemeral in a ring, but it was a very small one. This one was as big as a star and far more beautiful.

(V)

As the morning lengthened whole parties appeared over the sand-hills and came down on the beach to bathe. It was understood that at eleven o'clock the women and children of the summer colony had the sea to themselves. First the women undressed, pulled on their bathing dresses and covered their heads in hideous caps like sponge-bags; then the children were unbuttoned. The beach was strewn with little heaps of clothes and shoes; the big summer hats, with stones on them to keep them from blowing away, looked like immense shells. It was strange that even the sea seemed to sound differently when all those leaping, laughing

figures ran into the waves. Old Mrs Fairfield, in a lilac cotton dress
and a black hat tied under the chin, gathered her little brood and got
them ready. The little Trout boys whipped their shirts over their
heads, and away the five sped, while their grandma sat with one
hand in her knitting-bag ready to draw out the ball of wool when
she was satisfied they were safely in.

The firm compact little girls were not half so brave as the tender,
delicate-looking little boys. Pip and Rags, shivering, crouching
down, slapping the water, never hesitated. But Isabel, who could
swim twelve strokes, and Kezia, who could nearly swim eight,
only followed on the strict understanding they were not to be
splashed. As for Lottie, she didn't follow at all. She liked to be left
to go in her own way, please. And that way was to sit down at the
edge of the water, her legs straight, her knees pressed together, and
to make vague motions with her arms as if she expected to be
wafted out to sea. But when a bigger wave than usual, an old
whiskery one, came lolloping along in her direction, she scrambled
to her feet with a face of horror and flew up the beach again.

'Here, mother, keep these for me, will you?'

Two rings and a thin gold chain were dropped into Mrs
Fairfield's lap.

'Yes, dear. But aren't you going to bathe here?'

'No-o,' Beryl drawled. She sounded vague. 'I'm undressing
further along. I'm going to bathe with Mrs Harry Kember.'

'Very well.' But Mrs Fairfield's lips set. She disapproved of Mrs
Harry Kember. Beryl knew it.

Poor old mother, she smiled, as she skimmed over the stones.
Poor old mother! Old! Oh, what joy, what bliss it was to be
young. . . .

'You look very pleased,' said Mrs Harry Kember. She sat
hunched up on the stones, her arms round her knees, smoking.

'It's such a lovely day,' said Beryl, smiling down at her.

'Oh, my *dear*!' Mrs Harry Kember's voice sounded as though she
knew better than that. But then her voice always sounded as
though she knew something more about you than you did yourself.
She was a long, strange-looking woman with narrow hands and
feet. Her face, too, was long and narrow and exhausted-looking;
even her fair curled fringe looked burnt out and withered. She was
the only woman at the Bay who smoked, and she smoked
incessantly, keeping the cigarette between her lips while she talked,
and only taking it out when the ash was so long you could not
understand why it did not fall. When she was not playing bridge –
she played bridge every day of her life – she spent her time lying in
the full glare of the sun. She could stand any amount of it; she never

had enough. All the same, it did not seem to warm her. Parched, withered, cold, she lay stretched on the stones like a piece of tossed-up driftwood. The women at the Bay thought she was very, very fast. Her lack of vanity, her slang, the way she treated men as though she was one of them, and the fact that she didn't care twopence about her house and called the servant Gladys 'Glad-eyes,' was disgraceful. Standing on the verandah steps Mrs Kember would call in her indifferent, tired voice, 'I say, Glad-eyes, you might heave me a handkerchief if I've got one, will you?' And Glad-eyes, a red bow in her hair instead of a cap, and white shoes, came running with an impudent smile. It was an absolute scandal! True, she had no children, and her husband . . . . Here the voices were always raised; they became fervent. How can he have married her? How can he, how can he? It must have been money, of course, but even then!

Mrs Kember's husband was at least ten years younger than she was, and so incredibly handsome that he looked like a mask or a most perfect illustration in an American novel rather than a man. Black hair, dark blue eyes, red lips, a slow sleepy smile, a fine tennis player, a perfect dancer, and with it all a mystery. Harry Kember was like a man walking in his sleep. Men couldn't stand him, they couldn't get a word out of the chap; he ignored his wife just as she ignored him. How did he live? Of course there were stories, but such stories! They simply couldn't be told. The women he'd been seen with, the places he'd been seen in . . . but nothing was ever certain, nothing definite. Some of the women at the Bay privately thought he'd commit a murder one day. Yes, even while they talked to Mrs Kember and took in the awful concoction she was wearing, they saw her, stretched as she lay on the beach; but cold, bloody, and still with a cigarette stuck in the corner of her mouth.

Mrs Kember rose, yawned, unsnapped her belt buckle, and tugged at the tape of her blouse. And Beryl stepped out of her skirt and shed her jersey, and stood up in her short white petticoat, and her camisole with ribbon bows on the shoulders.

'Mercy on us,' said Mrs Harry Kember, 'what a little beauty you are!'

'Don't!' said Beryl softly; but, drawing off one stocking and then the other, she felt a little beauty.

'My dear – why not?' said Mrs Harry Kember, stamping on her own petticoat. Really – her underclothes! A pair of blue cotton knickers and a linen bodice that reminded one somehow of a pillow-case. . . . 'And you don't wear stays, do you?' She touched Beryl's waist, and Beryl sprang away with a small affected cry. Then 'Never!' she said firmly.

'Lucky little creature,' sighed Mrs Kember, unfastening her own.

Beryl turned her back and began the complicated movements of someone who is trying to take off her clothes and to pull on her bathing-dress all at one and the same time.

'Oh, my dear – don't mind me,' said Mrs Harry Kember. 'Why be shy? I shan't eat you. I shan't be shocked like those other ninnies.' And she gave her strange neighing laugh and grimaced at the other women.

But Beryl was shy. She never undressed in front of anybody. Was that silly? Mrs Harry Kember made her feel it was silly, even something to be ashamed of. Why be shy indeed! She glanced quickly at her friend standing so boldly in her torn chemise and lighting a fresh cigarette; and a quick, bold, evil feeling started up in her breast. Laughing recklessly, she drew on the limp, sandy-feeling bathing-dress that was not quite dry and fastened the twisted buttons.

'That's better,' said Mrs Harry Kember. They began to go down the beach together. 'Really, it's a sin for you to wear clothes, my dear. Somebody's got to tell you some day.'

The water was quite warm. It was that marvellous transparent blue, flecked with silver, but the sand at the bottom looked gold; when you kicked with your toes there rose a little puff of gold-dust. Now the waves just reached her breast. Beryl stood, her arms outstretched, gazing out, and as each wave came she gave the slightest little jump, so that it seemed it was the wave which lifted her so gently.

'I believe in pretty girls having a good time,' said Mrs Harry Kember. 'Why not? Don't you make a mistake, my dear. Enjoy yourself.' And suddenly she turned turtle, disappeared, and swam away quickly, quickly, like a rat. Then she flicked round and began swimming back. She was going to say something else. Beryl felt that she was being poisoned by this cold woman, but she longed to hear. But oh, how strange, how horrible! As Mrs Harry Kember came up close she looked, in her black waterproof bathing-cap, with her sleepy face lifted above the water, just her chin touching, like a horrible caricature of her husband.

(VI)

In a steamer chair, under a manuka tree that grew in the middle of the front grass patch, Linda Burnell dreamed the morning away. She did nothing. She looked up at the dark, close, dry leaves of the manuka, at the chinks of blue between, and now and again a tiny yellowish flower dropped on her. Pretty – yes, if you held one of those flowers on the palm of your hand and looked at it closely, it was an exquisite small thing. Each pale yellow petal shone as if each was the careful work of a loving hand. The tiny tongue in the centre gave it the shape of a bell. And when you turned it over the outside was a deep bronze colour. But as soon as they flowered, they fell and were scattered. You brushed them off your frock as you talked; the horrid little things got caught in one's hair. Why, then, flower at all? Who takes the trouble – or the joy – to make all these things that are wasted, wasted. . . . It was uncanny.

On the grass beside her, lying between two pillows, was the boy. Sound asleep he lay, his head turned away from his mother. His fine dark hair looked more like a shadow than like real hair, but his ear was a bright, deep coral. Linda clasped her hands above her head and crossed her feet. It was very pleasant to know that all these bungalows were empty, that everybody was down on the beach, out of sight, out of hearing. She had the garden to herself; she was alone.

Dazzling white the picotees shone; the golden-eyed marigolds glittered; the nasturtiums wreathed the verandah poles in green and gold flame. If only one had time to look at these flowers long enough, time to get over the sense of novelty and strangeness, time to know them! But as soon as one paused to part the petals, to discover the under-side of the leaf, along came Life and one was swept away. And, lying in her cane chair, Linda felt so light; she felt like a leaf. Along came Life like a wind and she was seized and shaken; she had to go. Oh dear, would it always be so? Was there no escape?

. . . Now she sat on the verandah of their Tasmanian home, leaning against her father's knee. And he promised, 'As soon as you and I are old enough, Linny, we'll cut off somewhere, we'll escape. Two boys together. I have a fancy I'd like to sail up a river in China.' Linda saw that river, very wide, covered with little rafts and boats. She saw the yellow hats of the boatmen and she heard their high, thin voices as they called . . .

'Yes, papa.'

But just then a very broad young man with bright ginger hair walked slowly past their house, and slowly, solemnly even, uncovered. Linda's father pulled her ear teasingly, in the way he had.

'Linny's beau,' he whispered.

'Oh, papa, fancy being married to Stanley Burnell!'

Well, she was married to him. And what was more she loved him. Not the Stanley whom every one saw, not the everyday one; but a timid, sensitive, innocent Stanley who knelt down every night to say his prayers, and who longed to be good. Stanley was

13

simple. If he believed in people – as he believed in her, for instance – it was with his whole heart. He could not be disloyal; he could not tell a lie. And how terribly he suffered if he thought anyone – she – was not being dead straight, dead sincere with him! 'This is too subtle for me!' He flung out the words, but his open, quivering, distraught look was like the look of a trapped beast.

But the trouble was – here Linda felt almost inclined to laugh, though heaven knows it was no laughing matter – she saw *her* Stanley so seldom. There were glimpses, moments, breathing spaces of calm, but all the rest of the time it was like living in a house that couldn't be cured of the habit of catching fire, or a ship that got wrecked every day. And it was always Stanley who was in the thick of the danger. Her whole time was spent in rescuing him, and restoring him, and calming him down, and listening to his story. And what was left of her time was spent in the dread of having children.

Linda frowned; she sat up quickly in her steamer chair and clasped her ankles. Yes, that was her real grudge against life; that was what she could not understand. That was the question she asked and asked, and listened in vain for the answer. It was all very well to say it was the common lot of women to bear children. It wasn't true. She, for one, could prove that wrong. She was broken, made weak, her courage was gone, through child-bearing. And what made it doubly hard to bear was, she did not love her children. It was useless pretending. Even if she had had the strength she never would have nursed and played with the little girls. No, it was as though a cold breath had chilled her through and through on each of those awful journeys; she had no warmth left to give them. As to the boy – well, thank heaven, mother had taken him; he was mother's, or Beryl's, or anybody's who wanted him. She had hardly held him in her arms. She was so indifferent about him, that as he lay there . . . Linda glanced down.

The boy had turned over. He lay facing her, and he was no longer asleep. His dark-blue, baby eyes were open; he looked as though he was peeping at his mother. And suddenly his face dimpled; it broke into a wide, toothless smile, a perfect beam, no less.

'I'm here!' that happy smile seemed to say. 'Why don't you like me?'

There was something so quaint, so unexpected about that smile that Linda smiled herself. But she checked herself and said to the boy coldly, 'I don't like babies.'

'Don't like babies?' The boy couldn't believe her. 'Don't like *me*?' He waved his arms foolishly at his mother.

Linda dropped off her chair on to the grass.

'Why do you keep on smiling?' she said severely. 'If you knew what I was thinking about, you wouldn't.'

But he only squeezed up his eyes, slyly, and rolled his head on the pillow. He didn't believe a word she said.

'We know all about that!' smiled the boy.

Linda was so astonished at the confidence of this little creature. . . . Ah no, be sincere. That was not what she felt; it was something far different, it was something so new, so . . . The tears danced in her eyes; she breathed in a small whisper to the boy, 'Hallo, my funny!'

But by now the boy had forgotten his mother. He was serious again. Something pink, something soft waved in front of him. He made a grab at it and it immediately disappeared. But when he lay back, another, like the first, appeared. This time he determined to catch it. He made a tremendous effort and rolled right over.

(VII)

The tide was out; the beach was deserted; lazily flopped the warm sea. The sun beat down, beat down hot and fiery on the fine sand, baking the grey and blue and black and white-veined pebbles. It sucked up the little drop of water that lay in the hollow of the curved shells; it bleached the pink convolvulus that threaded through and through the sand-hills. Nothing seemed to move but the small sand-hoppers. Pit-pit-pit! They were never still.

Over there on the weed-hung rocks that looked at low tide like shaggy beasts come down to the water to drink, the sunlight seemed to spin like a silver coin dropped into each of the small rock pools. They danced, they quivered, and minute ripples laved the porous shores. Looking down, bending over, each pool was like a lake with pink and blue houses clustered on the shores; and oh! the vast mountainous country behind those houses – the ravines, the passes, the dangerous creeks and fearful tracks that led to the water's edge. Underneath waved the sea-forest – pink thread-like trees, velvet anemones, and orange berry-spotted weeds. Now a stone on the bottom moved, rocked, and there was a glimpse of a black feeler; now a thread-like creature wavered by and was lost. Something was happening to the pink, waving trees; they were changing to a cold moonlight blue. And now there sounded the faintest 'plop'. Who made that sound? What was going on down there? And how strong, how damp the seaweed smelt in the hot sun. . . .

The green blinds were drawn in the bungalows of the summer colony. Over the verandahs, prone on the paddock, flung over the fences, there were exhausted-looking bathing-dresses and rough striped towels. Each back window seemed to have a pair of sand-shoes on the sill and some lumps of rock or a bucket or a collection of paua shells. The bush quivered in a haze of heat; the sandy road was empty except for the Trouts' dog Snooker, who lay stretched in the very middle of it. His blue eye was turned up, his legs stuck out stiffly, and he gave an occasional desperate sounding puff, as much as to say he had decided to make an end of it and was only waiting for some kind cart to come along.

'What are you looking at, my grandma? Why do you keep stopping and sort of staring at the wall?'

Kezia and her grandmother were taking their siesta together. The little girl, wearing only her short drawers and her under-bodice, her arms and legs bare, lay on one of the puffed-up pillows of her grandma's bed, and the old woman, in a white ruffled dressing-gown, sat in a rocker at the window, with a long piece of pink knitting in her lap. This room that they shared, like the other rooms of the bungalow, was of light varnished wood and the floor was bare. The furniture was of the shabbiest, the simplest. The dressing-table, for instance, was a packing-case in a sprigged muslin petticoat, and the mirror above was very strange; it was as though a little piece of forked lightning was imprisoned in it. On the table there stood a jar of sea-pinks, pressed so tightly together they looked more like a velvet pin-cushion, and a special shell which Kezia had given her grandma for a pin-tray, and another even more special which she had thought would make a very nice place for a watch to curl up in.

'Tell me, grandma,' said Kezia.

The old woman sighed, whipped the wool twice round her thumb, and drew the bone needle through. She was casting on.

'I was thinking of your Uncle William, darling,' she said quietly.

'My Australian Uncle William?' said Kezia. She had another.

'Yes, of course.'

'The one I never saw?'

'That was the one.'

'Well, what happened to him?' Kezia knew perfectly well, but she wanted to be told again.

'He went to the mines, and he got a sunstroke there and died,' said old Mrs Fairfield.

Kezia blinked and considered the picture again. . . . A little man fallen over like a tin soldier by the side of a big black hole.

'Does it make you sad to think about him, grandma?' She hated her grandma to be sad.

It was the old woman's turn to consider. Did it make her sad? To look back, back. To stare down the years, as Kezia had seen her doing. To look after *them* as a woman does, long after *they* were out of sight. Did it make her sad? No, life was like that.

'No, Kezia.'

'But why?' asked Kezia. She lifted one bare arm and began to draw things in the air. 'Why did Uncle William have to die? He wasn't told.'

Mrs Fairfield began counting the stitches in threes. 'It just happened,' she said in an absorbed voice.

'Does everybody have to die?' asked Kezia.

'Everybody!'

'*Me*?' Kezia sounded fearfully incredulous.

'Some day, my darling.'

'But, grandma.' Kezia waved her left leg and waggled the toes. They felt sandy. 'What if I just won't?'

The old woman sighed again and drew a long thread from the ball.

'We're not asked, Kezia,' she said sadly. 'It happens to all of us sooner or later.'

Kezia lay still thinking this over. She didn't want to die. It meant she would have to leave here, leave everywhere, for ever, leave – leave her grandma. She rolled over quickly.

'Grandma,' she said in a startled voice.

'What, my pet!'

'*You're* not to die.' Kezia was very decided.

'Ah, Kezia' – her grandma looked up and smiled and shook her head – 'don't let's talk about it.'

'But you're not to. You couldn't leave me. You couldn't not be there.' This was awful. 'Promise me you won't ever do it, grandma,' pleaded Kezia.

The old woman went on knitting.

'Promise me! Say never!'

But still her grandma was silent.

Kezia rolled off the bed; she couldn't bear it any longer, and lightly she leapt on to her grandma's knees, clasped her hands round the old woman's throat and began kissing her, under the chin, behind the ear, and blowing down her neck.

'Say never . . . say never . . . say never – ' She gasped between the kisses. And then she began, very softly and lightly, to tickle her grandma.

'Kezia!' The old woman dropped her knitting. She swung back in the rocker. She began to tickle Kezia. 'Say never, say never, say never,' gurgled Kezia, while they lay there laughing in each other's arms. 'Come, that's enough, my squirrel! That's enough, my wild pony!' said old Mrs Fairfield, setting her cap straight. 'Pick up my knitting.'

Both of them had forgotten what the 'never' was about.

(VIII)

The sun was still full on the garden when the back door of the Burnells' shut with a bang and a very gay figure walked down the path to the gate. It was Alice, the servant girl, dressed for her afternoon out. She wore a white cotton dress with such large red spots on it, and so many that they made you shudder, white shoes and a leghorn turned up under the brim with poppies. Of course she wore gloves, white ones, stained at the fastenings with iron-mould, and in one hand she carried a very dashed-looking sunshade which she referred to as her *perishall*.

Beryl, sitting in the window, fanning her freshly washed hair, thought she had never seen such a guy. If Alice had only blacked her face with a piece of cork before she started out the picture would have been complete. And where did a girl like that go to in a place like this? The heart-shaped Fijian fan beat scornfully at that lovely bright mane. She supposed Alice had picked up some horrible common larrikin and they'd go off into the bush together. Pity to make herself so conspicuous; they'd have hard work to hide with Alice in that rig-out.

But no, Beryl was unfair. Alice was going to tea with Mrs Stubbs, who'd sent her an 'invite' by the little boy who called for orders. She had taken ever such a liking to Mrs Stubbs ever since the first time she went to the shop to get something for her mosquitoes.

'Dear heart!' Mrs Stubbs had clapped her hand to her side. 'I never seen anyone so eaten. You might have been attacked by canningbals.'

Alice did wish there'd been a bit of life on the road though. Made her feel so queer, having nobody behind her. Made her feel all weak in the spine. She couldn't believe that someone wasn't watching her. And yet it was silly to turn round; it gave you away. She pulled up her gloves, hummed to herself and said to the distant gum tree, 'Shan't be long now.' But that was hardly company.

Mrs Stubbs's shop was perched on a little hillock just off the road. It had two big windows for eyes, a broad verandah for a hat, and the sign of the roof, scrawled MRS STUBBS'S, was like a little card stuck rakishly in the hat crown.

On the verandah there hung a long string of bathing-dresses, clinging together as though they'd just been rescued from the sea rather than waiting to go in, and beside them there hung a cluster of sand-shoes so extraordinarily mixed that to get at one pair you had to tear apart and forcibly separate at least fifty. Even then it was the rarest thing to find the left that belonged to the right. So many people had lost patience and gone off with one shoe that fitted and one that was a little too big. . . . Mrs Stubbs prided herself on keeping something of everything. The two windows, arranged in the form of precarious pyramids, were crammed so tight, piled so high, that it seemed only a conjuror could prevent them from toppling over. In the lefthand corner of one window, glued to the pane by four gelatine lozenges, there was – and there had been from time immemorial – a notice:

LOST! HANSOME GOLE BROOCH
SOLID GOLD
ON OR NEAR BEACH
REWARD OFFERED

Alice pressed open the door. The bell jangled, the red serge curtains parted, and Mrs Stubbs appeared. With her broad smile and the long bacon knife in her hand she looked like a friendly brigand. Alice was welcomed so warmly that she found it quite difficult to keep up her 'manners'. They consisted of persistent little coughs and hems, pulls at her gloves, tweaks at her skirt, and a curious difficulty in seeing what was set before her or understanding what was said.

Tea was laid on the parlour table – ham, sardines, a whole pound of butter, and such a large johnny cake that it looked like an advertisement for somebody's baking powder. But the Primus stove roared so loudly that it was useless to try to talk above it. Alice sat down on the edge of a basket-chair while Mrs Stubbs pumped the stove still higher. Suddenly Mrs Stubbs whipped the cushion off a chair and disclosed a large brown paper parcel.

'I've just had some new photers taken, my dear,' she shouted cheerfully to Alice. 'Tell me what you think of them.'

In a very dainty, refined way Alice wet her finger and put the tissue back from the first one. Life! How many there were! There were three dozzing at least. And she held hers up to the light.

Mrs Stubbs sat in an arm-chair, leaning very much to one side. There was a look of mild astonishment on her large face, and well there might be. For though the arm-chair stood on a carpet, to the left of it, miraculously skirting the carpet border, there was a dashing waterfall. On her right stood a Grecian pillar with a giant fern tree on either side of it, and in the background towered a gaunt mountain, pale with snow.

'It is a nice style, isn't it?' shouted Mrs Stubbs; and Alice had just screamed 'Sweetly' when the roaring of the Primus stove died down, fizzled out, ceased, and she said 'Pretty' in a silence that was frightening.

'Draw up your chair, my dear,' said Mrs Stubbs, beginning to pour out. 'Yes,' she said thoughtfully, as she handed the tea, 'but I don't care about the size. I'm having an enlargemint. All very well for Christmas cards, but I never was the one for small photers myself. You get no comfort out of them. To say the truth, I find them dis'eartening.'

Alice quite saw what she meant.

'Size,' said Mrs Stubbs. 'Give me size. That was what my poor dear husband was always saying. He couldn't stand anything small. Gave him the creeps. And, strange as it may seem, my dear' – here Mrs Stubbs creaked and seemed to expand herself at the memory – 'it was dropsy that carried him off at the larst. Many's the time they drawn . one and a half pints from 'im at the 'ospital. . . . It seemed like a judgmint.'

Alice burned to know exactly what it was that was drawn from him. She ventured, 'I suppose it was water.'

But Mrs Stubbs fixed Alice with her eyes and replied meaningly, 'It was *liquid*, my dear.'

Liquid! Alice jumped away from the word like a cat and came back to it, nosing and wary.

'That's 'im!' said Mrs Stubbs, and she pointed dramatically to the life-size head and shoulders of a burly man with a dead white rose in the button-hole of his coat that made you think of a curl of cold mutton fat. Just below, in silver letters on a red cardboard ground, were the words, 'Be not afraid, it is I.'

'It's ever such a fine face,' said Alice faintly.

The pale-blue bow on the top of Mrs Stubbs's fair frizzy hair quivered. She arched her plump neck. What a neck she had! It was bright pink where it began and then it changed to warm apricot, and that faded to the colour of a brown egg and then to a deep creamy.

'All the same, my dear,' she said surprisingly, 'freedom's best!' Her soft, fat chuckle sounded like a purr. 'Freedom's best,' said Mrs Stubbs again.

Freedom! Alice gave a loud, silly little titter. She felt awkward. Her mind flew back to her own kitching. Ever so queer! She wanted to be back in it again.

(IX)

A strange company assembled in the Burnells' wash-house after tea. Round the table there sat a bull, a rooster, a donkey that kept forgetting it was a donkey, a sheep and a bee. The wash-house was the perfect place for such a meeting because they could make as much noise as they liked and nobody ever interrupted. It was a small tin shed standing apart from the bungalow. Against the wall there was a deep trough and in the corner a copper with a basket of clothes-pegs on top of it. The little window, spun over with cobwebs, had a piece of candle and a mouse-trap on the dusty sill. There were clotheslines criss-crossed overhead and, hanging from a peg on the wall, a very big, a huge, rusty horseshoe. The table was in the middle with a form at either side.

'You can't be a bee, Kezia. A bee's not an animal. It's a ninseck.'

'Oh, but I do want to be a bee frightfully,' wailed Kezia. . . . A tiny bee, all yellow-furry, with striped legs. She drew her legs up under her and leaned over the table. She felt she was a bee.

'A ninseck must be an animal,' she said stoutly. 'It makes a noise. It's not like a fish.'

'I'm a bull, I'm a bull!' cried Pip. And he gave such a tremendous bellow – how did he make that noise? – that Lottie looked quite alarmed.

'I'll be a sheep,' said little Rags. 'A whole lot of sheep went past this morning.'

'How do you know?'

'Dad heard them. Baa!' He sounded like the little lamb that trots behind and seems to wait to be carried.

'Cock-a-doodle-doo!' shrilled Isabel. With her red cheeks and bright eyes she looked like a rooster.

'What'll I be?' Lottie asked everybody, and she sat there smiling, waiting for them to decide for her. It had to be an easy one.

'Be a donkey, Lottie.' It was Kezia's suggestion. 'Hee-haw! You can't forget that.'

'Hee-haw!' said Lottie solemnly. 'When do I have to say it?'

'I'll explain, I'll explain,' said the bull. It was he who had the cards. He waved them round his head. 'All be quiet! All listen!' And he waited for them. 'Look here, Lottie.' He turned up a card. 'It's got two spots on it – see? Now, if you put that card in the middle and somebody else has one with two spots as well, you say "Hee-haw," and the card's yours.'

'Mine?' Lottie was round-eyed. 'To keep?'

'No, silly. Just for the game, see? Just while we're playing.' The bull was very cross with her.

'Oh, Lottie, you *are* a little silly,' said the proud rooster.

Lottie looked at both of them. Then she hung her head; her lip quivered. 'I don't not want to play,' she whispered. The others glanced at one another like conspirators. All of them knew what that meant. She would go away and be discovered somewhere standing with her pinny thrown over her head, in a corner, or against a wall, or even behind a chair.

'Yes, you *do*, Lottie. It's quite easy,' said Kezia.

21

And Isabel, repentant, said exactly like a grown-up, 'Watch *me*, Lottie, and you'll soon learn.'

'Cheer up, Lot,' said Pip. 'There, I know what I'll do. I'll give you the first one. It's mine, really, but I'll give it to you. Here you are.' And he slammed the card down in front of Lottie.

Lottie revived at that. But now she was in another difficulty. 'I haven't got a hanky,' she said; 'I want one badly, too.'

'Here, Lottie, you can use mine.' Rags dipped into his sailor blouse and brought up a very wet-looking one, knotted together. 'Be very careful,' he warned her. 'Only use that corner. Don't undo it. I've got a little star-fish inside I'm going to try and tame.'

'Oh, come on, you girls,' said the bull. 'And mind – you're not to look at your cards. You've got to keep your hands under the table till I say "Go".'

Smack went the cards round the table. They tried with all their might to see, but Pip was too quick for them. It was very exciting, sitting there in the wash-house; it was all they could do not to burst into a little chorus of animals before Pip had finished dealing.

'Now, Lottie, you begin.'

Timidly Lottie stretched out a hand, took the top card off her pack, had a good look at it – it was plain she was counting the spots – and put it down.

'No, Lottie, you can't do that. You mustn't look first. You must turn it the other way over.'

'But then everybody will see it the same time as me,' said Lottie.

The game proceeded. Mooe-ooo-er! The bull was terrible. He charged over the table and seemed to eat the cards up.

Bss-ss! said the bee.

Cock-a-doodle-do! Isabel stood up in her excitement and moved her elbows like wings.

Baa! Little Rags put down the King of Diamonds and Lottie put down the one they called the King of Spain. She had hardly any cards left.

'Why don't you call out, Lottie?'

'I've forgotten what I am,' said the donkey woefully.

'Well, change! Be a dog instead! Bow-wow!'

'Oh yes. That's *much* easier.' Lottie smiled again. But when she and Kezia both had one Kezia waited on purpose. The others made signs to Lottie and pointed. Lottie turned very red; she looked bewildered, and at last she said, 'Hee-haw! Ke-zia.'

'Ss! Wait a minute!' They were in the very thick of it when the bull stopped them, holding up his hand. 'What's that? What's that noise?'

'What noise? What do you mean?' asked the rooster.

'Ss! Shut up! Listen!' They were mouse-still. 'I thought I heard a
– a sort of knocking,' said the bull.

'What was it like?' asked the sheep faintly.

No answer.

The bee gave a shudder. 'Whatever did we shut the door for?' she
said softly. Oh, why, why had they shut the door?

While they were playing, the day had faded; the gorgeous sunset
had blazed and died. And now the quick dark came racing over the
sea, over the sand-hills, up the paddock. You were frightened to
look in the corners of the wash-house, and yet you had to look with
all your might. And somewhere, far away, grandma was lighting a
lamp. The blinds were being pulled down; the kitchen fire leapt in
the tins on the mantelpiece.

'It would be awful now,' said the bull, 'if a spider was to fall from
the ceiling on to the table, wouldn't it?'

'Spiders don't fall from ceilings.'

'Yes, they do. Our Min told us she'd seen a spider as big as a
saucer, with long hairs on it like a gooseberry.'

Quickly all the little heads were jerked up; all the little bodies
drew together, pressed together.

'Why doesn't somebody come and call us?' cried the rooster.

Oh, those grown-ups, laughing and snug, sitting in the
lamp-light, drinking out of cups! They'd forgotten about them.
No, not really forgotten. That was what their smile meant. They
had decided to leave them there all by themselves.

Suddenly Lottie gave such a piercing scream that all of them
jumped off the forms, all of them screamed too. 'A face – a face
looking!' shrieked Lottie.

It was true, it was real. Pressed against the window was a pale
face, black eyes, a black beard.

'Granma! Mother! Somebody!'

But they had not got to the door, tumbling over one another,
before it opened for Uncle Jonathan. He had come to take the little
boys home.

(X)

He had meant to be there before, but in the front garden he had
come upon Linda walking up and down the grass, stopping to
pick off a dead pink or give a top-heavy carnation something to
lean against, or to take a deep breath of something, and then
walking on again, with her little air of remoteness. Over her
white frock she wore a yellow, pink-fringed shawl from the
Chinaman's shop.

'Hallo, Jonathan!' called Linda. And Jonathan whipped off his

23

shabby panama, pressed it against his breast, dropped on one knee, and kissed Linda's hand.

'Greeting, my Fair One! Greeting, my Celestial Peach Blossom!' boomed the bass voice gently. 'Where are the other noble dames?'

'Beryl's out playing bridge and mother's giving the boy his bath. . . . Have you come to borrow something?'

The Trouts were for ever running out of things and sending across to the Burnells' at the last moment.

But Jonathan only answered, 'A little love, a little kindness'; and he walked by his sister-in-law's side.

Linda dropped into Beryl's hammock under the manuka tree and Jonathan stretched himself on the grass beside her, pulled a long stalk and began chewing it. They knew each other well. The voices of children cried from the other gardens. A fisherman's light cart shook along the sandy road, and from far away they heard a dog barking; it was muffled as though the dog had its head in a sack. If you listened you could just hear the soft swish of the sea at full tide sweeping the pebbles. The sun was sinking.

'And so you go back to the office on Monday, do you, Jonathan?' asked Linda.

'On Monday the cage door opens and clangs to upon the victim for another eleven months and a week,' answered Jonathan.

Linda swung a little. 'It must be awful,' she said slowly.

'Would ye have me laugh, my fair sister? Would ye have me weep?'

Linda was so accustomed to Jonathan's way of talking that she paid no attention to it.

'I suppose,' she said vaguely, 'one gets used to it. One gets used to anything.'

'Does one? Hum!' The 'Hum' was so deep it seemed to boom from underneath the ground. 'I wonder how it's done,' brooded Jonathan; 'I've never managed it.'

Looking at him as he lay there, Linda thought again how attractive he was. It was strange to think that he was only an ordinary clerk, that Stanley earned twice as much money as he. What was the matter with Jonathan? He had no ambition; she supposed that was it. And yet one felt he was gifted, exceptional. He was passionately fond of music; every spare penny he had went on books. He was always full of new ideas, schemes, plans. But nothing came of it all. The new fire blazed in Jonathan; you almost heard it roaring softly as he explained, described and dilated on the new thing; but a moment later it had fallen in and there was nothing but ashes, and Jonathan went about with a look like hunger in his black eyes. At these times he exaggerated his absurd manner of speaking, and he sang in church – he was the leader of the choir – with such fearful dramatic intensity that the meanest hymn put on an unholy splendour.

'It seems to me just as imbecile, just as infernal, to have to go to the office on Monday,' said Jonathan, 'as it always has done and always will do. To spend all the best years of one's life sitting on a stool from nine to five, scratching in somebody's ledger! It's a queer use to make of one's . . . one and only life, isn't it? Or do I fondly dream?' He rolled over on the grass and looked up at Linda. 'Tell me, what is the difference between my life and that of an ordinary prisoner. The only difference I can see is that I put myself in jail and nobody's ever going to let me out. That's a more intolerable situation than the other. For if I'd been – pushed in, against my will – kicking, even – once the door was locked, or at any rate in five years or so, I might have accepted the fact and begun to take an interest in the flight of flies or counting the warder's steps along the passage with particular attention to variations of tread and so on. But as it is, I'm like an insect that's flown into a room of its own accord. I dash against the walls, dash against the windows, flop against the ceiling, do everything on God's earth, in fact, except fly out again. And all the while I'm thinking, like that moth, or that butterfly, or whatever it is, "The shortness of life! The shortness of life!" I've only one night or one day, and there's this vast dangerous garden, waiting out there, undiscovered, unexplored.'

'But, if you feel like that, why – ' began Linda quickly.

'*Ah*!' cried Jonathan. And that 'Ah!' was somehow almost exultant. 'There you have me. Why? Why indeed? There's the maddening, mysterious question. Why don't I fly out again? There's the window or the door or whatever it was I came in by. It's not hopelessly shut – is it? Why don't I find it and be off? Answer me that, little sister.' But he gave her no time to answer.

'I'm exactly like that insect again. For some reason' – Jonathan paused between the words – 'it's not allowed, it's forbidden, it's against the insect law, to stop banging and flopping and crawling up the pane even for an instant. Why don't I leave the office? Why don't I seriously consider, this moment, for instance, what it is that prevents me leaving? It's not as though I'm tremendously tied. I've two boys to provide for, but, after all, they're boys. I could cut off to sea, or get a job up-country, or – ' Suddenly he smiled at Linda and said in a changed voice, as if he were confiding a secret, 'Weak . . . weak. No stamina. No anchor. No guiding principle, let us call it.' But then the dark velvety voice rolled out:

25

>   Would ye hear the story
>   How it unfolds itself . . .

and they were silent.

The sun had set. In the western sky there were great masses of crushed-up rose-coloured clouds. Broad beams of light shone through the clouds and beyond them as if they would cover the whole sky. Overhead the blue faded; it turned a pale gold, and the bush outlined against it gleamed dark and brilliant like metal. Sometimes when those beams of light show in the sky they are very awful. They remind you that up there sits Jehovah, the jealous God, the Almighty, Whose eye is upon you, ever watchful, never weary. You remember that at His coming the whole earth will shake into one ruined graveyard; the cold, bright angels will drive you this way and that, and there will be no time to explain what could be explained so simply. . . . But to-night it seemed to Linda there was something infinitely joyful and loving in those silver beams. And now no sound came from the sea. It breathed softly as if it would draw that tender, joyful beauty into its own bosom.

'It's all wrong, it's all wrong,' came the shadowy voice of Jonathan. 'It's not the scene, it's not the setting for . . . three stools, three desks, three inkpots and a wire blind.'

Linda knew that he would never change, but she said, 'Is it too late, even now?'

'I'm old – I'm old,' intoned Jonathan. He bent towards her, he passed his hand over his head. 'Look!' His black hair was speckled all over with silver, like the breast plumage of a black fowl.

Linda was surprised. She had no idea that he was grey. And yet, as he stood up beside her and sighed and stretched, she saw him, for the first time, not resolute, not gallant, not careless, but touched already with age. He looked very tall on the darkening grass, and the thought crossed her mind, 'He is like a weed.'

Jonathan stooped again and kissed her fingers.

'Heaven reward thy sweet patience, lady mine,' he murmured. 'I must go seek those heirs to my fame and fortune. . . . ' He was gone.

(XI)

Light shone in the windows of the bungalow. Two square patches of gold fell upon the pinks and the peaked marigolds. Florrie, the cat, came out on to the verandah and sat on the top step, her white paws close together, her tail curled round. She looked content, as though she had been waiting for this moment all day.

26

'Thank goodness, it's getting late,' said Florrie. 'Thank goodness, the long day is over.' Her greengage eyes opened.

Presently there sounded the rumble of the coach, the crack of Kelly's whip. It came near enough for one to hear the voices of the men from town, talking loudly together. It stopped at the Burnells' gate.

Stanley was half-way up the path before he saw Linda. 'Is that you, darling?'

'Yes, Stanley.'

He leapt across the flower-bed and seized her in his arms. She was enfolded in that familiar, eager, strong embrace.

'Forgive me, darling, forgive me,' stammered Stanley, and he put his hand under her chin and lifted her face to him.

'Forgive you?' smiled Linda. 'But whatever for?'

'Good God! You can't have forgotten,' cried Stanley Burnell. 'I've thought of nothing else all day. I've had the hell of a day. I made up my mind to dash out and telegraph, and then I thought the wire mightn't reach you before I did. I've been in tortures, Linda.'

'But, Stanley,' said Linda, 'what must I forgive you for?'

'Linda!' – Stanley was very hurt – 'didn't you realise – you must have realised – I went away without saying good-bye to you this morning? I can't imagine how I can have done such a thing. My confounded temper, of course. But – well' – and he sighed and took her in his arms again – 'I've suffered for it enough to-day.'

'What's that you've got in your hand?' asked Linda. 'New gloves? Let me see.'

'Oh, just a cheap pair of wash-leather ones,' said Stanley humbly. 'I noticed Bell was wearing some in the coach this morning, so, as I was passing the shop, I dashed in and got myself a pair. What are you smiling at? You don't think it was wrong of me, do you?'

'On the *con*-trary, darling,' said Linda, 'I think it was most sensible.'

She pulled one of the large, pale gloves on her own fingers and looked at her hand, turning it this way and that. She was still smiling.

Stanley wanted to say, 'I was thinking of you the whole time I bought them.' It was true, but for some reason he couldn't say it. 'Let's go in,' said he.

(XII)

Why does one feel so different at night? Why is it so exciting to be awake when everybody else is asleep? Late – it is very late! And yet every moment you feel more and more wakeful, as though you were slowly, almost with every breath, waking up into a new, wonderful, far more thrilling and exciting world than the daylight one. And what is this queer sensation that you're a conspirator? Lightly, stealthily you move about your room. You take something off the dressing-table and put it down again without a sound. And everything, even the bedpost, knows you, responds, shares your secret. . . .

You're not very fond of your room by day. You never think about it. You're in and out, the door opens and slams, the cupboard creaks. You sit down on the side of your bed, change your shoes and dash out again. A dive down to the glass, two pins in your hair, powder your nose and off again. But now – it's suddenly dear to you. It's a darling little funny room. It's yours. Oh, what a joy it is to own things! Mine – my own!

'My very own for ever?'

'Yes.' Their lips met.

No, of course, that had nothing to do with it. That was all nonsense and rubbish. But, in spite of herself, Beryl saw so plainly two people standing in the middle of her room. Her arms were round his neck; he held her. And now he whispered, 'My beauty, my little beauty!' She jumped off her bed, ran over to the window and kneeled on the window-seat, with her elbows on the sill. But the beautiful night, the garden, every bush, every leaf, even the white palings, even the stars, were conspirators too. So bright was the moon that the flowers were bright as by day; the shadow of the nasturtiums, exquisite lily-like leaves and wide-open flowers, lay across the silvery verandah. The manuka tree, bent by the southerly winds, was like a bird on one leg stretching out a wing.

But when Beryl looked at the bush, it seemed to her the bush was sad.

'We are dumb trees, reaching up in the night, imploring we know not what,' said the sorrowful bush.

It is true when you are by yourself and you think about life, it is always sad. All that excitement and so on has a way of suddenly leaving you, and it's as though, in silence, somebody called your name, and you heard your name for the first time. 'Beryl!'

'Yes, I'm here. I'm Beryl. Who wants me?'

'Beryl!'

'Let me come.'

It is lonely living by oneself. Of course, there are relations, friends, heaps of them; but that's not what she means. She wants someone who will find the Beryl they none of them know, who will expect her to be that Beryl always. She wants a lover.

'Take me away from all these other people, my love. Let us go far away. Let us live our life, all new, all ours, from the very beginning. Let us make our fire. Let us sit down to eat together. Let us have long talks at night.'

And the thought was almost, 'Save me, my love. Save me!'

. . . 'Oh, go on! Don't be a prude, my dear. You enjoy yourself while you're young. That's my advice.' And a high rush of silly laughter joined Mrs Harry Kember's loud, indifferent neigh.

You see, it's so frightfully difficult when you've nobody. You're so at the mercy of things. You can't just be rude. And you've always this horror of seeming inexperienced and stuffy like the other ninnies at the Bay. And – and it's fascinating to know you've power over people. Yes, that is fascinating. . . .

Oh why, oh why doesn't 'he' come soon?

If I go on living here, thought Beryl, anything may happen to me.

'But how do you know he is coming at all?' mocked a small voice within her.

But Beryl dismissed it. She couldn't be left. Other people, perhaps, but not she. It wasn't possible to think that Beryl Fairfield never married, that lovely, fascinating girl.

'Do you remember Beryl Fairfield?'

'Remember her! As if I could forget her! It was one summer at the Bay that I saw her. She was standing on the beach in a blue' – no, pink – 'muslin frock, holding on a big cream' – no, black – 'straw hat. But it's years ago now.'

'She's as lovely as ever, more so if anything.'

Beryl smiled, bit her lip, and gazed over the garden. As she gazed, she saw somebody, a man, leave the road, step along the paddock beside their palings as if he was coming straight towards her. Her heart beat. Who was it? Who could it be? It couldn't be a burglar, certainly not a burglar, for he was smoking and he strolled lightly. Beryl's heart leapt; it seemed to turn right over and then to stop. She recognised him.

'Good evening, Miss Beryl,' said the voice softly.

'Good evening.'

'Won't you come for a little walk?' it drawled.

Come for a walk – at that time of night! 'I couldn't. Everybody's in bed. Everybody's asleep.'

'Oh,' said the voice lightly, and a whiff of sweet smoke reached her. 'What does everybody matter? Do come! It's such a fine night. There's not a soul about.'

Beryl shook her head. But already something stirred in her, something reared its head.

The voice said, 'Frightened?' It mocked, 'Poor little girl!'

'Not in the least,' said she. As she spoke that weak thing within

29

her seemed to uncoil, to grow suddenly tremendously strong; she longed to go!

And just as if this was quite understood by the other, the voice said, gently and softly, but finally, 'Come along!'

Beryl stepped over her low window, crossed the verandah, ran down the grass to the gate. He was there before her.

'That's right,' breathed the voice, and it teased, 'You're not frightened, are you? You're not frightened?'

She was; now she was here she was terrified and it seemed to her everything was different. The moonlight stared and glittered; the shadows were like bars of iron. Her hand was taken.

'Not in the least,' she said lightly. 'Why should I be?'

Her hand was pulled gently, tugged. She held back.

'No, I'm not coming any further,' said Beryl.

'Oh, rot!' Harry Kember didn't believe her. 'Come along! We'll just go as far as that fuchsia bush. Come along!'

The fuchsia bush was tall. It fell over the fence in a shower. There was a little pit of darkness beneath.

'No, really, I don't want to,' said Beryl.

For a moment Harry Kember didn't answer. Then he came close to her, turned to her, smiled and said quickly, 'Don't be silly! Don't be silly!'

His smile was something she'd never seen before. Was he drunk? That bright, blind, terrifying smile froze her with horror. What was she doing? How had she got here? The stern garden asked her as the gate pushed open, and quick as a cat Harry Kember came through and snatched her to him.

'Cold little devil! Cold little devil!' said the hateful voice.

But Beryl was strong. She slipped, ducked, wrenched free.

'You are vile, vile,' said she.

'Then why in God's name did you come?' stammered Harry Kember.

Nobody answered him.

A cloud, small, serene, floated across the moon. In that moment of darkness the sea sounded deep, troubled. Then the cloud sailed away, and the sound of the sea was a vague murmur, as though it waked out of a dark dream. All was still.

MAN'S INHUMANITY TO MAN

John A. Lee

The sun was fierce and the sweat ran down the Shiner's face. His singlet was glued to his back although it kept climbing. His celluloid collar was slippery with sweat. The moisture from his brow was moistening the bleached dusty band of his straw boater and another layer of dust was gathering. It was a day, hot, fierce heat, clear but too hot for a man warmly clad to be on the road carrying a swag and a heavy swag.

Harvest was coming at a rush. As he walked the road it seemed that the blue green of the wheat and oats turned to silver green, the silver green to yellow ears and straw. Two or three days and the farmers would be in the fields with their reapers and binders, working the clock around to get the wheat and oats in sheaf before a dry wind shook half the crop to the floor of the paddock. Man and beast would drive until the flesh was sore in those days before tractors eased the tension for the lovely horses.

In a few days he would go into the field himself. He always did respond to the call for harvest labour for a day or two. When everyone crowded into the fields to race the wind and the rain the social adventure of it all compelled a few days' loyalty from the most incorrigible of vagabonds. He would stook and he would help to stack and he would discourse learnedly on the quality and quantity of the harvest. He had better memory of such things than most of the farmers who were too busy fighting debt, whose noses were too near the soil for academic comparison of harvest with harvest.

Work was not so bad when it had a measure of novelty, of society, when man's race to gather the harvest before it was spoiled by the elements had a touch of adventure. But work for wages day after day, dull, unremitting, backbreaking, who wanted to work for wages when the glory had departed? So at every harvest he heeded the call. He spent a few days in the fields and then collected his money and hurried on, and that was the only time when he felt a trifle ashamed as he ran from the group who already had more than they could do, a group who on Monday were inclined to think him a good fellow and on Friday chased his back up the road with curses and sneers as though they were kicking a dog in the tail.

Later, when the mills were coming out to thresh, he would throw his swag in again with a team and for a day or two be a man amongst men in the yearly novelty of the job, the whirr of the machinery, the vagabondage of other men. For half the mills recruited their crews off the road, men and swags.

He could fork from a stack to a mill with any man on earth when he was in the mood. It was because of his prowess that he achieved the pinnacle of notoriety as a loafer. He could and he wouldn't. The mood to show the world would come to him as he stood on a stack and looked down upon the mill feeder who, knowing the Shiner held the fork would have for him a measure of contempt. The attitude and tones of the mill feeder would say: 'Huh, the Shiner. Easy to keep ahead of this bird!'

So the Shiner would shower the sheaves down on him, or pile them up around him. The feeder had to set a fast pace for the mill. The Shiner would start to set an impossible pace for the feeder. The feeder would smile contemptuously at the start of the day but be a beaten man before the day was out, never quite able to win a fraction of a second between the arrival of the sheaves. And then the Shiner would smile even as he sweated, and maybe even as his hands blistered. And the feeder at last might be the one to plead for mercy.

'Steady!'

'You can't keep ahead of the Shiner!'

'Easy, easy.'

'When I was a lad feeders were feeders!'

But by the time the Shiner had convinced the feeder he was the greatest forker from the stack in New Zealand, a sorely libelled man, he was getting toward the mood to loaf as prodigiously as he had worked. From then on he had to be coaxed, he could not be driven for he was the most imperturbable loafer in the land. He would slow up his delivery and the mill would pour out a diminishing stream of grain, and when the feeder called for speed he had been known to lean on the fork and ask the feeder if he had heard this one, until at last the millowner paid the Shiner off and sent him packing.

There were millowners who had been known to keep him hard at work for a couple of days, or until some other had come carrying his swag along the road, by sheer flattery. The Shiner would stay on the stack, in the spotlight as it were. But no engine driver could stand for a whole season gazing in admiration at the Shiner's prowess. There were jobs to do. Flattery can become real hard work.

Nevertheless the Shiner was feeling the call of harvest again as he tramped the road on this hot sweaty day. But he had a prior call. The road was dusty, his palate was dusty, his tongue was dusty, his lips were cracking like the mud in the drying creeks. This was no place where he could find cool shade in pine trees and pitch a tent, and loaf, and feed upon the country until the silver green straw and heads of wheat and oats turned to hard yellow, even if that moment was only a couple of days ahead. This was bad country for him to forage in. This was country in which he had played too many tricks, country in which he possessed notoriety and not fame.

He wanted liquor as he hadn't wanted it in a decade. And he did not want the bite but the bitterness of alcohol. He wanted beer, long bitter beer, not whiskey. He wanted alcohol and a sense of having alcohol, the gradual lubrication and easement of malt and hops and not the warm mellow forgetfulness of spirits. Oh for a beer, for a long, long, long, bitter, bitter, bitter beer. 'B-e-e-r.' He said the word with a long deep 'e' and his desire became a fanaticism. 'Be-e-e-e-r.'

The idea was getting hold of him so thoroughly that he was in grave danger of being driven to work to secure the price. But the job would have to yield the price in advance. He couldn't wait!

'Be-e-e-r!'

He wanted beer so much that he felt sinful at the lack of it. He was an inferior. Without a pint in his hand he was conscious of an awful blasphemous nakedness. Beer he wanted until he was prepared to work for beer. And in the Shiner could there be greater proof of the intensity of craving? And he couldn't get beer anywhere. Along the road, and the country was thick with pubs, he tried to scrounge the bitter foaming liquor.

'How about a beer, boss?'

'It's the Shiner himself! Well, I'll make a bargain. Go out the back and chop wood for a couple of hours and I'll give you two beers and dinner.'

'One now. Can't you see I'm perishing?'

'You'll last it out. No one will give you anything around here in advance.'

It was as if the Shiner had got a craving for a brewery in the Sahara. Except that this Sahara was due to his own past bad behaviour. Be sure your peccadillos will find you dry.

'Look, one glass!'

'The axe is sharp.'

'You can go to hell, you miserable cow!' The Shiner picked up his swag.

'I'll be seeing you, Shiner!'

Publicans. They had no sense of the fitness of things. Such a

33

thirst derived from publicans and yet they baulked at a little human charity. They had no milk of human kindness, or could not understand that sometimes the milk of human kindness was a long beer. 'I haven't any money but will you take stamps?'

Alas, the story of the great stamp trick travelled so fast that he could not work it again. There are no copyrights about vagabondage. Publicans told the story and thought it wonderful because it celebrated the downfall of people easy to deceive like Mick Scanlan and Paddy Griffen. To demonstrate superiority to those weaklings was a point of honour.

'Now, if you wanted a feed, Shiner.'

Beer. That was what he wanted. Bitter. Something to stimulate the glands that moistened the palate and something that would take aridity out of the soul. A feed. Who wanted a pie? Who wanted roast mutton, and baked potatoes, and bread and gravy, and cabbage and tea? He wanted beer. And there was no substitute.

'Just one long beer and I'll call back and pay you after harvest.'

'You fooled me once, Shiner!'

'But this is a pledge between gentlemen.'

'Gentlemen, indeed!'

Vagabond's thirst countered by publican's memory. What an awful predicament for a thirsty soul on a dry scorching day, on a day when the temperament is as parched as the throat. Publican's memory is as much an occupational disease as alcoholic's thirst.

Two, three, four hotels he tried in four or five miles. And all the publicans were scornful, even hilarious. They all knew him and had given the dog his bad name. No one begrudged the beer as much as they feared they would live to regret the slightest weakening.

'Give him a pint and he'll drink the pub dry!'

Not as bad as that but all had pitched him, neck and crop, into the dusty road on other days when he had quartered himself on the neighbourhood. You could never tell with that one. Treat him kindly, and end by a declaration of war, and maybe a storm of abuse before he walked down the road. And good customers would sometimes go to other places rather than be plagued with his insistence on free drink.

'I haven't had a beer for weeks!'

'Thought you were looking well.'

'You could stand me a beer.'

'I could. But I won't. Stick it out for another week and it'll become a habit. Never let it be said I started you again on the downward path.'

'Oh hell, I want a be-e-e-r!'

'I believe in helping a man to go straight when he's been trying.'

'Man, I'll die of thirst!'

'The only time my conscience ever pricked me was when a man died of beer in my own pub.'

'Have you no feeling for one of your victims?'

'Victim. You!'

For publicans from end to end of the country had been the Shiner's victims. And there were no men loitering around the hotels from whom he could cadge. They were out in the fields doing the work of the world. They were getting their reapers and binders turned over and ready. Nowhere was there someone with cash and his resistance half lowered and his geniality exaggerated by the goods he had imbibed.

'It's hell!' the Shiner said as he walked.

He always knew what hell would be like, for he was a believer and paid a measure of attention to the observance of his faith. Hell would be a terrible place where everyone would be hot and sweaty and would work on hot plates. They would be furry of tongue, and cracked of lip, and dry of throat. And Satan would be a fat leering publican. A fellow in shirtsleeves and bowler and pasty of face and fishy of eye, and with a waistcoat that had to reach around twice as much circumference to cover the abdomen as to cross the chest. And in hell Satan would have vats of foaming cold bitter, and clean wide deep glasses. And the swine would laugh at the thirsty. Already on this day he was in purgatory. No. Satan would be no saturnine fellow with horns. He would be a hog fat publican, dull and mean.

The craving grew as the Shiner walked. At the start of the day his flesh had been parched. By late afternoon he could feel his soul being dehydrated.

'Sure I'm shrinking up and I won't expand until I can drink a bucket!'

He stood on a bridge over the muddy waters of a dredge-dirtied river and recited to himself: 'Water water everywhere, and all the boards did shrink; water, water everywhere, and not a drop to drink.'

His thirst became as sizzling as a hot plate as he walked on. He failed to take his usual draughts of spring water and that made his plight worse. Nostalgia for beer and repugnance for water developed simultaneously. If he could only get fourpence for a pint. If he had threepence a publican would oblige, and when he had nothing and was known he had no chance. But he had an idea. There were four hotels in the town ahead and he would get a penny subsidy in all. They would go a penny but not a pint. He entered the first.

35

'I'm dying of thirst. If you'd give me a penny I'd have enough for a pint.'

'Give me the threepence then, Shiner.'

'No. Give me the penny and let me pay in full.'

'What's the game?'

'It's my dignity. I want to pay in full. Humour an old man!'

The publican opened the till and threw him a penny.

'Thanks.'

'What'll you have?'

'I've still got to get the other threepence.'

'You scoundrel!'

'You lent me a penny, didn't you. What are you screaming about?' the Shiner walked out.

'You thief.'

Let him bawl. He managed to work the trick in the next two hotels. Yes, it worked each time. They were all prepared to advance a penny to catch threepence. He didn't mind the abuse. His standing was at that zero at which beer freezes. He entered the last hotel. The publican, wonder of wonders, was a new fellow. An old enemy of the Shiner had moved on. The bar was empty.

'Good-day to you.'

'Good-day. Come far?'

'I'm really very sorry. I want a pint of beer and I've only got threepence.' He laid the pennies along the bar. 'Three pennies. Faith. Hope. Charity. Could you trust me with a penny? Faith. Hope. Charity. Benevolence, would be your penny.'

'Going to work in the neighbourhood?'

'Harvest. I'm the best forker in Otago and Canterbury.'

The publican filled out the glass and the Shiner pushed the three pennies across.

'Ah.' The Shiner sipped. Never let it be said he swallowed his beer at a draught. He wanted to taste and loiter over the wetness and bitterness of each drop. He had walked miles to win a pint. 'Ah.' A teaspoonful at a time. 'Ah. You keep the best beer around here.'

'You think so?' the publican was pleased.

'I don't think. I know. I'm an authority. Don't I bust my harvest cheque every year in this town?'

'You do? Have another!'

'Yes. The reapers and binders'll be going in a few days. Yes. Very good beer. I'll come here when I'm through.' As the Shiner sipped and sighed and ummed and ahed he saw a rat run out of a hole in the corner of the bar where someone had dropped a fragment of water biscuit.

'Rats. Cheeky. Ah.'

'There's dozens of them around here. I wish I could get rid of them!'

'You should see me kill rats.'

'Go on.'

'There isn't another ratter my equal in the whole country.'

'And you've got nothing to do for a couple of days until the harvest starts?'

'Nothing. I'm broke. Me time's all me own.'

'I'll tell you what. Pull into the hut at the back. You can have your food and there's a bed there. You kill the rats.'

'There'll be never a rat left.' The Shiner drank his beer at a draught. 'Give me another beer and put it on the slate. I'll square after a few days at harvest.'

'You can kill rats, you say?' The publican filled the glass again. He had to make a good impression as a newcomer to the district and was prepared for a little generosity as a business investment. Set a beer and catch a boozer.

'I'll clear them all out for you.' The Shiner meant what he said. He was the greatest ratter on earth. He knew it.

'Anything you want to clean them out?'

'Look. I'll tell you what. I'll get it from you. Cheese. And a quart of beer. No rat can resist – '

'Cheese and beer! It sounds as if you wanted to catch a man!'

'Rats are human. Feed them on what they're used to. They live like humans around here. Cheese attracts. But Welsh rarebit!'

'I'll put some in a bottle.'

'No. Put a drop in my billy.'

'You're sure?'

'Of course. Rats get used to beer and cheese around a hotel. Now if you make what they're used to savoury – '

'It sounds alright to me.'

The Shiner didn't loaf around. Someone might come in who knew him and that would spoil the place for him. He retreated to the hut and unrolled his swag. He walked all round and through the hotel, into every room and every shed, made a great show of finding the holes in the walls. He baited a few rabbit traps with cheese and left them about. The publican left him alone.

He retired to his hut at sundown. He did not want to be around the hotel when the evening customers came around. Someone would be sure to know him. He lay down to rest with the billy by his side. He was serene after nearly a day's frustration. Calm and cool after heat and storm. He lifted the billy to his lips and had a mouthful and said, 'ah', and smiled at the roof of the hut. Good

37

beer. Welsh rarebits for rats. Why should he teach hotel rats bad habits. If the rats got drunk it would take a policeman and not the Shiner to arrest them. And what were a few rats around the pub? They ate the crumbs and that saved a lot of sweeping. And they got many a customer used to what he was going to see anyhow. That was all to the good. In fact, it might be better for some of the fellows if there were a few snakes around for the same reason. His mind retraced the events of the day as he sipped. It had been started in the desert but had ended in an oasis.

'Be-e-e-er!'

Yes. Good beer. Homeopathy worked wonders with the Shiner. A couple of quarts of bitter in the stomach dissolved a lot of bitterness in the heart. He would have to deliver some dead rats on the morrow, but who organised life that far in advance? And, wonder of wonders, most of the rats seemed to come from the store where the publican kept the bottled spirits; they seemed to come from there even when a man was sober. That was an inducement to go ratting.

In the morning he fooled around and fooled around. He had a couple of rats to show, caught in his cheese baited rabbit traps.

'There are rats in the bottle store, dozens of them!'

'I know.'

'Well, let me in.'

'Have a glass of beer.'

'No thanks. You can't mix work and drink. I always believe in getting my job done first. Mind you, it's kind of you, and I'm not saying I wouldn't like it, the good beer you keep. When I get the harvesting done I'll bring a dozen fellows down here. It's the best pub in town!'

'Just a glass?'

'No. Work first. You just lock me into that store. I'll shut the door tight so that nothing can get out and I'll move all the boxes. I'll find out where all the holes are.'

'Right-oh.' He let the Shiner in.

'Lock me in. I'll knock when I want to come out.' The Shiner had a little parcel in his hand.

'Sure you won't have a glass?'

'When I come out.'

When the door was pulled shut and locked, the Shiner put a couple of cases against it. It opened inward so he would be safe. He opened his little parcel. It contained the two rats he had already caught. 'Two and two make four,' he said sweetly. He had to make some sort of showing.

He was in that store a long time and there was a great banging and rattling as he bumped the floor and made pretence of a great shifting. And long spells of silence as he sat quietly waiting for the rats. In truth he was soon sitting on a case making an odd bump on the floor and drinking whiskey from the neck of a flask he had opened, a flask of the real mackay. He sat and he drank, as fast as he could drink. And then he slipped a quart bottle in his hip pocket. He scattered a few baits around before he shifted the cases and knocked again on the door.

'Look. I caught two myself while I was in there. I'll catch a hundred tonight now I know where they all are. With the bait.'

'You'll have a beer now?'

'Never a drop till my task is done.' The Shiner didn't want to kill the spirits with the ferment.

'A cup of tea,' said the publican's wife.

'Sure. It's a lady after me own heart that you are. And are these your own scones made hot from your own hands?'

'Yes, they're mine.'

'Me own mother never made better scones and she could make scones.'

'A nice man,' said the wife to the husband.

'Steady fellow,' said the publican. 'He refuses to touch a drop while he's working.'

So the Shiner had a cup of tea and hot buttered scones and went back to his hut 'to give the bait a chance to work'. He took some water in his billy and thought he would have a dram. And since he hadn't been drinking spirits for many weeks the liquor made way with his caution. He had many drams. Although there was one precaution he never forgot to take. He filled the whiskey into his pannikin, enough for a dram or two, and always rolled up the quart bottle in his swag. If he was forced to retreat and went with his swag retreat had compensations. He had learned that trick across the years. Soon whiskey got the better of all but that one discretion. The descent was easy and glorious.

A customer came from the bar around the house to a place marked 'gents'. He heard a raucous voice singing.

> I'm out in the cruel world
> Out in the street
> I'm asking a penny
> From each one I meet
> I'm fatherless, motherless
> Sadly I roam
> What will become of me
> I have no home.

The customer looked into the hut.

'Well, if it isn't the Shiner!'

'Hullo. Hullo. Hullo.'

'What are you doing Shiner?'

'Catching rats.'

'Catching rats! Ha, ha. Seems to me as if you will soon catch rats alright. Watch you don't catch a few snakes too. Ha, ha.'

'I'm out in the cruel world.' The Shiner was more interested in himself than in his visitor and started to sing again.

'Come and have a drink with me, Shiner.'

'Sorry. But I never drink during working hours.' He was expansive, engaging, apologetic.

'What work are you doing?'

'I told you. I'm catching rats.'

'Catching rats, ha, ha, ha.'

His interrogator went back to the bar while the Shiner changed his song.

> Only a leaf
> Oh but what grief
> It caused in the
> Dim long ago
> Once it was red
> Now faded and dead
> And the woman
> Who wore it lies low.

'See you've got the Shiner in the hut out there,' said the customer to the publican.

'The Shiner. Where? Where?'

'Out in the hut. Drunk. Singing like mad. Says he's catching rats. He's making a good start. Watch he doesn't put a trick across you.'

'Is that the Shiner? What's the Shiner like?'

'Tall. Straw boater tied to the coat with a bootlace. Celluloid collar. I thought everyone around here knew the Shiner!'

'Drunk as a lord you say? On what?'

'Smells like whiskey.'

'Come on.'

'They stood outside the hut listening.

> It is ten weary years
> Since I left England's shores
> In a far distant country to roam
> How I long to return to my own native land
> To my friends and the old folks at home.
> Last night as I slumbered
> I had a strange dream –

40

'You'll have a nightmare tonight, Shiner,' the publican put his head around the door. 'You won't have a drink?'

'Not during working hours,' said Shiner. 'One that seemed to bring distant friends near,' he went back to his singing.

'Good-day, Mister Shiner,' the publican moved in. A dark, tough looking little cuss when he was riled.

'It is that. It is that.'

'Drunk. Where did you get it? You wouldn't have any beer. You didn't sneak any whiskey by any chance did you?'

'It's me rheumatic fever,' the Shiner grinned.

'Seen any rats yet?'

'Easy now. Easy. Can't you take a joke?'

'You promised to kill the rats.'

'Sure.'

'Well, kill them, or I'll kill the ratter!'

'Come on,' said the Shiner, unsteady on his feet but determined to carry it off, 'come on.' He walked out of the hut to the wood pile. 'Did I say how I would kill them? Did I now?'

'Welsh rarebit,' the publican was mumbling.

'Can't you see they are not water rats.'

'Welsh rarebits,' the publican was glowering. 'Well, get busy.'

'Sure I can kill all the rats,' the Shiner bent and lifted up a billet of wood. 'I'm ready to perform me contract now. You bring the rats out and hold their heads on the block and I'll knock the brains out of everyone of them. Bring out your rats.'

There was an audience of three now and they were tittering. The publican might have considered his experience cheap at the price had it not been for the audience, but he had some dignity too. He hit the Shiner in the stomach and doubled him over. And as the Shiner doubled he let him have a boot in the exposed haunches. The Shiner sat amid the sawdust and the chips gasping for breath.

'You — wind — ed — me.'

'Let me wind you again.'

'Sure you can't take a joke.'

'Stand up.' The publican was small but he had been a champion wrestler at Caledonian sports gatherings for years. 'Stand up!'

'If I stand up you'll knock me down.'

'If you don't stand up I'll knock you down just the same.'

'Publicans,' said the Shiner mournfully, 'are losing their sense of humour.'

'Stand up!'

'Not again.'

'Well I'll knock you flat if you don't.'

'I won't have so far to fall.'

41

The audience was laughing. The Shiner looked at them accusingly and recited –

'Man's inhumanity to man makes countless thousands mourn.'

The publican dragged the Shiner to his feet, picked him up, carried him to the road, and threw him urgently in the dustiest spot he could find.

His wife called to him and the publican turned to talk to her. The Shiner jumped and scrambled through the fence into the field opposite, leaving his boater in the dust. The publican sent it after him with a couple of kicks, one of which sent a toe through the crown. He went to the hut and got the swag and the billy and brought them and threw them across the fence. And the swag didn't leak. The bottle didn't break. The Shiner sat looking out on to the road mournfully, his straw boater with its ruptured top on his head.

'Now go catching your rats,' the publican went back to his bar followed by his customers. 'And if ever you want the Shine taken out of the Shiner call in on me. I'll oblige you.'

'Publicans without humour,' said the Shiner to his back as he sat looking through the fence.

But the sun was shining and the birds were twittering and harvest was coming, and there was half a quart of whiskey in the swag. And half a quart and a flask in the Shiner, so he mellowed after a mournful inspection of his hat. He unrolled his swag and took out the bottle. There would be no rain for weeks and the ground was dry. And in his progress he had brought his billet of wood with him, grasping at it when he had been picked up, as he would have grasped at anything in reach. He drank and he sat in the field and bawled.

'Bring out your rats! Bring out your rats!'

Later in the day when twilight came he sat singing –

> I'm out in the cruel world
> I'm out in the street
> I'm asking a penny
> From each one I meet.
> Fatherless, motherless,
> Sadly I roam
> What will become of me
> I have no home.

'The poor man,' said the publican's wife and she took him some tea and scones.

'Your scones are better than the ones me mother used to make.'

She gave him half a crown as well, but never told her husband.

'Man's inhumanity to man,' he said to her as he handed back the jug and took the coin, 'makes countless thousands mourn.'

That publican never did any good anyhow. His wife took pity on too many customers.

THE TOTARA TREE

Roderick Finlayson

People came running from all directions wanting to know what all the fuss was about. 'Oho! it's crazy old Taranga perching like a crow in her tree because the Pakeha boss wants his men to cut it down,' Panapa explained, enjoying the joke hugely.

'What you say, cut it down? Cut the totara down?' echoed Uncle Tuna, anger and amazement wrinkling yet more his old wrinkled face. 'Cut Taranga down first!' he exclaimed. 'Everyone knows that totara is Taranga's birth tree.'

Uncle Tuna was so old he claimed to remember the day Taranga's father had planted the young tree when the child was born. Nearly one hundred years ago, Uncle Tuna said. But many people doubted that he was quite as old as that. He always boasted so.

'Well it looks like they'll have to cut down both Taranga *and* her tree,' chuckled Panapa to the disgust of Uncle Tuna who disapproved of joking about matters of tapu.

'Can't the Pakeha bear the sight of one single tree without reaching for his axe?' Uncle Tuna demanded angrily. 'However, this tree is tapu,' he added with an air of finality, 'so let the Pakeha go cut down his own weeds.' Uncle Tuna hated the Pakehas.

'Ae, why do they want to cut down Taranga's tree?' a puzzled woman asked.

'It's the wires,' Panapa explained loftily. 'The tree's right in the way of the new power wires they're taking up the valley. Ten thousand volts, ehoa! That's power, I tell you! A touch of that to her tail would soon make Taranga spring out of her tree, ehoa,' Panapa added with impish delight and a sly dig in the ribs for old Uncle Tuna. The old man simply spat his contempt and stumped away.

'Oho!' gurgled Panapa, 'now just look at the big Pakeha boss down below dancing and cursing at mad old Taranga up the tree; and she doesn't know a single word and cares nothing at all!'

And indeed Taranga just sat up there smoking her pipe of evil-smelling torori. Now she turned her head away and spat slowly and deliberately on the ground. Then she fixed her old half-closed eyes on the horizon again. Aue! how those red-faced Pakehas down below there jabbered and shouted! Well, no matter.

Meanwhile a big crowd had collected near the shanty where Taranga lived with her grandson, in front of which grew Taranga's totara tree right on the narrow road that divided the straggling little hillside settlement from the river. Men lounged against old sheds and hung over sagging fences; women squatted in open doorways or strolled along the road with babies in shawls on their backs. The bolder children even came right up and made marks in the dust on the Inspector's big car with their grubby little fingers. The driver had to say to them, 'Hey there, you! Keep away from the car.' And they hung their heads and pouted their lips and looked shyly at him with great sombre eyes.

But a minute later the kiddies were jigging with delight behind the Inspector's back. How splendid to see such a show – all the big Pakehas from town turned out to fight mad old Taranga perching in a tree! But she was a witch all right – like her father the tohunga. Maybe she'd just flap her black shawl like wings and give a cackle and turn into a bird and fly away. Or maybe she'd curse the Pakehas, and they'd all wither up like dry sticks before their eyes! Uncle Tuna said she could do even worse than that. However, the older children didn't believe that old witch stuff.

Now as long as the old woman sat unconcernedly smoking up the tree, and the Pakehas down below argued and appealed to her as unsuccessfully as appealing to Fate, the crowd thoroughly enjoyed the joke. But when the Inspector at last lost his temper and shouted to his men to pull the old woman down by force, the humour of the gathering changed. The women in the doorways shouted shrilly. One of them said, 'Go away, Pakeha, and bully city folk! We Maoris don't yet insult trees or old women!' The men on the fences began grumbling sullenly, and the younger fellows started to lounge over toward the Pakehas. Taranga's grandson, Taikehu, who had been chopping wood, had a big axe in his hand. Taranga may be mad but after all it was her birth tree. You couldn't just come along and cut down a tree like that. Ae, you could laugh your fill at the old woman perched among the branches like an old black crow, but it wasn't for a Pakeha to come talking about pulling her down and destroying her tree. That smart man had better look out.

The Inspector evidently thought so too. He made a sign to dismiss the linesmen who were waiting with ladders and axes and ropes and saws to cut the tree down. Then he got into his big car, tight-lipped with rage. 'Hey, look out there, you kids!' the driver shouted. And away went the Pakeha amid a stench of burnt benzine leaving Taranga so far victorious.

'They'll be back tomorrow with the police all right and drag old Taranga down by a leg,' said Panapa gloatingly. 'She'll have no chance with the police. But by golly! I'll laugh to see the first policeman to sample her claws!'

'Oho! they'll be back with sodjers,' chanted the kiddies in great excitement. 'They'll come with machine guns and go t-t-t-te at old Taranga, but she'll just swallow the bullets!'

'Shut up, you kids,' Panapa commanded.

But somehow the excitement of the besieging of Taranga in her tree had spread like wildfire through the usually sleepy little settlement. The young bloods talked about preparing a hot welcome for the Pakehas tomorrow. Uncle Tuna encouraged them. A pretty state of affairs, he said, if a tapu tree could be desecrated by mere busybodies. The young men of his day knew better how to deal with such affairs. He remembered well how he himself had once tomahawked a Pakeha who broke the tapu of a burial ground. If people had listened to him long ago all the Pakehas would have been put in their place, under the deep sea – shark food! said Uncle Tuna ferociously. But the people were weary of Uncle Tuna's many exploits, and they didn't stop to listen. Even the youngsters nowadays merely remarked 'oh yeah?' when the old man harangued them.

Yet already the men were dancing half-humorous hakas around the totara tree. A fat woman with rolling eyes and a long tongue encouraged them. Everyone roared with laughter when she tripped in her long red skirts and fell bouncingly in the road. It was taken for granted now that they would make a night of it. Work was forgotten, and everyone gathered about Taranga's place. Taranga still waited quietly in the tree.

Panapa disappeared as night drew near but he soon returned with a barrel of home-brew on a sledge to enliven the occasion. That warmed things up, and the fun became fast and more furious. They gathered dry scrub and made bonfires to light the scene. They told Taranga not to leave her look-out, and they sent up baskets of food and drink to her; but she wouldn't touch bite nor sup. She alone of all the crowd was now calm and dignified. The men were dancing mad hakas armed with axes, knives and old taiahas. Someone kept firing a shot-gun till the cartridges gave out. Panapa's barrel of home-brew was getting low too, and Panapa just sat there propped up against it and laughed and laughed; men and women alike boasted what they'd do with the Pakehas tomorrow. Old Uncle Tuna was disgusted with the whole business though. That was no way to fight the Pakeha, he said; that was the Pakeha's own ruination. He stood up by the meeting-house and harangued the mob, but no one listened to him.

The children were screeching with delight and racing around the bonfires like brown demons. They were throwing fire-sticks about here there and everywhere. So it's no wonder the scrub caught fire, and Taikehu's house beside the tree was ablaze before anybody noticed it. Heaven help us! but there was confusion then! Taikehu rushed in to try and save his best clothes. But he only got out with his old overcoat and a broken gramophone before the flames roared up through the roof. Some men started beating out the scrub with their axes and sticks. Others ran to the river for water. Uncle Tuna capered about urging the men to save the totara tree from the flames. Fancy wasting his breath preaching against the Pakeha, he cried. Trust this senseless generation of Maoris to work their own destruction, he sneered.

It seemed poor old Taranga was forgotten for the moment. Till a woman yelled at Taikehu, 'What you doing there with your old rags, you fool? Look alive and get the old woman out of the tree.' Then she ran to the tree and called, 'Eh there, Taranga! don't be mad. Come down quick, old mother!'

But Taranga made no move.

Between the woman and Taikehu and some others, they got Taranga down. She looked to be still lost in meditation. But she was quite dead.

'Aue! she must have been dead a *long* time – she's quite cold and stiff,' Taikehu exclaimed. 'So it couldn't be the fright of the fire that killed her.'

'Fright!' jeered Uncle Tuna. 'I tell you, pothead, a woman who loaded rifles for me under the cannon shells of the Pakeha isn't likely to die of fright at a rubbish fire.' He cast a despising glance at the smoking ruins of Taikehu's shanty. 'No! but I tell you what she died of,' Uncle Tuna continued. 'Taranga was just sick to death of you and your Pakeha ways. Sick to death!' The old man spat on the ground and turned his back on Taikehu and Panapa and their companions.

Meanwhile the wind had changed, and the men had beaten out the scrub fire, and the totara tree was saved. The fire and the old woman's strange death and Uncle Tuna's harsh words had sobered everybody by now, and the mood of the gathering changed from its former frenzy to melancholy and a kind of superstitious awe. Already some women had started to wail at the meeting-house where Taranga had been carried. Arrangements would have to be made for the tangi.

'Come here, Taikehu,' Uncle Tuna commanded. 'I have to show you where you must bury Taranga.'

Well, the Inspector had the grace to keep away while the tangi was on. Or rather Sergeant O'Connor, the chief of the local police and a good friend of Taranga's people, advised the Inspector not to meddle until it was over. 'A tangi or a wake, sure it's just as sad and holy,' he said. 'Now I advise you, don't interfere till they've finished.

But when the Inspector did go out to the settlement afterwards – well! Panapa gloatingly told the story in the pub in town later. 'O boy!' he said, 'you should have heard what bloody Mr Inspector called Sergeant O'Connor when he found out they'd buried the old woman right under the roots of the bloody tree! I think O'Connor like the joke though. When the Inspector finish cursing, O'Connor say to him, "Sure the situation's still unchanged then. Taranga's still in her tree".'

Well, the power lines were delayed more than ever and in time this strange state of affairs was even mentioned in the House of Parliament, and the Maori members declared the Maoris' utter refusal to permit the desecration of burial places, and the Pakeha members all applauded these fine orations. So the Power Board was brought to the pass of having to build a special concrete foundation for the poles in the river bed so that the wires could be carried clear of Taranga's tree.

'Oho!' Panapa chuckles, telling the story to strangers who stop to look at the tomb beneath the totara on the roadside. 'Taranga dead protects her tree much better than Taranga alive. By golly she cost the Pakeha thousands *and* thousands I guess!'

THE HOLE THAT JACK DUG

Frank Sargeson

Jack had got a pretty considerable hole dug in the backyard before I knew anything about it. I went around one scorching hot Saturday afternoon, and Jack was in the hole with nothing on except his boots and his little tight pair of shorts. Jack is a big specimen of a bloke, he's very powerfully developed, and seeing he's worked in the quarry for years in just that rigout, he's browned a darker colour than you'd ever believe possible on a white man. And that afternoon he was sweating so much he had a shine on as well.

Hello Jack, I said, doing a spot of work?

And Jack leaned on his shovel and grinned up at me. The trouble with Jack's grin is that it shows too many teeth. It's easy to pick they're not the real thing, and I've always thought they somehow don't fit in with the rest of him. Also his eyes are sky-blue, and it almost scares you to see them staring out of all that sunburn. I don't say *they* don't fit in though. They always have a bit of a crazy look about them, and even though Jack is my closest cobber I will say that he'll do some crazy things.

Yes Tom, he said, I'm doing a job.

But it's hot work, I said.

I've said it was scorching hot and it was. We'd been having a good summer, the first one after the war broke out. You'd hear folks say what lovely days we were having, and you'd be somehow always telling yourself you just couldn't believe there was any war on, when everything round about you looked so fine and dandy. But anyhow, I was just going to ask Jack if he wanted a hand, when his missis opened the back door and asked if I'd go in and have a cup of tea.

No thanks, Mrs Parker, I said, I've only just had one.

She didn't ask Jack, but he said he could do with one, so we both went inside and his missis had several of her friends there. She always has stacks of friends, and most times you'll find them around. But I'm Jack's friend, about the only one he has that goes to the house. I first ran across Jack in camp during the last war, though I only got to be cobbers with him a fair while after, when we lived at the same boardinghouse and worked at the same job, shovelling cement. In those days he hadn't started to trot the sheila he eventually married, though later on when he did I heard all about it. It knocked Jack over properly. He was always telling me about how she was far too good for him, a girl with her brains and refinement. Before she came out from England she'd been a governess, and I remember how Jack said she'd read more than ten books by an author called Hugh Walpole. Anyhow Jack was knocked over properly, and I reckon she must have been too. Or why did she marry him? As for me, I reckon it was because she did have the brains to tell a real man when she saw one, and hook on to him when she got the chance. But all that must be well over twenty years ago now, and it's always a wonder to me the way Jack still thinks his missis is the greatest kid that ever was, even though she couldn't make it plainer than she does, without a word said, that she's changed her mind about him. Not that you can altogether blame her of course. Just about any man, I should say, would find it awfully trying to be a woman married to Jack. But for a cobber you couldn't pick on a finer bloke.

One thing Mrs Parker's always had against Jack is that he's stayed working in the quarry year after year, instead of trying to get himself a better job. Meaning by a better job one that brings in more pay, without it mattering if it's only senseless and stupid sort of work you have to do. Of course, Jack knows that to run the house, with the snooks growing up fast, his missis could have always done with considerably more money than he's able to let her have. He lets her have the lot anyway, he never would smoke or drink or put money on a horse. But he isn't the sort that's got much show of ever being in the big money, and any case it would need to be pretty big, because his missis is always coming to light with some big ideas. Not to mention a car, one thing she's always on about is a refrigerator. It would save money in the long run is what she reckons, and maybe she's right, but it's always seemed too much of a hurdle to Jack.

Do you know dear, I heard him say once, when I was a little boy, and my mother opened the safe, and there was a blowfly buzzing about, it sometimes wouldn't even bother to fly inside.

And Mrs Parker said, What's a blowfly (or your mother for that matter) got to do with us having a refrigerator? And Jack went on grinning until she got cross and said, Well, why *wouldn't* it fly inside?

Because dear, Jack said, it knew it was no good flying inside.

And you could tell it annoyed his missis because she still couldn't work it out, but she wasn't going to let on by asking Jack to explain.

But I was telling about that Saturday afternoon when we went inside, and Jack had his cup of tea and I wouldn't have one.

Well, do sit down, Mrs Parker said to me, but I stayed standing. It sounds dirty I know, but I'd had years of experience behind me. I've only got a sort of polite interest in Jack's missis and those friends of hers. They're always talking about books and writers, but never any I know anything about. Henry Lawson now, that would be different. Though I've always remembered that name Hugh Walpole, and once I started one of his, I forget the name, but I never got past the first chapter. I only go there because I'm Jack's cobber, but Mrs Parker is a mighty good-looking woman, so I suppose she's always naturally expected everybody of the male sex to be more interested in her than in her old man. Everybody is anyhow, except me. But still she's never seemed satisfied. And with things that way I've usually always picked on fine weekends to go round and see Jack, because then the pair of us can work in the garden, and I don't have to listen to his missis all the time nipping at him. And times when it comes on wet I've usually shoved off, though sometimes we've gone and sat yarning on the camp stretcher in the little room off the back verandah where Jack sleeps. Jack mightn't have the brains that his missis has but he isn't dumb, and I've always liked to hear him talk. He's such a good-natured cuss, always wanting everything in the garden to be lovely for everybody that walks the earth, and he'll spout little pieces of poetry to show what he means. Years before the war broke out I was listening to him talking about the way things were going with the world, and saying what he thought was going to happen. After all, the pair of us had been in the last war, and I agreed when Jack said he could see it all coming again. And he had more to worry about than I had, because his eldest one was a colt. (I say was, because later on it was rotten to get the news from Italy about him.)

Anyhow, one reason I stayed standing when Mrs Parker asked me to sit down, was because I thought I'd get Jack back into the garden sooner if I didn't sit down. And although he grinned round at the company, looking awfully hairy and sweaty though not too naked on account of his dark colour, and even spouted one of his pieces of poetry (which his missis several times tried to interrupt), he was all the time gulping several cups of tea down hot, and I reckoned he had that hole he was digging on his mind, which as it turned out he had.

That hole!

It was right up against the wash-house wall, and we went out and looked at it, and Jack said it would take a lot of work but never mind. He said he hadn't thought about me giving him a hand, but

51

never mind that either. We could widen it another four feet so the pair of us could work there together. And he went and got the spade, and I began by taking the turf off the extra four feet, while Jack got down below again with the shovel.

Now I've known Jack a longer time than his missis has, so maybe that's the reason why I know it's never any good pestering him with straightout questions, because if you do you only get an answer back like the one I'd heard his missis get over the refrigerator. Only seeing Jack knows me pretty thoroughly, he'll probably make it a lot more difficult to work out than that one was. So if he wanted to dig a hole that was all right with me, and I thought if I just kept my mouth shut I'd find out in plenty of good time what he was digging it *for*. To begin with though, I don't know that I thought about it much at all. It was Jack's concern, and he didn't have to tell me.

But I admit it wasn't long before I began wondering. You see, when we finished up that Saturday afternoon Jack said we'd done a good job of work, but how about if I came round and we carried on one night during the week? And that was all right, I said for one night I could cut out taking a few bob off the lads that were learning to play billiards along at the room, and I'd make it Wednesday. And Wednesday after work I had my wash but didn't change out of my working clothes, and after dinner I got on my bike and went round to Jack's place and found him hard at it. Also it was easy to tell this wasn't the only night he'd been working because already by now it was a whopping great hole he was working in. Anyhow we had our usual yarn, then the pair of us got to work and kept on until it was too dark to see any more. And just about then Jack's missis came round the corner of the wash-house.

Whatever are you two boys doing? she wanted to know.

We've been working Mrs Parker, I said.

Yes, she said, but what are you digging that hole for?

You see dear, Jack said, some people say they don't like work, but what would we ever have if we didn't work? And now the war's on we've all got to do our share. Think of the soldier-boys. Fighting's hard work, and Tom and me want to do our bit as well.

But before he'd finished Mrs Parker had gone inside again. I was putting my bicycle clips on my trousers, but Jack was still down the hole, and he asked if I'd mind handing him down a box with a candle and matches that I'd see in the wash-house. I watched while he lit up and fixed the box so the light shone where he wanted to work. And for a few minutes I stayed watching, the shovel going in deep each time under his weight, the candle-light showing up the hollows and curves made by his big muscles, and the sweat making him look as if he was all covered with oil. I left him to it, but said I'd be round again Saturday afternoon, and going home I thought perhaps it was a septic tank he was putting in. Or was it an asparagus bed? Or was he going to set a grape vine. It was evidently going to be a proper job any way, whatever it was.

Well. The job went on for weeks. As far as I could make out Jack must have come home and worked at it every night until late. He didn't like taking time off to shift away the spoil from the edge, so that was the job I took on, and I must have shifted tons of the stuff down to the bottom of the garden in the wheelbarrow. Nor would Jack let me go down the hole any more, he said it was too dangerous, and it certainly looked like it. Because once he'd got down deep he started to under-cut in all directions, particularly on the wash-house side, which seemed pretty crazy to me. Once he struck rock, so brought some gelly home from the quarry and plugged a bit in and set it off, and it brought a lot of earth down on the wash-house side. Then he had to get to work and spend a lot of time rigging up props in case the blocks that were holding the wash-house up came through. I was hanged if I could get a line on what it was all about, and it was beginning to get me worried. His missis didn't ask any more questions, not while I was there anyhow, but I noticed she was getting round with a worried look, and I'd never felt that way before but I did feel a bit sorry for her then. About the only ones that got a kick out of the business were Jack's youngest snooks. The gelly he set off had been a real bit of fun for them, and they and their cobbers were always hanging around in the hope of another explosion. One that would finish off the wash-house, no doubt. Another thing was that for several weeks Jack hadn't done a tap of work in the garden, and one afternoon when Mrs Parker came out with cups of tea for us, she said he must be losing his eyesight if he couldn't see there was plenty just crying out to be done.

Yes dear, Jack said, in that good-natured sort of loving tone he always uses to her. Things being what they are between them, I can understand how it must make her want to knock him over the head. Yes dear, he said, but just now there are other things for Tom and me to do.

He was sitting on the edge of the hole, and after the strain of a long bout of shovelling his chest was going like a big pair of bellows worked by machinery. The day was another scorcher but blowy as well, and the dust had stuck to him, and run and caked, and stuck again, until about all you could see that was actually him was those eyes of his. And the bloodshot white and pure blue staring out of all that was something you almost couldn't bear to look at.

Yes dear, he repeated, we have other things to do.

And it was just then that half a dozen planes flying down quite low happened to suddenly come over. And of course we all of us stared up at them.

You see dear, Jack went on saying, though you could hardly hear him for the noise of the planes. You see dear, he said, we have more important things to do than those boys flying up there. Or at any rate, he went on, just as important.

But since we were watching the planes we didn't pay much attention to him. And it wasn't until they were nearly out of sight that I realised he'd disappeared down the hole again. You could tell he was there all right. The shovelfuls of spoil were coming flying up over the edge at a tremendous rate. And it was only afterwards, thinking it over, that I remembered what he'd been saying.

Well. This is the end of my yarn about Jack and the hole he dug. Next time I went round he was filling it in again, and he'd already got a fair bit done. All he said was that if he didn't go ahead and get his winter garden in he'd be having the family short of vegetables. And his missis had told him he'd got to do something about the hole because it was dangerous when there were kids about. So I took over wheeling the stuff up from the bottom of the garden, and Jack rammed it back in so tight that by the time he was up to ground level again there was practically nothing left over.

I must end up with a joke though. It was only a few summers later we had the Jap scare, and Jack earned a considerable amount of money digging shelters for people who were wanting them put in in a hurry, and weren't so particular how much they paid to get the work done. His missis appreciated the extra money, but she was always on to him to dig one for the family. All her friends agreed it was scandalous, the callous way he didn't seem to care if his own wife and children were all blown to bits!

As for me, I'm ready to stick up for Jack any time. Though I don't say his missis is making a mistake when she says that some day he'll end up in the lunatic asylum.

AFTER THE EARTHQUAKE

James Courage

The earthquake happened late on a Saturday night in summer and shook all that coast by the sea and the coastal farms and townships for twenty miles inland, as far as the mountains. At the Blakiston homestead everyone had gone to bed and was asleep, but the shake woke Mr Blakiston immediately. When it was over he sat up in bed, lit his candle, and looked about him at the bedroom walls and ceiling. Nothing seemed to be cracked or damaged, though the quake had been a sharp one and had heaved the house up for a moment or two and worried it as a dog worries a rabbit's pelt he cannot swallow.

'Are you all right?' Mr Blakiston asked his wife, who was now awake beside him in the double bed.

'Yes, dear, but you'd better find out if Walter's awake. The quake may have scared him.' She had been a good deal scared herself, waking from a dream of ships on the sea.

Her husband leaned up on one elbow, staring at the yellow candle-flame and listening so as to hear any sound from his son's room along the passage. Walter was six and had a room to himself near the head of the stairs.

'He'd call out if he'd been frightened,' said Mr Blakiston, hearing no sound in the house. He blew out the candle and lay back beside his wife. 'A nasty little quake, all the same,' he added. 'A hell of a nasty little quake.' Presently he was asleep again, lying on his back, snoring softly.

In the morning nothing was found damaged about the homestead, except for the old wash-house chimney, out at the back, which had collapsed on to the roof. Indoors, however, in Mr Blakiston's smoking-room, a thin china vase in which he kept hen-feathers for cleaning his pipe had fallen from the edge of the mantelpiece and shattered itself on the brick hearth. At breakfast-time he brought the pieces of the vase to the table, in his hand, to show his wife and son.

'English china,' he explained to the boy, pointing to a delicate capital D on what had been the base of the vase. 'You don't get fine stuff like that made in this corner of the world. D stands for Doulton, the people who fired it.'

But Walter was less interested by the vase than by the news of the earthquake which had not wakened him in the night. 'Did the whole house rock?' he asked his father.

'Rocked a bit, yes, and rose a bit.'

'Will the quake have shaken down any houses we know?'

'Not many, I should think. A few ceilings and chimneys down, maybe.'

Walter ate his porridge. 'I'd like to see an earthquake shake down a lot of houses,' he said presently, 'then all the people in them'd get a good fright.'

'Walter,' said his mother, who sat with her back to the windows, at the end of the table, 'you oughtn't to say things like that, without thinking first. It's very selfish.'

'I did think first,' said Walter softly, to his plate.

'What did you say?' asked his mother. 'You know I've told you not to mumble.'

'I only said I wished I'd wakened up in the earthquake,' he said loudly.

That day was a Sunday. Mr Blakiston was a farmer and though there are jobs to be done on a farm all seven days of the week he usually spent Sundays near the homestead and in the home stables and paddocks, resting himself. On one Sunday out of every four the family went to church in the township below the hills of the farm. Today, however, Mr Blakiston, willingly helped by Walter, put on an old dungaree suit and set to to clear the bricks from the roof of the wash-house, where the chimney had fallen in the night.

Walter always had questions to ask when he worked with his father. 'Do earthquakes happen in England?' he demanded.

'Yes,' said Mr Blakiston shortly, 'but not often.' He was a practical man, enjoying the manual work, and slightly bored by the way his son always wanted to talk. The breaking of the vase that held his pipe-cleaners, the vase of English china, had taken his thoughts back to the Old Country and he would have preferred to think about it in silence.

He had farmed in New Zealand for nearly twenty years but he still thought of England as home, his father's country, the original pattern. Colonial life was freer, less stiff, he liked it better, nevertheless something of the subtle flavour of the English way of living on which it had originally been founded was vanishing fast. The new climate was changing it, adapting its laws and forms to a younger society. And he himself had changed, and was changing, with it.

Now, as he worked at heaving bricks from the wash-house roof to the ground, he realised that he would never go back to England, as he had once intended to. He was a colonial farmer for life. He was as pleased as though he himself, and not the years, had made the decision.

'Can I drive to the township with Mum in the morning?' asked Walter, beside him on the roof.

'Yes, if you want to. Ask her yourself. Now get down that ladder and pile those bricks by the wall, shipshape.'

The following morning at eleven o'clock Mrs Blakiston had the horse and gig brought round to the front door by the odd-jobs man who was also the cowman and gardener at the homestead. Every fine week-day at eleven, wearing a flat grey hat with a veil tied under her chin, she drove to the township, four miles away, to collect the mail and the newspaper and to shop at the store. Summer or winter, she wore long elegant leather gloves to hold the reins.

On this Monday morning Walter went with her, happily hopping down from the gig to open the gates on the road as they came to them. On either side of the road lay wide flat paddocks of tussock-grass, divided by wire fences and burnt yellow by the sun. In the distance, in the summer haze, a mirage of heat flickered along the ridges of the hills. The blue reflection of the sea was on the sky.

When they reached the township, Mrs Blakiston drove the gig along the straggling street of one- and two-storeyed buildings and pulled up before the verandah of Lakin's General Store.

'Can I go in?' asked Walter, preparing to jump down.

'Mr Lakin will be out in a moment,' said his mother. She opened her purse and found the list of groceries she wanted. 'We'll wait till he comes.'

Presently the storekeeper, wearing a white apron, came out from the shop door under the verandah. He shaded his eyes against the morning glare and looked up at the gig. 'Glad to see you're all right after the quake, Mrs Blakiston,' he said in a high tinny voice.

'I'm very well, Mr Lakin, but it did frighten us a little, so late at night. Did you have any damage?'

'I slept through it, myself. A few broken bottles on the floor of the shop yesterday morning, though.'

Mrs Blakiston handed over her list. 'Have you heard about old Mrs Duncaster?' asked the storekeeper.

'Heard about her?' Mrs Blakiston was uncertain.

'The quake brought the plaster of the ceiling down on her. She died of shock, they say, early yesterday.'

'Oh, but what a dreadful thing, Mr Lakin – ' said Mrs Blakiston. Walter saw her face tighten and her lips twitch in the sunlight. 'I'd no idea – '

57

'Well, it was a sudden end,' said the storekeeper, looking vaguely up the street. 'I thought I'd better tell you,' he added. 'I don't like my old customers dying.'

'Yes,' said Mrs Blakiston. 'Thank you, Mr Lakin. I hadn't heard about it, of course. I'll go and call on Miss Duncaster this morning.'

The storekeeper nodded and disappeared into the shop, Mrs Blakiston's list in his hand.

'The Mrs Duncaster who's dead,' said Walter, 'is she the one I know?'

'Yes,' said his mother. 'I'd no notion,' she added quietly. 'Yesterday being Sunday, of course, we didn't hear.'

'Did the roof fall right on her face in bed?' 'I don't know, Walter. Don't ask silly questions. You heard what Mr Lakin said.'

'If she'd been properly under the blankets the plaster wouldn't have hit her.'

'She was very old. It's very sad that she's dead,' said Mrs Blakiston. She tilted his sun-hat down over his eyes and made him sit up straight on the hot leather seat of the gig.

'Are we going to visit Miss Duncaster?' he asked, after a moment.

'Yes, we must go and see her. She was very fond of her mother.'

After Mr Lakin had put a tin of biscuits, a bottle of methylated spirits and some smaller parcels into the back of the gig, under the seat, Mrs Blakiston drove up the street to the post office and collected the mail and the newspaper. She then drove straight to the northern end of the township, where the Duncasters lived in one of the oldest homes in the district.

Made of cob and with a wooden roof, the small squat cottage was hidden by pine and eucalyptus trees from the road. Inside the fringe of trees a lawn of wild hay-like grass, burnt almost red by the sun, bordered the short curving driveway that led up to the verandah.

'Somebody else is here too,' said Walter. He pointed to a saddled horse hitched by the bridle-reins to a hook in one of the verandah posts. The horse was a bay, roughly groomed and shaggy, a farmer's hack.

Mrs Blakiston looked at the horse for a moment as she drove up, then, carefully holding her long skirt, got down from the gig, and knocked at the door of the cottage. She knocked twice, in the hot summer silence, before the door was opened by a tall woman wearing a dark grey dress with a white lace collar.

Walter watched his mother greet Miss Duncaster and kiss her on the cheek. He had hoped that Miss Duncaster might have tears in her eyes for a mother killed in an earthquake: he was disappointed

58

that the light blue eyes and the long pink cheeks of Annie Duncaster looked as ordinary as ever.

'You must come in and have tea,' said Miss Duncaster's deep voice to his mother. 'And Walter with you. Please, please do. I'd like it.'

'But you have a visitor already,' hesitated Mrs Blakiston.

Miss Duncaster threw a quick glance at the saddled horse swishing its tail before the verandah. 'Nobody's here,' she said. 'Nobody at all. Do please come in.'

So Mrs Blakiston took the gig into the shade of the eucalyptus trees, tied up the horse, and took Walter with her into the cottage. 'You must be quiet,' she whispered to the boy in the doorway, 'and not ask questions.'

The inside of the cottage was dark and smelt cool after the hot morning. The tiny sitting-room behind the verandah was made even smaller by the glass cases of china and the shelves of books against the walls. A large, creamy-white ostrich egg hung by a string in a corner, by far the most interesting thing, to Walter, in the whole room. When Miss Duncaster had brought in the tea, he sat himself down so that he could gaze at this amazing egg while his mother talked.

'I've only just heard about your mother, Annie,' said Mrs Blakiston. 'I'm so very sorry.'

'Mother hated earthquakes,' Miss Duncaster said evenly. 'We had a bad one here, you know, just after father and she had first come from England. She'd always been frightened of them since then.'

'They frighten me too. Did your mother die quite suddenly?'

'A little of the ceiling fell, you know, in her room. I got her out of bed and into a chair and ran downstairs to make her a cup of tea. When I got back she was dead.' Miss Duncaster put down her cup and gazed out of the window. 'It was all a great shock. The earthquake itself and then my mother dead.'

'I slept all through the earthquake,' put in Walter, 'didn't I, Mum?' Mrs Blakiston ran her fingers over the gloves in her lap. 'Yes, dear, luckily,' she said.

Miss Duncaster, who had begun to sniffle, suddenly cheered up and said, 'Of course, my mother was no longer a young woman. Still, even at sixty, one likes to live. And she had had a wonderful life, you know. Young people like me can't hope for nearly so much.'

'Yes, Annie, I know,' said Mrs Blakiston, who knew also that old Mrs Duncaster had been seventy if she'd been a day and that her daughter was thirty-five. 'It is hard for you, being left alone,' she added.

Miss Duncaster got up, fumbling in her belt for her handkerchief. 'Oh, thank you, thank you. But I shan't let myself be lonely.' She glanced quickly out of the window, then moved to the door. 'I'd like you to come and see my mother now,' she said. 'She's lying upstairs in father's old room. She looks beautiful.'

'Yes, of course I'll come up,' said Mrs Blakiston. 'Walter, you stay down here for a few minutes.'

'Oh, but I want Walter to see her too,' said Miss Duncaster. 'She always loved children, you know.'

The stairs were almost as narrow as a ladder and so dark that Miss Duncaster lit a candle to usher the boy and his mother round the stair-head and along the upper passage. The air, close under the roof, was as warm as the inside of a bird's nest.

'In here,' said Miss Duncaster, opening a door. She made Mrs Blakiston and Walter go in first, while she blew out the candle.

The small bedroom was crowded with dark furniture and lit only by a window in the slope of the roof. The bed was against the wall by the door, and on the bed, covered by a sheet up to her chin, lay the dead Mrs Duncaster. Walter was startled: the creamy-white, oval face was like the ostrich-egg downstairs, he thought, except that somebody had pinched into it a nose and mouth and drawn a grim line down each cheek. He hadn't remembered that old Mrs Duncaster looked so severe: she had always laughed at him and given him jujubes.

On a table at the head of the bed stood a vase full of green leaves and large open milky flowers that gave out a thick smell of lemons into the room.

'Magnolias,' said Mrs Blakiston gently, her head on one side. She loved flowers. 'Beautiful,' she added.

'I picked them from the garden,' said Miss Duncaster. 'Mother planted the tree the year I was born. It has grown up with me. I felt she'd like to have the flowers beside her now.'

'Yes,' said Mrs Blakiston, 'yes, Annie, of course.'

Walter turned aside from the bed to look at a box made of dark polished wood. It stood on the floor by the window, with brass handles and a lock of inlaid steel.

'That was father's instrument case,' explained Miss Duncaster, beside him. 'He was a doctor, you know – the first doctor the district had. All his scalpels and things are in that box.'

'Did he come from England?' asked Walter.

'A long time ago, in a sailing-ship, with my mother. Mother was homesick all her life for England, but she didn't go back, even when father died.'

At that moment Walter saw that one of old Mrs Duncaster's hands was showing under the edge of the sheet on the bed and that the hand held a book with an animal of some sort printed in gold on the black cover. 'What's that?' he asked, pointing.

'My mother's Bible,' said Miss Duncaster.

'No, I meant the – '

'Oh, the crest on the cover? That's a griffin, my mother's family crest. She was proud of that.' Miss Duncaster sighed, and added, to Walter's mother: 'I never knew any of the English family, of course. They meant nothing to me. I'm a colonial.' She pulled the sheet over the dead hand and straightened the magnolias in their vase by the bed. 'The funeral is the day after tomorrow,' she finished in a firm voice.

Presently they went downstairs. Mrs Blakiston said that she and Walter must be going home.

'You have been so kind,' said Miss Duncaster, smoothing her fair, fluffy hair. She seemed to be looking round the sitting-room for something to give them as a reward. 'Wait now and I'll cut you some magnolias from the garden, before you go. Yes, let me.'

The huge magnolia tree, with dark leaves shining in the sun and with white flowers high up like sea-birds in the branches, grew at the back of the house. While Mrs Blakiston and Walter stood and watched, Miss Duncaster made big agile leaps to get at the flowering branches. She dragged them down and broke off the creamy heads, careful not to bruise the petals.

'They go brown so easily,' she explained. She laughed, with flushed and untidy face, handing over the bouquet to Walter. 'He's amazed I can jump so high,' she said to Mrs Blakiston, laughing again, this time at the boy's face.

'I only jump like that when I'm jumping for joy,' said Walter. 'Don't I, Mum? I can jump a hell of a height.'

'What did I hear you say, Walter?'

He had picked up the bad expression from his father. 'I can jump as high as my belt,' he amended softly, swinging the bunch of magnolias in his hand.

They walked round to the front of the house. While Mrs Blakiston went into the shade of the trees to fetch the gig, Walter was left with Miss Duncaster. He looked round and saw that the riding horse that had been tied to the verandah post was no longer there.

'Where's the horse gone?' he asked.

'What a funny boy you are,' said Miss Duncaster. 'What horse?'

He pointed with the magnolias. 'It was over by the verandah,' he said. 'We saw it.'

61

Miss Duncaster bent down and gave him a sudden sharp slap on the arm. 'You're bruising the flowers,' she snapped. 'There was no horse.'

Mrs Blakiston drove up with the gig. 'Come along, Walter. Say goodbye nicely to Miss Duncaster.'

On the way home from the township with his mother, Walter said: 'I didn't ask too many questions, did I?'

'No,' said his mother doubtfully, 'not as many as I expected.'

'Then why did she slap me?'

'I don't believe she did. You invent such things.'

That evening when Mr Blakiston came in from the farm to a late tea he glanced at the big bowl of magnolias in the middle of the dining-room table.

'Not ours, are they?' he asked.

'No.' His wife told him of their morning visit to the Duncasters and of Mrs Duncaster's death in the earthquake. While she talked she fiddled on the table with the broken pieces of the vase of English china that had held her husband's pipe-cleaners and that had fallen during the night. She was sticking them together with glue. Walter, his own tea finished, watched her and listened to her talking.

'Of course it's terrible for Annie, being left alone in that old cottage,' he heard her say presently to his father, 'though I must say she seemed very brave about it.'

'Brave?' Mr Blakiston paused. 'I should think she's damn well delighted! For ten years and more she's been cooped up at home looking after that old woman. She'll have a chance to marry now.'

'I don't think she's the marrying kind.'

'Don't you believe it. I hear more than you do.'

'Does Joe Sleaver ride a bay horse?' Walter put in suddenly.

Mr Blakiston looked surprised. He took his pipe from between his lips and studied the bowl of it before answering. 'Yes,' he said, 'now I come to think of it, he does ride a bay.'

'Walter,' interposed Mrs Blakiston warningly to the boy, 'you know what I said to you today, about not asking questions, don't you?'

'I only meant – ' began Walter, and stopped.

'I wish,' said Mr Blakiston, 'I wish I knew what the devil you were both talking about. Why shouldn't Joe Sleaver ride a bay horse if he wants to?'

'Walter thinks he saw a bay horse tied up to the Duncasters' verandah this morning,' explained Mrs Blakiston.

'I did see it,' cried Walter. 'Mum saw it too!'

His father and mother exchanged a glance. Then, with his pipe in his mouth, Mr Blakiston leaned forward and lightly took up from the table a piece of the vase his wife was mending. 'Well,' he said offhandedly, grinning as he spoke, 'well, we don't have earth-quakes every night.'

'I did see the horse,' insisted Walter, and felt that like all older people his parents were in some sort of conspiracy against his finding things out. 'I did see the horse.'

'Of course you saw the damned horse,' said his father suddenly. 'Shut up about it, that's all.' And he went on, to his wife, evenly: 'I was thinking yesterday, you know, I shall probably never go back to the Old Country. It's too far away now, too long ago.'

THE QUIET ONE

Dan Davin

The band concert was over and three of us came out of the Regent into Dee Street with the rest of the crowd.

'I could swear she gave me the eye,' Sid said.

'I'll bet she did,' Wally said. 'One look'd be all she'd need, too. Who did, anyway?'

'That sheila with the black hat on that was in front of us about two seats away. You'd be too busy looking at the statue of the naked Greek dame to notice, I expect. Anyhow she was just in front of me when we were coming out and when I pushed the swing door open for her she turned round and gave me a real grin. Look, there she goes.'

He pointed the way we were going, and, sure enough, we could see a black hat bobbing along a bit in front where the crowd wasn't so thick.

'Come on, boys,' said Wally, 'Here we go.'

'But, look here,' I said, 'I thought we were going to the Greek's.' All the same, I changed my pace to keep up with theirs.

'To hell with the Greek's. Who wants to be sitting down to eggs and chips when there's a chance of picking up a sheila, eh, Sid?'

Sid just grunted. You couldn't see the girl because of the crowd and he was staring straight down the footpath, towards where we'd last seen her. You wouldn't have needed to know him as well as I did to guess from the sour way his mouth was closed that he didn't fancy the shape things were taking much. Wally was a tiger for the girls, and a good-looking joker, too. And old Sid hadn't had the same confidence in himself since the dentist made him have all his top teeth out. Wally didn't give him much chance to forget about it, either, calling him Gummy all the evening.

Not that there was anything in it for me, anyway. If there was only one girl I wouldn't be the chap who got her, that was certain. And, as a matter of fact, though I'd have been the last to say so, I'd have been scared stiff if there'd been the least danger of me being the one. I never really knew why I tagged along with them those Sunday evenings. I must have hoped some sort of miracle would happen, I suppose, and that some sheila or other would fall for me and put me into a position where one move had to follow the other

64

in such a way that my mind'd be made up for me. At the same time I was terrified that just that would happen, knowing in advance that at close quarters with a girl I'd be like a cow with a musket. Anyhow, I needn't have worried. Nothing ever did happen and by this time I think I was getting to realise, only I wouldn't admit it, that nothing ever would.

That didn't stop me, though, from putting off going home till the last possible moment in case some sort of miracle turned up and when I finally left Wally or Sid at Rugby Park corner of a Saturday or Sunday night I'd trudge the rest of the way home in the rain or the moonlight, cursing myself and the town and everything in it and wondering what the hell was the matter with me, whether I was a different breed or what, and why it was always me that was left, and thinking that in some other country somewhere things mightn't be like that at all and people would see what I really was instead of what I'd always been.

So, with all that at the back of my mind, and Wally rampaging alongside with about as many afterthoughts as a dog has after a rabbit, and Sid on the other side getting down in the mouth already at the thought that Wally was going to pinch his girl, I didn't think much of the night's prospects. The upshot'd be that Wally would get her all right and I'd have to spend what was left of the evening at the Greek's trying to cheer Sid up by encouraging him to skite about all the girls that had fallen for him and pretending not to notice how much Wally going off with this one had got under his skin.

Well, after a bit the crowd got thinner and most of them started to cross over to where the last tram was waiting, towards the Majestic side. So we could see better what was in front of us. And there was the girl all right, about twenty yards ahead, all by herself into the bargain, and pacing along at a fair bat. Good legs she had, too.

'I reckon she knows we're following her,' Wally said. 'The trouble is, there's too many of us.'

'That's right, Wally.'

It was very sarcastic the way Sid said it but that didn't worry Wally.

'Go on, Sid,' he said, 'don't be a dog in the manger. A fair fight and let the best man win, eh?'

Of course, that was just the trouble, the way Sid looked at it. It's always the best man who says these things.

Anyhow, before Sid could think of an answer, or before he could think of something that wouldn't have given away he knew he hadn't a hope against Wally whatever kind of fight it was, the girl started to cross the road and so, us too, we changed course like a school of sprats and over the road after her, only about ten yards behind by this time.

She stepped up on to the footpath on the opposite side of the road, us tagging behind like three balloons on a string. She looked behind just then and saw us.

'Now's our chance,' Sid said, getting quite excited and nervous, I could tell.

Wally didn't say anything but he took advantage of his long legs and he was up on the pavement a good yard in front of us.

It was darker on the footpath because of the shop verandahs and because the nearest street-lamp was a good distance away. At first I couldn't see what was happening, owing to the notion I had that if I wore my glasses when we were out on the pick up on nights like this I'd spoil my chances, such as they were; but I felt both Wally and Sid check. And then I saw what it was. The girl had stepped into a shop doorway and there was a chap there waiting for her.

The girl and her bloke came out of the doorway and walked off towards the other end of Dee Street, her hanging on his arm and talking a blue streak and laughing the way we could tell the joke was on us. And the bloke looked back, once as if he'd like to have come at us. But, seeing Wally and thinking he had the trumps anyway, I suppose, he turned round again and kept on going.

'Well, I'm damned,' Wally said.

'Foiled again,' Sid said. But he didn't sound narked at all, really, and I knew by his voice he'd sooner have had it that way so that the laugh was on Wally instead of on himself as it would have been if things had gone differently.

I was pleased, too, for that matter, though I couldn't help envying that bloke a bit with a good-looking girl on his arm and a nice new blue overcoat and Borsalino and never a doubt in his head as to where he was going and what he'd do when he got there.

Still, envying him made it easier to pretend I meant it when I cursed the girl up hill and down dale like the others. For it wouldn't have done for me to show I was really relieved. It was sort of understood that even if I didn't mean business like Wally and Sid I had to go through the motions just the same. They really weren't bad blokes in a way, Wally and Sid, because they knew all the time I wasn't a serious competitor and yet they always treated me as if I was, thinking I'd be hurt if they didn't, I suppose.

And I would have been hurt, too. Somehow, if there hadn't been this kind of agreement about the way we were all to behave, I'd have had to drop the game altogether. I could tell that, because when, as happened sometimes, other blokes joined us who didn't know the rules or didn't care if there were any and they began to pull my leg, I always pushed off after a while. Which was what these other chaps wanted, I expect. 'The Wet Napkin', I heard one of them, Ginger Foyle it was, say once after I'd gone and he didn't think I could hear him, because I hadn't got my glasses on, perhaps.

No, Wally and Sid weren't like that, especially Wally. They knew I was all right once you got to know me and, besides, I used to be able to make them laugh when we were by ourselves and get them to see the funny side of things they'd never have noticed if it hadn't been for me.

Well, anyway, there we were left standing in the middle of Dee Street and all cursing our heads off in the same way.

'Nothing for it but to go over to the Greek's,' I said.

'Listen to him, will you, Sid,' Wally said. 'Him and his bloody Greek's. And us all whetted up for a bite of something tastier than old Harry could ever put under our noses.'

I felt a fool immediately, because I might have known that was the wrong thing to say, the way they were feeling. Once Wally had got the idea of skirt into his head it wasn't easy to put him off. And Sid, for all I don't think he really liked Wally, would trail along with him all right, knowing that was his best chance. That was what fascinated him about Wally, he could always have what Wally didn't want. But it was what made him hate Wally's guts, too.

Besides, I suppose they felt I'd sort of broken the rules by not being keen enough and waiting a bit longer before giving up what we all knew was a bad job.

'Well, what'll we do now, Wally?' Sid said.

'Let's take a stroll as far as the Civic and back,' I chipped in, trying to establish myself again. 'You never know, we might pick up something.'

'That's more like it,' Wally said. And then, because he wasn't a bad bloke, a better chap in many ways than Sid would ever be, he added: 'After all, if there's nothing doing, we can always go over to have a feed at the Greek's later on.' Which showed he wasn't really fooled by what I'd said.

So away we went, down past the Majestic where Len Parry and Alec Haynes and all that bunch were as usual, pretending they were talking about who was going to win the Ranfurly Shield when all they were interested in really was the girls who kept scuttling by on their way back from the band concert. I took a look at the Town Clock on the other side as we went by and there it was, half-past ten already, one more Sunday evening just about over and nothing happening, only the same old thing. Already everyone who had anywhere to go was going there and soon the only people left in the streets would be chaps like us who couldn't think of anything better to do and soon we'd be gone home too and the streets would be empty and another night would be gone out of a man's life and him none the wiser one way or the other.

'Was that your cousin Marty I saw all by himself in the doorway next that bloke who met the sheila, Ned?' Sid suddenly asked.

'I didn't notice.'

'It was him all right, poor bastard,' Wally said.

I pricked up my ears at that. My cousin Marty wasn't the sort of chap you talked about with that particular tone in your voice. He was rather a big shot in the eyes of our crowd. A good five or six years older than any of us, he must have been twenty-two or twenty-three, and he used to earn good money before the slump. A plasterer he was, by trade. But he'd been one of the first to be turned off when things got tough because, though he was good at his job, he had a terrible temper and was too handy with his fists. A big joker, he was, with reach and height, and they used to say that if only he'd do a bit more training there wasn't a pro in the business he couldn't have put on his back for the count. As it was he'd made quite a name for himself round the town as a fighter and once when I was at the barber's and got fed up with the way slick little Basset kept taking me for granted because I didn't know what was going to win the Gore Cup I'd managed to get in casually that Marty was my cousin and after that Basset could never do enough for me.

'What do you mean, "poor bastard"?' Sid was saying.

'Didn't you hear? The trouble with you, Sid, is you never hear anything now you've got your teeth out.'

'Come on, come on, know-all. What's it all about?'

'Yes, what was it, Wally?' I asked; for I could tell Wally was wishing he'd kept his mouth shut, knowing Marty was my cousin.

'Well, it's only what they're saying, Ned, and there mightn't be anything in it, though I have noticed Marty hasn't been about much lately. You know how you'd always see him and Dulcie Moore round together of a Saturday and Sunday night?'

'That's right,' Sid said, glad to get in on the inside again. 'I saw them coming out of the Rose Gardens about two in the morning the night of Ginger Foyle's keg-party and they were always at the Waikiwi dances together.'

'Well, they say he put her up the spout. And then he got some old dame who hangs out in Georgetown to fix her up. Of course, that's happening all the time all over the place, you know, and nobody ever thinks a thing about it as long as no one gets caught.' This was for me. 'But the trouble this time was that something went wrong and she got blood-poisoning or something, and now

68

she's in hospital and they say the johns have been at her all the time beside her bed trying to find out who did it and who was the man. But so far she won't say and the odds are she won't pull through.'

'Jesus,' said Sid. 'I thought he looked a bit down in the mouth.'

'Wouldn't you be?'

'But, look here, Wally,' I said, 'who told you all this?'

'I heard Marty's crowd, Jim Fergus and all that lot, talking about it yesterday after the game. And when I was shaving in the bathroom this morning and they didn't know I was there, I heard Mum telling the old man about it. It was her that told that bit about her not being expected to live.'

We'd got as far as the Civic and turned back by this time and the crowd was getting very thin by now, everybody making for home, feeling much the way I'd been feeling, I expect, that they might as well be in bed as hanging round. Only I didn't feel like that any more. Things happened, sure enough, and even to people you knew, even to your own family, near enough.

Sid and Wally kept talking about it all the way back up Tay Street. It was queer the way they seemed to get a sort of pleasure out of discussing it. And what was queerer still was that I liked hearing them talk about it. It must have been partly how old we were and partly the town we lived in. You felt the place wasn't quite such a dead-alive hole, after all, and you felt you really were grown up when things like that, terrible things but things all the same, happened to people you even knew.

Anyhow, just as we got to the Bank corner, two girls came round it the opposite way and we almost banged into them. While we were dodging around them to let them pass and show what gentlemen we were they cut through between me and Wally and we could hear them giggling as they went on.

'Sorry,' Wally called back in an extra-polite voice I hardly recognised, he could put on the gyver so well when he wanted to.

'Don't mention it,' one of the girls said and giggled again.

We stopped at that and Sid made a great show of lighting cigarettes for us while we all had a good dekko back to see what the girls were up to.

'They've stopped in the doorway next the jewellers,' Wally said. 'Come on, Sid, here we go. We're home and dry.' He was so excited he forgot to pretend I was in on it, too.

The two of them cut back the way we'd come, like a couple of whippets at first and then as they got closer with a sort of elaborate stroll as if they might just as well be walking that way as any other. I followed after them, trying to catch up and yet not to catch up. I knew I ought to have gone away. There was no good just tagging on, being a nuisance. But I kept following, all the same.

'Hello,' Wally was saying as I came up to the doorway. 'Going anywhere?'

'What's that got to do with you?' the girl who had called back to us said.

'Well,' Sid said, 'it's getting late for girls to be out by themselves with all the roughs there are about this time of night and we thought you might like to have an escort on the way home.'

Sid could always talk well when it came to the pinch, especially if he had Wally with him. I of course couldn't say a thing, being as nervous as a cat, although I knew already that it didn't matter much what I did, me being only the spare part.

'You know what thought did,' the girl said.

'Come on, Isobel,' the other girl said. 'It's getting late.'

'Will you have a cigarette, Isobel?' Wally said. And he took out his case. It was the one he kept his tailor-mades in, not the one he used for home-rolled ones and butts. In that light you'd have taken it for silver.

'Don't mind if I do.'

'Come on, Isobel,' the other girl said again.

'Now, Jean, don't be an old fusspot. There's heaps of time really. Why don't you have a cigarette, too.'

'That's right,' Wally said, and so Jean took one from the case, a bit nervously, I thought.

'We don't even know your names, do we, Jean?' said Isobel when Sid had flourished his lighter for them. You could see them trying to get a look at us while the flame was there. But of course we had our backs to the street-lights and they couldn't have made out much what we looked like.

'That's easy,' Wally said then. 'I'll introduce us. My name's Wally Radford and this is my friend Sid, Sid Cable. And this is Ned.'

'He's a quiet one, isn't he?' Isobel gave Jean a nudge and giggled at me.

I tried to think of something very witty to say, the sort of thing that would have come to Wally or Sid in a flash. But I couldn't think of anything at all and I could feel myself blushing. I hated that Isobel then. It was always the good-looking ones that made me feel most of a fool. The other one, Jean, I didn't mind so much because I could tell by her way of giggling that she was nervous, too. She wasn't anything like such a good-looker, though.

There was a bit of a silence then. They were all waiting for me to say something. When I still didn't say anything I felt them all just give me up. Wally got into the doorway close to Isobel and tried to get his arm round her. She kept fending him off and looking at him and then at Jean in a way that said as plain as a pikestaff: Wait till afterwards when we can get away by ourselves.

Sid was talking a blue streak to Jean so as to give her a chance to get over her shyness, I suppose, and to shut me out of it and make me see I was being the gooseberry, in case I didn't see it already.

There was nothing to do but leave them to it. I was only holding Wally and Sid back from doing their stuff, hanging round like that.

'Well, I must be getting along,' I said.

'Why don't you come with us?' Jean said. Her voice sounded quite scared. But I could tell Sid wasn't going to get anywhere with her and I wasn't going to have her use me as an excuse to keep him off and then have him putting the blame on me next day.

'I'd like to,' I said, 'but I live up the other end of the town.'

'OK, Ned, good night,' Wally said in an offhand sort of way and Sid said good night too, in the friendly voice he always used when you were doing something he wanted you to do. That was one of the things Sid liked about me, that I always did the expected thing. It wasn't one of the things I liked about him.

So I set off by myself up towards the Bank corner again, feeling like a motherless foal, as the old man would have said. I thought I'd better give them plenty of time to get clear and so I decided I'd walk a few blocks up Dee Street and back again.

The Town Clock was pointing to nearly eleven by now. All the crowd that'd been in front of the Majestic was gone and Dee Street was as empty as the tomb except for a bobby standing in the library doorway over the other side, just in case there should be a row at the Greek's, I expect.

Seeing the Greek's lighted windows gave me the idea of going in for a feed, after all. But it was pretty late and I couldn't face going in there all by myself, with the blokes eyeing me and guessing what had happened. So I crossed Esk Street and went straight on up.

But it wasn't nearly so bad being by yourself when the whole street was empty like that and you didn't have to wonder what people were thinking about you. I quite liked striding along under the shop verandahs as if I were going nowhere in a hurry and listening to my heels hammer on the asphalt and seeing my reflection pass dark on the windows. It was better feeling miserable by yourself and not having to put up a show any more. Or else the kind of show you put up when there was no one but yourself to watch was more convincing.

'Hullo, Ned.'

I stopped in my tracks and looked round to see where the voice

71

came from. Then I saw him. He was in the same doorway that the sheila had met her bloke in earlier on. He was standing there, all stiff like a sentry, and in that light you'd have thought his eyes were black they were so dark. A Spaniard, he might have been, with the long sideboards halfway down his cheeks and his straight, thin nose, that had never been broken for all the boxing he'd done.

'Hullo, Marty,' I said.

He didn't say any more, just went on looking at me. I didn't know quite what to do because it struck me it was probably only the suddenness of seeing someone he knew that had made him call out and probably he wished he hadn't now. Besides, knowing what I did, I felt uncomfortable.

I went up to him all the same, not knowing how to get away without it looking awkward and as if I'd heard about his trouble and was dodging off so as not to be seen with him.

'Have a cigarette,' I said and I produced a packet of ten Capstan.

'Thanks.'

I lit them for us both and when that was over there I was still stuck and unable to think of anything else to say. The only things that came into my head sounded quite hopeless compared with the things he must have on his mind.

'All the crowd gone home?' I said in the end, for lack of anything better.

'Suppose so,' he answered and took a puff of the cigarette. Then he added in a voice so savage that it gave me a real fright. 'Who the hell cares what they've done? Pack of bastards.'

I didn't say anything. I was trying to work out what he meant by that. Had they done the dirty on him and talked to the johns? Or was he just fed up with them?

He gave me a look just then, the first time he'd really looked at me since I stopped.

'You've heard all about it, I suppose?'

That stumped me properly. I didn't want him to get the idea the whole town was talking about him. Especially as that was what they were probably doing. I was scared of him, too. He'd be a bad bloke to say the wrong thing to.

'Heard about what?'

'You know.' He'd guessed by the time I took to answer. 'About Dulcie.'

There was no good pretending. 'Yes,' I said. 'How is she?'

He didn't answer but he kept on looking at me in the same queer way that he had been looking at me before. And then, as if he'd been sizing me up, he got down to what was on his mind.

'Look here, Ned,' he said. 'What about doing something for me?'

'All right,' I said. 'What do you want me to do?' My heart was in my boots because I didn't know much about the law but I felt sure this was going to be something against it.

'It's like this. I can't ring the hospital to see how she is because the johns are there and they keep asking me my name and they know my voice, too. What about you ringing for me?'

'All right, Marty,' I said. 'But what'll I say if they ask who I am? If I give my name they might come poking about home trying to find out what I know about it.'

'Say your name's Eddie Sharp. That's a friend of her young brother's and it'd be quite natural for him to ring. Will you do it?'

'I'll just see if I've got any pennies.'

We walked back towards the Post Office square. But the john was still in the library doorway and so I told Marty to go back to the place where I'd met him and wait for me there.

The john gave me that hard look that policemen give you but I went straight past him without giving a sign of how nervous I was. It was being so sorry for Marty that made me able to do it, I think.

'Southland Hospital,' a woman's voice answered when I'd got the number.

'I want to inquire about a patient, Miss Moore, Miss Dulcie Moore.'

'Will you hold on, please?'

There was a lot of clicking at the other end and I could hear whispering. Then a man's voice answered.

'The patient died an hour ago. Who is that speaking?'

I didn't answer. I just rang off and came out of the phone box.

How was I going to tell him, I kept asking myself as I went back past the john, hardly noticing him this time.

Marty was standing in the doorway, just as he had been the first time.

'How was she?'

There was nothing else I could do. I out with it.

'She died an hour ago.'

He stood there without saying a thing, just looking at me and yet not seeing me. Then he took a deep breath and his chest came out and he stood even straighter.

'So that's how it is,' he said. 'She's dead.'

I didn't say anything. I just stood there, wishing I was anywhere else in the world.

'If only I'd known,' he said. 'Christ, man. I'd have married her a hundred times, kid and all.'

He stopped. His mind must have been going over and over this ground for days.

73

He gave a laugh suddenly, such a queer, savage sort of a laugh that I jumped.

'If it d been twins, even,' he said.

I had enough sense not to think that I was meant to laugh at that one.

'And those bloody johns sitting by the bed.'

'Did she come to?' I asked.

'Yes, she was conscious a lot of the time. But she wouldn't talk, not Dulcie. Not her. She was all right, Dulcie.'

Then there was silence again. I didn't know what to do or say. It was getting late. They'd have locked the door at home and there'd be a rumpus if they knew what time it was when I came in. How queer it was: here I was in the middle of something that really mattered and worrying about what my mother would say if she heard me climbing in the window.

All the same I wanted to get home. And then I had to admit to myself it wasn't really that. It was that I wanted to get away from Marty. I think it must have been the first time I was ever with someone who felt as badly as he was feeling.

'I remember her,' I said. 'She was a stunner to look at.'

'Wasn't she?' Marty said. And the way he said it made the tears come into my eyes.

'Why don't you walk my way?' I asked him. If he did that I could be making towards home and at the same time wouldn't feel I was ratting on him.

'No, I'm not going home yet,' he said.

I shuffled from one foot to the other, wondering what to do next and a bit worried what he would do after I'd gone.

'We always used to meet here,' he said. 'In this doorway.'

'Oh,' I said. 'Well, look here, Marty, I've got to be getting home now.'

'That's all right.'

I tried to think of some way of saying how sorry I was. But there was no way of saying it.

'Good night, Ned,' he said, and then, as I began to walk away, he called out: 'Thanks for doing that for me.'

So that's how it is, I was saying to myself all the way home. That's the sort of thing that happens once the gloves are off. And by the time I'd got to the front gate and opened it with one hand on the latch to stop it clicking and sat on the front verandah to take my shoes off I think I'd taken it all into myself and begun to wake up to how we only kid ourselves we can tell the good things from the bad things when really they're so mixed up that half the time we're thinking one thing, feeling another, and doing something else altogether.

ALL PART OF THE GAME

A. P. Gaskell

The Sockburn tram clanked away. I picked up my suitcase and walked along to their gate.

Well, there it was again, all just the same as I'd remembered it from last year; the long straight gravelled drive, the brick and roughcast house with the rose bushes over on the left, and down at the end of the drive the high brick stables with the loft above. Somebody led a horse out of the stable doorway as I watched, and took it round to the paddocks at the side. I couldn't see who he was. He didn't look like Cliff, but the shed under the windmill stopped my view before I had a good look at him. Perhaps he was a stable-boy. He looked small leading that high green-covered horse. Perhaps he'd been rubbing it down and was just going to turn it out. I couldn't see properly at that distance.

Down right at the back was the row of poplars beside the water-race. The ground was flat for miles and miles, the soil was grey and glittered in the sun, the grass in the paddocks behind the gorse fence was burnt brown, people rode their bikes on the footpath, everybody had a windmill, and in town, the trams were green and white, the pictures kept open continuously all day, clear water ran along in the gutters, and, of course, there was the Avon. It was all so different from New Plymouth. We had hills all around there, and the Mountain too, but here I could look across flat country, away beyond the rows of trees, and see the Southern Alps right over by the sky. I liked holidays in Christchurch very much, even the air smelled different, and nearly always I used to cry on my last morning before I got up, because I didn't want to go home again. Of course other times Mum had come with me, but this time I had come the whole way by myself, except that Dad's cousin had seen me from the train to the boat in Wellington.

I opened the gate, picked up my bag, and went in. I started to walk along the drive, but someone in the shadow down by the stables yelled, 'Get off the drive.' I saw that the drive had just been raked so I walked on the strip of grass along the side. That sounded like Cliff who shouted, though I wasn't sure of his voice after a year. I suppose he'd just raked the drive. I couldn't help smiling as I walked along. It felt so good to be coming here again.

75

I went up the steps to the back porch and knocked. 'It's me, auntie,' I called.

'Is that you Gordon? Step over the step.' My auntie always kept the doorstep scrubbed very clean. I went in, and there was the smell of their place again, quite different from at home. My uncle kept a cow, and I could smell the big basin of milk that would be sitting in the pantry, and scrubbed wood, and cooking, and their own warm smell that came from the people who lived in the kitchen. My auntie was down on her knees polishing the range. She smiled up at me. 'Hello Gordon. My word you've grown. Give us a kiss, you're not too big for that are you?'

I bent and kissed the faint dark moustache above her mouth. She was very dark and good-looking, and her eyebrows met faintly above her thin straight nose. She had dark brown eyes like Mum's. I noticed she had her hair short in a buster-cut.

'Mum told me you'd got your hair cut,' I said.

'Do you like it? It's the latest. Hasn't she got hers done yet?'

'No. She says she will if many more people do.'

She told me to take my coat off and sit down, then she asked me all about the trip and about Mum and Dad, and told me about the wins they'd had lately with Red Wing, and about the nor-wester they'd had that she was still cleaning up after. She kept rubbing at the range until it shone. She was very particular about her house. All the time I was wanting to get away down to the stables and see Cliff and the horses and my uncle and Mary.

'Would you like a cup of tea?' auntie asked. 'They always want one after they've finished mucking out. They'll be up soon.'

'I think I'll go down and say hello to them.'

'Well you can take your things down. I've put you in the whare with Cliff and Norman.'

'Who's Norman?'

'He's the new boy working for your uncle. He's a steeplechase jockey.'

'I think I saw him. Does he get many wins?'

'He used to be very good, but he had a bad fall last year and he's just getting his nerve back. Your uncle thinks he'll be good again if he just has a win or two. He's a nice wee chap.' I picked up my bag and coat. 'If you want a wash, you know where the wash-house is. Or you can wash in the sink if you don't make a mess. I don't want you mucking up my bathroom. I've just cleaned it out.'

'Righto,' I said. I had looked in her bathroom once the last time I was there. It was corker and clean and shiny. But last year, when Mum was there, I used to roll up my pants and sit on the bench and wash my legs in the sink. Some of the water would run down under my pants and not get dried properly and make my legs sore.

I took my stuff and went smiling down to the stables.

I looked in at the whare door and sniffed the familiar smell of tobacco smoke and grey blankets. Someone was lying on one of the bunks reading. My shadow on the floor made him look up. 'Hello,' he said. He had a smooth round little face.

'Hello.' This would be Norman, the steeplechase jockey. 'Where's Cliff?'

'He's mucking out. In the stable.'

I went through the big doorway on to the concrete floor. The air was full of the smell of straw and horses and leather. Someone was hissing through his teeth, and a horse stamped with a hollow sound on the packed earth in the loosebox. 'Stand still, blast you,' said a voice. I looked in over the lower half of the door, and there was Cliff, hissing as he brushed down the horse's legs. The horse was flicking his tail and gnawing the edge of his manger and stamping. 'Oh you bad-tempered bastard,' said Cliff. He was thin-faced and dark, and a few years older than me.

'Good-day there,' I said. I could feel my face cracking, I was so pleased.

He smiled up at me with his cheeky sort of smile, and came reaching over the door to shake hands. I was too slow and he got the grip on me and squeezed. 'Hello Gordon,' he smiled, squeezing, 'how are you?'

'Ow, Cliff,' I said. 'Cut it out. You're hurting. Oo. Dicken.'

He let me go. 'I've just got to wash his face,' he said. 'Like to come in and do it?'

'What's his name?'

'Gloaming,' he grinned at me. He had dust caked round his mouth and it made his teeth look white. 'I'll just finish him and then I'm set. How about getting me some water in that bucket.'

'How many horses have you got now?' I asked, handing him the bucket.

'Five. There's this one, he's Scallywag, and you know old Red Wing, and three others.

'They're not all yours though?'

'Oh no. Only Red Wing. Scallywag's running at the next meeting. Haven't I got him looking good?'

When he had finished we went into the whare at the end of the stables. 'Norm, this is Gordon.' Norman got off the bunk to shake hands. He was just about the same height as me and he was a grown man. He had funny little legs. 'Pleased to meet you,' he said, and he didn't squeeze my hand. When he smiled he looked like a little round-faced boy and he had a high sort of voice.

'See what happens to you if you start smoking too soon,' said Cliff. He was a good bit taller than Norman.

'Pity you didn't start a bit sooner,' said Norman bitterly. 'You've grown out of a job.'

'Don't worry about me, I can get a job all right.' Cliff took out a packet of Yellows. 'Have one?' He held them out to me.

'Have you started smoking?' I asked. 'Does auntie let you?'

Norman laughed. 'She makes him. He's nearly ten stone now.'

'Some people never grow up,' said Cliff airily.

'Not in the head they don't.' Norman went and lay down again.

'I had a cigarette the other day after school,' I said. 'Another kid and I smoked one in the woodshed.'

'Did it make you sick?'

'No, but afterwards we ate all sorts of things to take the smell away, cabbage leaves and raw onion.'

'Chewing gum's best,' said Cliff. 'Or Smokers.'

'Where's uncle and Mary?'

'They've gone down to the store,' said Norman. 'Hang up your coat. There's a hook.'

'Which will be my bunk?' I asked.

'Do you wet the bed?' Cliff asked. 'Well you can sleep above me.' Cliff was a hard case. He knew lots of yarns too. He'd always start by saying 'Did you hear the one about . . . ?' He didn't seem to like telling them when Norman was there, but he told me some corkers after. He was a real wag. It was good fun going round with him.

By and by, we went up for a cup of tea. Uncle had been a jockey once and he was short too, only he had got a lot thicker now. He was fair and red-faced with little veins on his cheeks, and he always had to wear a hat outside because he sunburned very easily. He never used to talk much to me because I didn't know about horses, so he kept asking 'How's your Mum and Dad?' and 'What class are you in now?' When Mary came in from the front, I noticed straight away that she had her hair up. She looked just about grown-up like that. I thought she was very pretty too, because she took after uncle and her face was fair and smooth and she looked corker when she smiled.

'Hello Gordie,' she cried, and grabbed hold of me and started hugging and kissing me a lot before I could get away. It was hard to know how to struggle with her because Mum had told me never to punch girls in the chest. It was funny too because when she kissed me she would look over at Norman to see if he was watching, and he turned very red.

'Here here here,' said auntie. 'That's enough of that in my clean kitchen. Mary, don't be such a damn fool. It's just as well for you my lady you didn't bump the table.'

'Yah, you big sissy,' said Cliff. 'Always kissing the girls.'

'You'll change your tune one of these days, smarty,' said Mary. 'What about Doreen?'

'Her!' said Cliff. 'Why I – '

'That's enough,' said auntie. 'Gordon you get round there behind the table. Sit in your usual place Norman.'

Gee it was good fun there with them all, talking about the horses and everything. I thought I'd better remember later on to ask Cliff about Doreen. He was a hard case with girls.

Afterwards, auntie told me I'd better go and change my clothes. 'Can you unpack your own things?'

'I'll come down and do them for him,' said Mary. 'I'll be his mother while's he's here and make him wash his neck.'

'You'll do these dishes first. You haven't done a hand's turn all morning. Plenty girls are out working long before your age.'

'Now now,' said uncle. 'We've been over all that. Mary's work is around here, helping me with the horses. Isn't it, Mary?'

'Too right. Gordon, did you know I ride work now in the mornings?'

'Yes, on Red Wing,' Cliff broke in. 'That old thing. You try it on Scallywag. I bet you wouldn't stay long on him.'

'Cliff sometimes doesn't stay very long on him either,' said Norman in his soft little voice, smiling.

'Cliff got dumped the other morning,' said auntie. 'He's getting too long in the legs. We might have to find another job for him.'

'He won't dump me again,' said Cliff darkly. 'I made him feel sorry for it.' He took out his packet and lit a cigarette.

'Started smoking yet Gordon?' asked uncle. He took out a wooden match, split it with his thumbnail and started picking a place in his teeth. He opened the paper at the racing page.

'I've got to go to High School after I finish primary,' I said. 'You can't smoke there either, though some of the boys do.'

'More school yet!' Cliff blew a smoke ring. 'Don't you get sick of it? You wouldn't catch me going there.'

'Everybody isn't – ' Norman started to say, then he stopped and went red. 'I'll dry the dishes for you Mary.'

'See if you can put them away in the right places this time.' Auntie was smiling at him. She liked anyone who did things for her. Last time, she asked me to pluck and clean a fowl for her. It was a hell of a job, and I got in an awful mess. Mum was very annoyed with auntie over that, but auntie just laughed. I suppose Norman was doing things for her now. I didn't mind doing them really because if she was around she would talk about people and crack jokes about them and make the time pass. She knew some yarns too, but she didn't tell very bad ones. She did enjoy a bit of fun though, like the time years ago when she was staying at our place and she came out all dressed up in Dad's clothes and bowler hat that he wore on Sundays, with a wee mou drawn with chalk, and said she was going down to work with him. She went right out the gate and along the street a bit. Dad didn't like it much, but Mum and I nearly died laughing at her the tricks she got up to. Mum used to say it was a different story in her own place though.

Down in the whare again, Cliff stretched out on the bunk while I took the things out of my bag and changed my clothes.

'That little runt. He's always hanging round Mary these days. Mum lets him take her to dances, too.'

'Who?'

'Norman. If I catch him up to any monkey business with my sister I'll bash him.'

'Could you fight him? He must be pretty strong.'

'Him? Course I could. That little squirt. You just let him try anything on and you'll see. I don't like Mary going out with the stable-boy.'

'But isn't he a jockey?'

'He's a jockey when anyone gives him a mount, but he's our stable-boy most of the time. He's half crazy too.'

'Crazy? He looks all right to me.' I began to feel a bit uneasy.

'Course he's crazy. He got dumped at the board fence last year and kicked on the head. You never know what he's going to do. He's moody as hell. If I was Dad I'd give him the sack. I could work Red Wing out over the jumps. I'm a damn sight better rider than he is. It's only that they skite him up, and he's a bit smaller.'

I didn't like to say what about getting dumped off Scallywag the other morning because Cliff knew some corker tortures. One of them he tried last time was to stick his finger in under your ears, or he'd get you down on the floor and kneel on your arm and roll back and forth.

'What books have you got there?' I asked.

'I'm reading a beaut now, *Drag Harlan*. Just when he's going to draw he stops and lets the other joker draw first, and then he flashes it out. There's another one there by the same author, *Square Deal Sanderson*. Have you read it?'

'I've read *Bar 20*,' I said, 'and *Bar 20 Days* and *The Bar 20 Three* and *Johnny Nelson*.'

'He's a wag,' said Cliff, 'that Johnny Nelson. He's like Hoot Gibson in the pictures.'

'He gets married in the last book,' I said.

'Does he? Aw hell, I hate that mushy stuff.'

'Have you read *The Three Musketeers*?' I asked. 'It's a corker, all sword fights. Like Doug Fairbanks.'

'No, I don't like that old-fashioned stuff. Give me quick on the draw.'

After dinner, everybody had a lie-down. They said it was because they got up so early in the morning to ride work. Norm was there reading a book called *My Man Jeeves*. He said he hadn't read any cowboy books for years. Sometimes he read Nat Gould, but he liked adventure stories best, or funny ones. Cliff had just put down his book and was going to have a doss when there was the sound of wheels on the drive. From the window you could see right up the drive past the house. It was a big two-horse wagon loaded with bales of straw.

'It's Charlie,' said Cliff. 'Blast him. What's he want to come now for? We only ordered the bloody stuff this morning. A man never gets any peace round this place.' He began slipping on his shoes.

The two big heavy horses stopped just outside the door, and threw out their heads to loosen the reins. You could hear their teeth chewing on their bits. One of them lifted his tail and dropped some dung. Charlie, high on his seat, leaned away down to look under the doorway. 'Anyone home?' He wore a waistcoat and his shirtsleeves were rolled up showing freckly forearms. It was hard to tell what his face was like because it was almost upside-down looking under the doorway. I went out to see him. He was thin with a big sandy moustache and big eyebrows, and was wearing an old bun hat. 'I drove 'em nice and straight down the drive,' he said to Cliff. 'Look at it. Two nice straight marks down the middle. Decorate it for you. Bet you I can drive back on the same marks. Couldn't I girls?' he said to the horses. 'I could draw flowers for you along the edge with this pair.'

'One of them's not very well-behaved,' I said.

'Haw, haw, haw,' he went, 'that Bessie, she just don't like the job Cliff made of the drive, do you Bess?' He put his hand on her rump and jumped down.

'You can bloody well clear up that mess before you go,' said Cliff.

'Haw, haw, haw. He's a hard case our Cliff. She's thinking your skinny racehorses don't do much of a job so she's giving you some good manure.' He became very businesslike. 'Where will you have it? Up aloft?' He backed the wagon to the doorway of the stables. The horses moved stiffly backwards, chipping their shoes down on the drive and scattering the gravel.

I went with Cliff up the steep narrow stairs into the loft. It was warm and dusty up there under the roof. There were some bales of hay and straw, and sacks of chaff, and some horse covers, and dry-looking cobwebby bits of harness hanging from nails. Three or four cats scampered out of sight. Cliff opened the door at the front and the light poured in. There was a little platform, and a beam above it with a pulley. Cliff fed a rope through, with a hook on the end, and we hauled the bales up, swung them in to the platform, and rolled them over into the loft.

'That's the lot,' called Charlie. 'See you some more. Tell your Dad I got a good line of oats now. Come on girls. Giddap.' We watched him go away down the drive.

'I'll tell you what,' I said to Cliff. 'I'll go down and you haul me up.'

'To hell with that for a joke. Do you think I like work? I'll tell you what,' he said. 'I'll tie this end and you can slide down the rope.'

'I don't know how to hold it with my legs.'

'What, aren't you game? Go on. Look, I'll tie it here.'

'You go first.'

'Me? I could do it easy. I often do it. I'm sick of it.'

I went out on the platform, leaned out, and grabbed the rope, but it looked a long way down and the stones were sharp. Cliff gave me a push and before I knew where I was the rope was burning through my hands and I was waving with my legs to grab it, and just when I was getting it the ground hit under my feet and I went down on my knees on the gravel. There was Cliff's head sticking out over the platform, laughing. 'I knew you could do it. Easy, isn't it?'

I gulped a bit before I could smile back at him. It didn't look very high from the ground, but from up there the ground looked an awful long way down. I'd got a bit of a fright and felt shaky so I went to sit on the whare step and look at my knees. One was bleeding.

Norman came over to me. 'You be careful with him or he'll hurt you,' he said. 'He's got no common sense at all, especially when it doesn't concern himself. He's just at the awkward age.'

'I'm all right,' I said. 'I just wasn't expecting it that's all.'

Cliff came in. 'Well, now you know how it's done.'

'I thought you'd have more sense than let Gordon do that,' said Norman.

'You mind your own bloody business,' Cliff blazed at him.

'This is my business. I'm in charge of the stables when your father's not here.'

'Then why weren't you hauling up that straw?'

'Oh, I let the stropper do jobs like that. I'm a jockey. And I don't want anyone hurt around here. You be more careful.' He stood there with his round little face looking up at Cliff, standing up straight, looking very light and quick. His eyes didn't blink at all but his face got red. I thought Cliff was going to hit him, but Norman smiled and said, 'There's enough mess to clear up as it is.' He got a shovel and a handful of straw and picked up the dung.

Cliff came back from the dressing-table with some ointment. 'Here rub this on.' It had a corker clean smell. Then he lay down on his bunk and didn't say anything for a long time.

That night after tea, uncle got up with the match between his teeth and took his hat. 'Better see Harry about those acceptances,' he said and went out.

'Are there races soon?' I asked.

'Too right,' said Mary. 'Red Wing's going to win the steeplechase, isn't he Norman?'

'He's getting a bit old now.' Norman was smiling at her. 'He might win if I get off and lift him over some of those fences.'

'I'll lift you,' said Mary, returning his smile, 'right under the ear. If he doesn't win it's because his rider's no good.'

'He won't win then,' said Cliff, lying back on the sofa.

'Are you going to ride him, Norman?' I asked.

'If Mary'll let me. I'll tell you where I'd like to ride him, and that's down to the glue factory.' Norman looked corker with that wee cheeky smile. You couldn't help liking him, though sometimes it seemed funny for him to be acting like a grown man when he was so small.

'What are your colours?' I asked.

'Sky blue. A nice clear colour. Like Mary's eyes.' Norman and Mary both went red when he said that, but I thought Mary was quite pleased about it.

Cliff snorted and auntie looked up. 'Here here you two. That's enough of that damn silly nonsense. Just as well your father's not here my lady.' They were both uncomfortable, looking down at the table. 'Well, what about these dishes?' said auntie. 'A woman's work is never done.' She was looking at Norman but he didn't move. 'Norman, will you give me a hand?' She was smiling nicely at him, but his face had a funny closed look.

'Not tonight,' he said. 'I want to take some books back to the Ellis's.' He started to get up.

'You men are all the same,' said auntie. 'Big ones and small ones you're all the same. Who'd be a woman?'

'You've got a big one lying there on the sofa doing nothing.'

83

'Never you mind about him,' said auntie sharply. 'I'll see he does his share.'

'If it goes according to size,' said Norman, 'he ought to do them a good bit more often than I do.'

'Leave his size out of it. We can't all be as small as you.' Auntie did look fierce when she was angry. She was so dark.

'I suppose it's just as well,' said Norman. 'Quality before quantity.' He stood leaning his hands on the table as though he wanted to get away but was making himself stand and face her.

'You leave him out of it,' said auntie. 'Just leave my family out of it. When you get a family of your own you can start bossing them around. Poor little beggars.' Then she seemed to realise she'd said too much because Norman was looking awful. His face had gone pale and thin-looking, as though he was very cold.

'Now Norman, let's not quarrel again,' she said. 'My tongue runs away with me. Sit down for a while and we'll have a game of cards.'

'It's all right,' he said stiffly, and went out looking very small.

'Mum, you've hurt him. You are a devil,' said Mary. 'You know he's awfully sensitive about being so small.'

'You needn't start telling me what's right and what's wrong. I've got along so far without your advice, thank you.'

'But Mum, you must remember he's not right yet. Just when he's getting along nicely you have to go and upset him again.'

'I go and upset him. I like that. If he's so damned thin-skinned he can't take a bit of a joke he deserves to be upset. What he needs is a good hard kick on the backside to wake him up a bit.'

'Oh don't be so childish. He's not a little boy. You can't smack him to smack him better.'

'I can still smack you, my lady. Not so much of your back-chat. It's all your fault anyway. If you didn't encourage him, he wouldn't – '

'I don't encourage him. I like him, that's all, and I felt sorry for him.'

'Oh, you feel sorry for him. So that's why you're always down at the stables instead of doing your room out. That's why you're off to dances with him every night of the week. That's why you're always talking about him. You better watch your step, my lady. He's not your class and you better let him know it, the sooner the better.'

'There's nothing the matter with him. He's always perfectly all right with me. I know how to treat him. And I like him. So there.' Mary stood up and started clearing the table. She didn't look like a girl at all. She'd grown up a lot in the last year. Auntie was glaring at her.

'You watch yourself,' said Cliff from the sofa. 'I don't want any half-wits in our family.'

Auntie rushed across to him and gave him such a box on the ear that his cigarette went flying out of his mouth. 'If you don't get up off your backside and help your sister this minute and stop smoking those damned cigarettes I'll knock you into the middle of next week,' she yelled.

Cliff got up, whimpering. I was too scared to do anything. I didn't know what to do. If I went down to the whare Norman would be there. I just sat and shivered.

The other three got busy on the dishes. After a time, auntie turned and smiled at me. 'Well Gordon, you'll be able to tell your mother I'm having trouble with my family.' I tried to smile back. That was one good thing about auntie, she would flare up suddenly, but she got over it just as quickly. She was right back to ordinary things again now. 'Has your mother got any new hats lately?' she asked.

'She's got a wee one,' I said. 'A high sort of a one with a narrow brim. She says she'll have to have her hair cut before she can wear it properly. It's not round, it's – you know – oval.'

'Mary and I are going to get new ones like that if Red Wing wins this race. They're the latest.'

'You won't know me if we have a win,' said Mary. 'I'm getting a new dress, very short, nearly up to my knees, with a low waist, and some new gloves, and a new coat, aren't I Mum? I'll be really coming out in all the latest. And Mum and I might go up to Wellington for the races. Gee, I'm looking forward to that. I hope we get a win.'

'You better keep Norman sweet then,' said Cliff. 'Shall I go and see if he's there?'

'No, I'll go.' And Mary was out the door before anyone could say a word.

Auntie put the red cloth on the table and we sat down. Cliff handed me the cards. 'Let's see if you can shuffle any better than last time you were here.' I tried it, but we didn't play cards much at home, and my fingers were too short and stiff. Bits of the pack kept falling on the floor. 'Look, I'll show you,' said Cliff. He took them and did it easily, and then put two lots down on the table and flipped their corners in together.

Auntie started laughing. 'Gordon, do you remember that time years ago at your place – perhaps you wouldn't remember it – we played strip poker and we had your father sitting with only his pants and socks on?'

'He doesn't play cards as a rule,' I said. 'I suppose that's why he wasn't much good.'

They were both laughing. 'I'll never forget that as long as I live. It was a cold night and he was sitting there shivering and looking miserable and he couldn't win anything back to put on.'

'And that Christmas a long time ago when we were staying at your place,' said Cliff, 'and we hopped out the bedroom window and sneaked round and looked in the sitting-room window and saw all the presents waiting to go in our stockings.'

'Yes, you little devils,' said auntie. 'You didn't deserve any presents after that.'

'Do you remember the time the pony chased you when you were eating a carrot?' Cliff was always reminding me about that. Cliff and Mary used to have a pony when they were in the old place, and it was dead keen on carrots. One day it followed me, trying to snatch one out of my hand. I ran inside and locked the door. I was small at the time of course, and not used to horses.

'Mary is a long time,' I said. 'Shall I go and tell her to hurry?'

Auntie nodded so I went out into the dark. I knew there was a clothes-prop leaning across the path so I was walking on the grass and not making any noise and I almost bumped into them. They were very close together, perhaps they were hugging, and Norman was saying, 'Please Mary. Will you? Please.' But she said, 'Not now, Norman. Perhaps if Red Wing wins.'

I said, 'Are you two going to play cards?'

They got a fright and stepped back. Norman said, 'Why, it's Gordon. How are you Gordon?'

'I'm all right thanks. Are you coming to play cards?'

'Not me,' said Norman. 'I've got to take these books back. You'd better go, Mary.'

As we walked back, Mary put her arm round my shoulders and took hold of my ear. 'I don't know what you saw. But not a word of this inside or Mum will hit the roof. It's our secret. Eh?' She squeezed my ear. I wanted to ask why auntie would hit the roof, but I forgot because I was measuring myself against her to see if she would be much taller than Norman. My head came up to her ear.

Gee, we had some fun that night. After we had played cards, we got to talking and laughing about things, and auntie took her teeth out, pulled her hair down over her face, and acted old mother Kennedy going into the store and trying to say, 'Three fresh sausages please.' Then Cliff put on some of auntie's old clothes, and Mary dressed me up in some of her things with a hat and powder and everything, and we pretended to be two girls. Mary got her father's suit and hat and then came out and pretended to be courting me. She took off her hat and asked me for a dance and wondered if she could see me home afterwards. She asked me to marry her, and auntie put some white paper round her neck and hung her top teeth down as though she was buck-toothed and pretended to be the parson. Gee, it was great fun. I nearly died laughing. We never had fun like that at home.

Uncle came in and said what a skinny girl I was, but he said Mary had a good backside on her for a man. He said to be careful she didn't bend or she'd burst his pants for him and then he'd have to wear hers. I think it was the best evening's fun I ever had. Norman came in later for a cup of tea, and he seemed all right again too. I always had corker fun at Christchurch.

Next morning I was tired and had a good sleep in, but later on in my stay I'd get up early and go over to the course to watch the horses working and rolling in the sand. I wasn't game to ride any of them. Cliff kept asking me to try, but they looked too tall. I used to help Cliff with the mucking-out. I could carry two buckets of water. Last time I was there I couldn't do that. Of course I slopped a bit, but still it showed I was getting stronger. Uncle wanted me to come and learn how to milk, but I liked the horses better. Besides there were plenty cows just over the road from our place at home, so I stayed in the stable. Up in the loft, there were bags of oats to dip your hands and arms down into and feel them dry and cold and slithery. One of the cats had kittens and they were a lot tamer than the mother, though the old mother didn't like you touching them, and she kept handy all the time. Sometimes uncle would let me sieve the chaff, but I couldn't make it curve up in the air the way he did. Sometimes in the mornings I'd take a book up in the loft and sit on the wee platform in the sun and hang my legs down. I could look down between my knees and there was the gravel away down below. I always took care Cliff wasn't in the loft when I sat there.

One morning when I was there, Mary came up and then called Norman to come and shift a bag of chaff for her. I don't think they knew I was there because they were talking quietly for a long time, and then there was a clatter and Mary said, 'You devil, you're stronger than I thought you were.' She didn't sound very annoyed though and Norman was laughing as they went down. I suppose he had hugged her or kissed her. I wondered for a while whether I should tell Cliff about it but I thought there might be a row, and anyway Mary hadn't seemed to mind. If it had been anything much Mary would have made a fuss. Besides, Norman was jolly nice to me. For a while I had been a bit nervous with him, and didn't like to say anything was very small or little in case he got offended, but I soon forgot about that. Sometimes he did get a bit moody and hard to please, and then he wouldn't answer and ask you to leave him alone and sit and look as though he was thinking of something unpleasant, but he never got as crabby as our school-teacher, although I suppose they're different. Most of the time he was corker and friendly, and he didn't try to play tricks on me at all.

One afternoon, Cliff and I went over to the water-race and caught some tadpoles. Cliff splashed me a bit of course, but I got him a beauty just at the end. He couldn't catch me either. I suppose the cigarettes made him short-winded.

Another day, I went into town with auntie and Mary, and we had a good look round the shops and the Square, and then Mary and I came home on the top deck of the trailer. That was corker and breezy. Another afternoon, Cliff and I went in to the pictures to see Doug Fairbanks in *The Mark of Zorro*. He was a stunner sword-fighter and he cut a Z on their faces. Cliff liked it too because Doug Fairbanks could ride so well. The girl in the picture said to him, 'You ride like a part of the horse.'

The next morning, when they all came riding back from the course, before they got off at the stables, Cliff called out to me, 'Look at me Gordon. I ride like a part of the horse.'

Norman started laughing so much he could hardly speak. 'Which part?' he said. 'When that tram passed and Scallywag started to play up, you were riding like a part of his neck.' He was laughing so much he could hardly get down. Poor Cliff just glared at him and moved his mouth, but he couldn't think of anything to say at all. It was funny, and good too, to see Cliff without an answer. He was still pretty wild afterwards, and kept swearing and muttering that he would get even with Norman if it was the last thing he did. I felt like laughing, but if I had it would have meant a long run so I kept quiet.

Well, by this time the races were only a day or two off, and we were all busy getting ready. Norman had washed his colours himself and Mary ironed them for him and they looked stunner. He was sitting in the sun on the doorstep of the whare cleaning his racing boots. They were very light and soft. I tried one on, but it was a little too small for me.

'Gee, I'm excited about these races Norman,' I said. 'Are you getting excited?'

'Not yet,' he said, 'but I will. I always get a bit windy just before a race starts. It's so long-drawn-out, you know, the way you have to hang about before you line up at the barrier. Most of the jocks get the wind up a bit.'

'Is Red Wing good at the barrier?'

'Oh yes. Most steeplechasers are pretty quiet. It's the sprints where they play up.'

'Do you think you'll win? Honestly, do you?' I asked.

'I hope so. Your uncle and auntie will be very pleased if I do. Your uncle's got old Red Wing in great nick.' He went on rubbing away at his boot. 'Do you want us to win?'

'Of course I do. If you win it'll be a sort of – you know the word, what it all works up to.'

'A climax?'

'Yes. It'll be the climax of my holiday. I'm going home next week.'

He asked me about home, and would I be sorry to go, and then he said, 'What about Mary? Does she want us to win?' I was surprised at that. I thought she would have told him. They were always talking about things and riding to the track together. She must have told him plenty times. It seemed funny he should ask me. But perhaps he didn't believe her.

'Too right she does,' I said. 'If you win she's going to do all sorts of things, get a lot of new dresses and gloves and things. She's going up to Wellington, too. She's dead keen on it. And she and auntie are going to get new hats.'

He looked a bit funny as though he was disappointed, and kept rubbing at a shiny place on his boot. 'I might get a new hat myself,' he said, and got up and went inside, leaving me wondering what was the matter.

'Yoo-hoo,' auntie was standing on the porch and waving. 'Yoo-hoo, Gordon.' When I got there, she had on her nice smile. 'Gordon, would you like to turn the wringer for me? It makes the job such a lot quicker.' The wash-house was full of steam, and the smell of soap and wet clothes. She was getting our things ready for the races.

When I started to turn the wringer, it squeaked a bit. 'Shall I get some oil? There's some down in the stables.'

'I'll oil you. Do you think I want oil on these clothes? Leave it just now.'

I remembered Mum telling me how particular auntie was. One time, when auntie had been away, uncle did all the washing just before she came back, but auntie said that it wasn't clean enough for her, and she did it all again. But that wasn't really what I was thinking about as I turned the wringer.

'Auntie, do you want Norman to win?' I asked.

'What a damn silly question. Would you like £800?'

'You bet. I'd get a motor-bike. We have motor-bike races on the race-course up home.'

'If we win,' said auntie, 'we get £800. And then there are our bets too. Besides, if your uncle wins, he'll get more horses to train.'

'What about Norman?' I asked. Auntie was sloshing the clothes in clean water. Her hands were all pale and wrinkled and very clean from the suds.

'It would do him good too,' she said. 'Not only his share of the money, but he'd get more mounts too. He's had rather a lean time since his spill. He used to be very good.'

'Auntie – '

'What?'

I was going to ask her if she'd let Mary marry Norman if he won, but she was looking at me and I wasn't game. I started to turn the wringer. 'He thinks an awful lot of Mary, doesn't he?'

'Who told you that tale? Did he?'

'No, but I mean – they go round a lot together, don't they?'

'Mary's a mile too young to think of settling down yet. She'll have plenty more boys before she strikes the right one. It's too risky marrying a jockey. You never know when they'll get hurt. Besides Norman's not her class.'

'But wasn't uncle a jockey when you married him?'

'That was quite a different matter. A flat jockey's quite a different matter. Your uncle was one of the leading jockeys. Come on, turn a bit faster.' She pushed the clothes in between the rollers. 'Has Norman been having any more of his moods lately?'

'No, he's corker. I think he only has the really bad ones about Mary. I've never seen him really bad. Cliff makes him wild sometimes but he doesn't get any moods over it. He just gets angry.'

'Cliff's just at the awkward age,' she said. 'He thinks he knows more about training horses than his own father. Your uncle's thinking of sending him away somewhere else to work for a while to see if he'll steady up a bit.'

That sank in. 'Won't he be here if I come another time?' That did knock the bottom out of things.

'Come on, turn the handle. We'll see about that.'

'But auntie, fair go, will he be here next year?'

'I suppose he will. Turn a bit faster or we'll never get to the races at this rate.'

That was news indeed. I wandered down to the stables to ask Cliff about it. Mary was there, cleaning Red Wing's bridle. 'Hello, sweetheart. Come to give me a kiss?'

'Don't be silly. Tarts are always silly when you're thinking about something.'

'None of your cheek now, young Gordon, or I'll rub my hands all over your face. Look at them.' She held them out for me to see.

'You'd have to catch me first. Where's Cliff?'

'He and dad have taken the horses down to have their racing

plates put on. They were looking for you. You could have gone on the bike.' I stood watching her for a while. 'The winner must have a clean bridle,' she said. 'What have you been doing to Norman? He's as miserable as a bandicoot. I'll have to go in and sweeten him up as soon as I finish this. Shall I give him a nice big kiss? Like this?' She went to grab me but I ducked out.

'Couldn't catch a flea,' I said. I went into the whare to ask Norman if it was all right for me to take the bike. He was standing looking at his face in the mirror, not doing his hair, or shaving, or anything, just looking at himself. His reflection had a sad sort of expression as though it was looking out and seeing Norman and not liking the sight of him very much. 'Norman,' I said. After a while he turned towards me, and his reflection looked away. 'Norman, can I have the bike?'

'Don't bother me,' he said as though he hadn't really listened to what I said. He went and lay down on his bunk, still with that same expression on his face.

I went to the shed under the windmill and got the bike and rode off to the blacksmith's. It was uncle's bike and I could reach the pedals by just stretching a little bit, and of course I rode on the footpath all the way. There were lots of horses and jockeys round the smithy, and there was the smell like burning toe-nails, and the hammering red-hot iron, and the smoke when they tried the shoes on. It was such good fun watching and listening to the talk that I forgot to ask Cliff.

When race morning came, I can tell you we did bustle round to get there for the first race. Gee, it was great. There were crowds and crowds of people, and cars going in one gate all the time, and trams with two trailers, and as soon as they stopped the people all made a rush for the gates. There were wee jockeys leading in horses, and some of the horses had covers right over their faces with just holes for their eyes and pointed things to fit their ears into. Men were yelling and trying to sell race-books, and round the back of the stand there were refreshment tents and places for hot water, and people carrying teapots, and the smell of hot pies and beer. It was a stunner day and the place was packed with people. I thought when we left auntie's place that she and Mary were all dolled up, but gosh, they were nothing to some of the sights. The men were just ordinary though.

We went down to the birdcage to see the horses. It was funny too. The birdcage had white iron posts all round, on this side and on the far side too, and when you walked past them they looked as though they were going backwards. Mary said it was like the wheels in the pictures. We got a good possie just as the horses were coming in. Auntie and uncle kept talking about their names and weights and riders, and how they ran at the last meeting, but I just watched them walking round. Gosh, they looked stunner when they had their covers off. So tall and shiny and proud, and they just sort of drifted round as though the grass was springy and they didn't need to touch it hard at all, and their skins fitted them perfectly without any wrinkles or baggy places, all just smooth and ripply and neat.

Uncle went away to have a bet, and Mary, auntie, and I went up to the stand. We had to go away up to the back to get a seat. It was high up and you could see for miles and miles right away over the smoky part of Christchurch. I could see auntie's place too. I could tell it by the loft above the stables. The horses started away over at the back of the course and when they got away it looked as though all the bright colours of the jockeys were sliding round on the railings. They soon swung into the straight and everybody stood up. I couldn't see very well, but auntie was yelling 'You beauty. You beauty,' and hammering my shoulder, and Mary rubbed her cheek against mine, so we were on a winner all right.

That made us all happy, it was such a good start. Mary kept saying, 'I've got a feeling this is going to be our lucky day. Don't you feel lucky, Gordon?' She looked lucky. She was smiling all the time and her eyes were bright, and when we met Norman at the corner of the stand, he couldn't help looking at her. He was all dressed up in a wee suit with his collar and tie and hat on, and he looked smaller than ever. I noticed that he went and stood on the uphill side of us, so that he could look down to us. Cliff and uncle were busy with the horses, so we went in for a cup of tea. When we found a table in all the crowd, Norman wouldn't have anything to eat, but he came and sat with us.

'Well Norman,' said auntie, 'how do you feel about it?'

'I'm beginning to feel a bit weak about the knees,' he said. Then he smiled. 'But Mary's my lucky charm. She says we'll be all right.'

'Too right you will. I'm sure you're going to win.' Mary patted his hand. I looked at auntie, but she was all smiles too. I was beginning to think they were a bit silly, and I wished Cliff was there. He'd lucky-charm them. I wanted to go and see him, but auntie said she couldn't be sure where he'd be, so I'd better stay with them or I'd get lost in the crowd.

When the steeplechase came on, we went to the birdcage to see the horses, and there was Norman in his sky-blue blouse and cap and clean boots perched away up high with his knees up. Old Red Wing was looking quite used to all this and not making any fuss at all. Norman looked pale. Auntie said the others did too. They were nervous because a steeplechase was a big risk.

'I can't bear to watch this all the way round,' said Mary. 'Let's go down by the rails and see the finish.'

Just as we got down there, a man in a blue suit began to stagger backwards and fell over, wallop. He just lay there. I was going over to look at him, but auntie caught my arm and dragged me up to the rails.

'Stay here,' she said. 'He's probably drunk or something.'

He was lying there on his back just a few yards away. His hat was off and his face was a funny purply colour, he still had a dead cigarette butt in his mouth, and he was making noises in his throat as he breathed. Lots of people were turning round to look at him, and then they'd look away as though they hadn't noticed him.

There was a roar, 'They're off,' from the crowd up in the stand. I couldn't see very well except when they went over the jumps, but blue seemed to be near the front, and auntie and Mary got over their fright about the man falling over and began to get excited. While we were waiting for the horses to come round for the first time, I had another look at the man. I could just see his legs between the people behind us. Nobody seemed to be helping him. They should have loosened his collar. Just then there was a beating sound and people began to shout. I leaned over the fence in front of Mary. I had a great view. And Red Wing was first over the hurdle into the straight. He was. He stuck his head and neck out and stretched out his front legs and there was Norman in blue and they were over the hurdle. 'Norman,' we yelled, 'Go it Norman,' and old Red Wing came striding past, nice and easy with about four others fairly close behind. Norman was very serious and he didn't look when we yelled. I suppose he couldn't hear us. He told me the wind roars in your ears so that you can't hear anything. Besides, there was the crowd.

Well, you can imagine how we felt after that. We couldn't see them after they'd gone round the turn. We could see little bits of colour hopping up and down over the jumps away at the back, and it looked as though blue was still in front. It took ages for them to go round the back stretch. My mouth got dry. I was holding tight to the railings. If I let them go, I felt Norman would get beaten. Mary was leaning on me all soft and hot and squashing me against the fence. 'What the hell's the matter with them,' said auntie. 'Have they fallen?'

'Mum, stop it,' said Mary, right beside my ear. 'Keep your fingers crossed.'

I thought they were never going to come round again.

Then the crowd at the back began to roar so loud you could tell it was going to be a close finish, and the yell got louder and more excited, and underneath it came that beating sound again. Over the top of the hurdle you could see heads bobbing, and then the first horse came up and over and it was Red Wing still. He landed with a jolt and Norman bounced in the saddle. The others poured over just behind him. Norman had lost his cap and he seemed to be riding lop-sided. 'He's lost a stirrup. He's lost a stirrup,' Mary yelled. 'Norman, Norman,' we screamed, but the whips were out and two or three others lashed their way past him just in front of us. The horses were running heavily with no spring, stretching out hard.

I felt like crying. I didn't want to turn round in case the others should see. I suddenly noticed the crowd was still cheering. Someone was pleased at any rate. My hands were stiff and I could hardly let go the rails. Mary leaned away and my back felt cold.

We watched the Clerk of the Course bring in the winner. Norman was fourth. Poor old Red Wing looked very tired. Norman had both feet in the stirrups now. 'Well that's that,' said auntie. We turned away and there was the man in the blue suit still lying there with the blackened cigarette butt still in his mouth. It seemed ages since he'd fallen over. His eyes had only the whites showing. The people all streamed round him, leaving a gap where he was lying. They looked away from him as though they were ashamed of him. One man stepped over and winked at me.

We just wandered along without saying much. We met uncle and he didn't seem to mind much. He said it was jolly hard luck Norman losing his iron like that. It was Red Wing landing with such a jolt over the last fence that did it. Norman did jolly well to stick on. He said Norman was very upset about it all.

Well, the rest of the afternoon I couldn't get excited. Norman didn't come to see us. There was some fun at the last race though. Scallywag came second. He wasn't really second, he was third, but there was a protest, and the winner was disqualified. When the winner came in, some of the crowd started to boo and others took it up. A fat old lady just in front of me was boo-ing away, pushing out her mouth and saying, 'Boo-o-o-o.' Then she turned to me and said, 'What are they boo-ing for son? What's it for? Boo-o-o-o.' Anyway they made Scallywag second. I don't know how uncle got on with the betting.

As we walked home, auntie was talking to people she knew. 'It would have been very nice if we'd won,' she said, 'but it's all part of the game. We'll be lucky some other time.' I was glad to get home again, I was tired of all the crowds and the pushing. Mary had hardly said a word since the steeplechase. She didn't seem to hear if I spoke to her. I suppose she was very disappointed at not getting the new clothes or the trip to Wellington or anything. And then she used to ride Red Wing to work, and she was fond of Norman, so I suppose just about everything had gone wrong.

Well, when we got home, there was Cliff looking as pleased as punch. 'What about Scallywag now,' he said. 'Eh? Who's the best trainer in this house?' He pushed his hat on to the back of his head and stuck his thumbs in the armholes of his waistcoat. 'Cleaned up the old man,' he said. 'The only one in the money all day. Think I'll leave you and set up as a trainer on my own. Got a second with my first start. Not bad, eh?' He was showing off in great style. 'How did you like him, Gordon? Didn't he finish well? Didn't I have him fit?'

Auntie was laughing at him. 'Oh, you were wonderful,' she said. 'We all thought that.'

'Except that you didn't really train him, and you didn't ride him,' said Mary. She was still in a bad mood. 'And it looks as if you've left Dad to bring him home.'

'I did a damn sight better than your wee joker,' said Cliff. 'Calls himself a jockey. Hell! Wait till I have a piece of him. Talk about riding like a part of the horse. Where is he? There's a few things I'd like to tell him about riding.'

But we didn't know where Norman was. Uncle came down the drive riding Scallywag and leading Red Wing, but he hadn't seen Norman either.

We all changed into our old clothes again except Mary. There was going to be a dance that night and she didn't know whether to go or not. She said she'd see how she felt after tea. She didn't feel much like going.

'Go along, Mary,' said auntie. 'It'll do you good. It might cheer you up a bit. You took this race too damned seriously. There'll be plenty more you know.'

'I'll see how I feel,' she said. I was just going out the door when I think she said, 'I won't go with Norman.' I think it was that. It sounded as though she was going to rub it in a bit. Poor old Norman.

'Where do you think Norman is?' I asked Cliff. We were down at the stables. Cliff was feeding the horses and uncle was out the back, milking.

'Blowed if I know.' Cliff was sieving chaff and hissing so the dust wouldn't get in his mouth. 'Here you are,' he said. 'No, wait on.' He put some oats in with it. 'Put that in Red Wing's manger.' Old Red Wing was waiting for it, and leaned down over my shoulder to eat before I had it all poured out. He kept snorting down his nose to blow the chaff away so that he could get at the oats.

'I should think most likely he's gone to the pub,' said Cliff.

'Who, Norman?'

'Yes. I thought I might drop in myself and celebrate, but old Harry knows I'm not near twenty-one. There'd be too many cops about there today.'

'Does Norman drink?'

'Does he what! I've seen him shickered two or three times since he's been here. He gets one of his moods, then off to the pub.'

'Why?'

'To get drunk of course. It cheers him up. You ought to see him trying to get to bed. He thinks he's hung his clothes up and they fall down and he just stands and looks at them as though he doesn't believe it. It's hellashin funny. One night I made his bed up on the top bunk for him, stripped everything off his bottom one. Laugh. I nearly burst trying to keep quiet. He couldn't climb up and in the end he just lay down on the wire mattress. Jesus I laughed.'

Well that was how Norman came home all right. We were all having tea and there was a knock at the door. Mary went and we heard Norman speaking. Auntie called out for Mary to tell him to come in and have his tea, but he said he didn't want any tea, he just wanted to talk to Mary. He'd only be a minute, he wouldn't keep her, he just wanted to talk to Mary.

Cliff winked at me, and I was going to go and see him but auntie made me stay in my place. It was a good while before Mary came back.

'He wants me to go to the dance with him,' she said. 'He's been pestering the life out of me. He's drunk too, and you can smell it a mile off.'

'Are you going?' asked auntie.

'Not with him like that. Not on your life. I think it's a damned insult him coming like that and expecting me to go with him. I thought he was a decent sort of a chap.'

'So he is,' said uncle. 'He's all right. Just had a few too many.'

'One over the eight,' said Cliff.

'I'm not going with him,' said Mary. 'He's just being damned silly, coming here like that and expecting me to go with him.'

'I thought I heard you a couple of days ago saying you'd go,' said auntie.

'I said I'd go if he won. I didn't say I'd go if he lost. I wouldn't have minded so much, but for him to come here stinking like that, and he's all untidy, it's a damned insult.'

96

'You're too touchy,' said uncle. 'Where is he? I'll get him to have a sleep for a couple of hours, and then a good wash and a cup of tea and he'll be all right.' He went out.

'You don't have to go out with him,' auntie told Mary. 'There's plenty more boys. As far as that goes, you could go with Mabel and get a partner there.'

'Go with Fred,' said Cliff. 'That'll teach his nibs a lesson. You've hardly looked at Fred for months. Show Norman he's not the only pebble on the beach. Fred rode a winner today too, and he's more your size.'

'I know that,' said Mary. 'You don't have to tell me.'

Uncle came in and said he couldn't find Norman.

Well in the end, both Cliff and Mary went to the dance. There wasn't much for me to do with Cliff away. Auntie and uncle talked about the races for a long time, and then auntie started to teach me how to play crib. We were all pretty tired and went to bed early. I wasn't very scared at going down to the whare by myself. Of course I was a bit nervous at the noises, but I knew they were only the horses stamping and moving about.

Cliff came in, I don't know what time it was, and woke me up when he put the light on. He said he had a hell of a lot of fun. She was a great show. He said if it hadn't of been for bringing Mary home he'd of been on to a good thing. He had a promise for another night.

'And you should of seen Norman,' he said. 'Did I rub it in to him. I paid him back for that "part of the horse" the other morning. I put a beaut across him.'

'How?' I said, struggling up in bed so that the light wouldn't get in my eyes. 'What did you do?'

'Well he came in about halfway through. He'd been drinking again and his coat was all dust. Mary was dancing with Fred and I said, "Mary only dances with jockeys who win," I said, "it's all over with you now. Especially coming along shickered like this," I said, "she's very offended over that. And who rides like the part of the horse now," I said. He didn't like that a bit.'

'Did Mary speak to him?'

'No, I don't think she saw him. We were just by the door. "Mary only likes big jokers," I said, and then I went away for a dance. He was standing there for a good while watching her. He looked pretty rough with his clothes all untidy and his face red and puffy. He didn't say a word after he saw she was dancing with Fred, he just stood there looking miserable as hell. I got my own back on him all right. "Who rides like part of the horse now?" I said.'

Cliff got into bed and I didn't hear Norman come in. In fact the next thing I knew it was morning and the sun was up. I was a bit dopey from waking up, but I thought I heard the lock rattling and uncle calling, 'Don't come out, Cliff, stay where you are.' Then the door opened and uncle reached round, took the key out and locked the door on the outside. That was so strange I thought I must have been dreaming because usually uncle had to yell at Cliff to get him up, and often Norman would call him too. Then there were quick steps scrunching on the gravel outside, and I twisted round and looked out the window. Uncle was running up the drive, taking fast little steps with his funny little jockey's legs. I heard the bunk below me squeaking, and Cliff said 'What the hell's all the fuss?' I peered down over the edge of my bunk at him and he was looking out the window too. 'Well, I'll be – . Look.' Uncle must have been in the shed under the windmill to get his bike, and now he was pedalling flat out up the drive. He skidded on the gravel, just about fell off at the gate, dragged his bike through, left the gate open and disappeared.

'What the hell do you make of that?' Cliff looked up at me with his mouth open. His hair was all over the place.

'Search me.'

Cliff got up and tried the door. 'He's locked us in,' he said. He scratched his chest, and rubbed one foot over the other. 'This floor is cold. Where's Norman?' Norman's bunk hadn't been slept in. His coat and hat were not on their pegs. 'Hell, he has had a bash,' said Cliff. 'Spent the whole night on the tiles, eh? I suppose he'll be asleep in a loosebox somewhere.' He tried the door again. 'I wonder why he locked us in?'

'I don't know. And where would he go on the bike?'

'I'm going to have a look.' He opened the window, jumped out, and went round to the door. 'He's got the key,' he called. 'You'll have to get out the window.'

I climbed down and jumped out. The gravel hurt on my bare feet. It was cold too. I hobbled round the front. 'Jesus Christ,' said Cliff in a funny voice. 'Oo-o-o-o.' He was looking up at the loft.

Norman was hanging from the beam above the platform. He had his overcoat on. His feet hung down pigeon-toed. The rope round his neck must have been very tight for his face was all blue and swollen and twisted. You could see his teeth. His neck seemed to twist up out of his coat collar and his face was round to one side. He was just swaying a little bit. His hat was down on the gravel in front of us.

I started to shiver and I couldn't get my breath. Cliff gulped and turned and pushed past me and got in the window. I followed. I didn't feel the gravel at all. We got back into bed, but I couldn't stop shivering. Cliff said 'Oo-o-o-o' again like a moan and started to cry. I was very frightened but I didn't cry.

Well of course the policemen came back with uncle, and a doctor came, and they got him down. They were talking and moving about just outside, but Cliff and I stayed in bed and pretended we didn't hear anything at all. We didn't know what to do. We didn't even talk to each other.

There were people coming and going all morning, and I didn't know what to do. I seemed to be getting in the way all the time and nobody wanted to talk to me. Cliff didn't get up, and kept crying when they asked him to. I didn't see Mary either. Auntie didn't know what to do about me. I didn't want to go down to the whare again once I got in the house. I kept shivering.

In the end uncle brought my clothes up, and auntie took me into town and managed to get me a berth on the boat for that night. She came right to Lyttelton to see me off. It was the first time she'd ever done that for any of us. She sent telegrams too, to Dad's cousin in Wellington, and to Mum. But it wasn't until the boat had pulled out and I was in my bunk, feeling it press up underneath my back and sink away again that I started to cry. I liked Norman, and it seemed so awfully sad to think that someone always had to be the loser.

SWANS

Janet Frame

They were ready to go. Mother and Fay and Totty, standing by the gate in their next best to Sunday best, Mother with her straw hat on with shells on it and Fay with her check dress that Mother had made and Totty, well where was Totty a moment ago she was here?

– Totty, Mother called. If you don't hurry we'll miss the train, it leaves in ten minutes. And we're not to forget to get off at Beach Street. At least I think Dad said Beach Street. But hurry Totty.

Totty came running from the wash-house round the back.

– Mum quick I've found Gypsy and her head's down like all the other cats and she's dying I think. She's in the wash-house. Mum quick, she cried urgently.

Mother looked flurried. Hurry up, Totty and come back Fay, pussy will be all right. We'll give her some milk now there's some in the pot and we'll wrap her in a piece of blanket and she'll be all right till we get home.

The three of them hurried back to the wash-house. It was dark with no light except what came through the small square window which had been cracked and pasted over with brown paper. The cat lay on a pile of sacks in a corner near the copper. Her head was down and her eyes were bright with a fever or poison or something but she was alive. They found an old clean tin lid and poured warm milk in it and from one of the shelves they pulled a dusty piece of blanket. The folds stuck to one another all green and hairy and a slater with hills and valleys on his back fell to the floor and moved slowly along the cracked concrete floor to a little secret place by the wall. Totty even forgot to collect him. She collected things, slaters and earwigs and spiders though you had to be careful with earwigs for when you were lying in the grass asleep they crept into your ear and built their nest there and you had to go to the doctor and have your ear lanced.

They covered Gypsy and each one patted her. Don't worry Gypsy they said. We'll be back to look after you tonight. We're going to the Beach now. Goodbye Gypsy.

And there was mother waiting impatiently again at the gate.

– Do hurry. Pussy'll be all right now.

Mother always said things would be all right, cats and birds and people even as if she knew and she did know too, mother knew always.

But Fay crept back once more to look inside the wash-house.

– I promise, she called to the cat. We'll be back, just you see.

And the next moment the three Mother and Fay and Totty were outside the gate and mother with a broom-like motion of her arms was sweeping the two little girls before her.

O the train and the coloured pictures on the station, South America and Australia, and the bottle of fizzy drink that you could only half finish because you were too full, and the ham sandwiches that curled up at the edges, because they were stale, Dad said, and he *knew*, and the rabbits and cows and bulls outside in the paddocks, and the sheep running away from the noise and the houses that came and went like a dream, clackety-clack, Kaitangata, Kaitangata, and the train stopping and panting and the man with the stick tapping the wheels and the huge rubber hose to give the engine a drink, and the voices of the people in the carriage on and on and waiting.

– Don't forget Beach Street, Mum, Dad had said. Dad was away at work up at six o'clock early and couldn't come. It was strange without him for he always managed. He got the tea and the fizzy drinks and the sandwiches and he knew which station was which and where and why and how, but Mother didn't. Mother was often too late for the fizzy drinks and she coughed before she spoke to the children and then in a whisper in case the people in the carriage should hear and think things, and she said I'm sure I don't know kiddies when they asked about the station, but she was big and warm and knew about cats and little ring-eyes, and father was hard and bony and his face prickled when he kissed you.

O look the beach coming it must be coming.

The train stopped with a jerk and a cloud of smoke as if it had died and finished and would never go anywhere else just stay by the sea though you couldn't see the water from here, and the carriages would be empty and slowly rusting as if the people in them had come to an end and could never go back as if they had found what they were looking for after years and years of travelling on and on. But they were disturbed and peeved at being forced to move. The taste of smoke lingered in their mouths, they had to reach up for hat and coat and case, and comb their hair and make up their face again, certainly they had arrived but you have to be neat arriving with your shoes brushed and your hair in place and the shine off your nose. Fay and Totty watched the little cases being snipped open and shut and the two little girls knew for sure that never would they grow up and be people in bulgy dresses, people knitting purl and plain with the ball of wool hanging safe and clean from a neat brown bag with hollyhocks and poppies on it. Hollyhocks and poppies and a big red initial, to show that you were you and not the somebody else you feared you might be, but Fay and Totty didn't worry they were going to the Beach.

The Beach. Why wasn't everyone going to the Beach? It seemed they were the only ones for when they set off down the fir-bordered road that led to the sound the sea kept making forever now in their ears, there was no one else going. Where had the others gone? Why weren't there other people?

– Why mum?

– It's a week-day chicken, said Mum smiling and fat now the rushing was over. The others have gone to work I suppose. I don't know. But here we are. Tired? She looked at them both in the way they loved, the way she looked at them at night at other people's places when they were weary of cousins and hide the thimble and wanted to go home to bed. Tired? she would say. And Fay and Totty would yawn as if nothing in the world would keep them awake and mother would say knowingly and fondly The dustman's coming to someone. But no they weren't tired now for it was day and the sun though a watery sad sun was up and the birds, the day was for waking in and the night was for sleeping in.

They raced on ahead of mother eager to turn the desolate crying sound of sea to the more comforting and near sight of long green and white waves coming and going forever on the sand. They had never been here before, not to this sea. They had been to other seas, near merry-go-rounds and swings and slides, among people, other girls and boys and mothers, mine are so fond of the water the mothers would say, talking about mine and yours and he, that meant father, or the old man if they did not much care but mother cared always.

The road was stony and the little girls carrying the basket had skiffed toes by the time they came to the end, but it was all fun and yet strange for they were by themselves no other families and Fay thought for a moment what if there is no sea either and no nothing?

But the sea roared in their ears it was true sea, look it was breaking white on the sand and the seagulls crying and skimming and the bits of white flying and look at all of the coloured shells, look a little pink one like a fan, and a cat's eye. Gypsy. And look at the seaweed look I've found a round piece that plops, you tread on it and it plops, you plop this one, see it plops, and the little girls running up and down plopping and plopping and picking and prying and touching and listening, and mother plopping the seaweed too, look mum's doing it and mum's got a crab.

102

But it cannot go on for ever.

– Where is the place to put our things and the merry-go-rounds and the place to undress and that, and the place to get ice-creams?

There's no place, only a little shed with forms that have bird-dirt on them and old pieces of newspapers stuffed in the corner and writing on the walls, rude writing.

– Mum, have we come to the wrong sea?

Mother looked bewildered. I don't know kiddies, I'm sure.

– Is it the wrong sea? Totty took up the cry.

It was the wrong sea. Yes kiddies, mother said now that's strange I'm sure I remembered what your father told me but I couldn't have but I'm sure I remembered. Isn't it funny. I didn't know it would be like this. Oh things are never like you think they're different and sad. I don't know.

– Look, I've found the biggest plop of all, cried Fay who had wandered away intent on plopping. The biggest plop of all, she repeated, justifying things. Come on.

So it was all right really it was a good sea, you could pick up the foam before it turned yellow and take off your shoes and sink your feet down in the wet sand almost until you might disappear and come up in Spain, that was where you came up if you sank. And there was the little shed to eat in and behind the rushes to undress but you couldn't go in swimming.

– Not in this sea, mother said firmly.

They felt proud. It was a distinguished sea oh and a lovely one noisy in your ears and green and blue and brown where the seaweed floated. Whales? Sharks? Seals? It was the right kind of sea.

All day on the sand, racing and jumping and turning head over heels and finding shells galore and making castles and getting buried and unburied, going dead and coming alive like the people in the Bible. And eating in the little shed for the sky had clouded over and a cold wind had come shaking the heads of the fir-trees as if to say I'll teach you, springing them backwards and forwards in a devilish exercise.

Tomatoes, and a fire blowing in your face. The smoke burst out and you wished. Aladdin and the genie. What did you wish?

I wish today is always but father too jumping us up and down on his knee. This is the maiden all forlorn that milked the cow.

– Totty, it's my turn, isn't it Dad?

– It's both of your turns. Come on, sacks on the mill and *more on still*. Not father away at work but father here making the fire and breaking sticks, quickly and surely, and father showing this and that and telling why. Why? Did anyone in the world ever know why? Or did they just pretend to know because they didn't like anyone else to know that they didn't know? Why?

They were going home when they saw the swans. We'll go this quicker way, said mother, who had been exploring. We'll walk across the lagoon over this strip of land and soon we'll be at the station and then home to bed. She smiled and put her arms round them both. Everything was warm and secure and near, and the darker the world outside got the safer you felt for there were mother and father always, for ever.

They began to walk across the lagoon. It was growing dark now quickly and dark sneaks in. Oh home in the train with the guard lighting the lamps and the shiny slippery seat growing hard and your eyes scarcely able to keep open, the sea in your ears, and your little bagful of shells dropped somewhere down the back of the seat, crushed and sandy and wet, and your baby crab dead and salty and stiff fallen on the floor.

– We'll soon be home, mother said, and was silent.

It was dark black water, secret, and the air was filled with murmurings and rustlings, it was as if they were walking into another world that had been kept secret from everyone and now they had found it. The darkness lay massed across the water and over to the east, thick as if you could touch it, soon it would swell and fill the earth.

The children didn't speak now, they were tired with the dustman really coming, and mother was sad and quiet, the wrong sea troubled her, what had she done, she had been sure she would find things different, as she had said they would be, merry-go-rounds and swings and slides for the kiddies, and other mothers to show the kiddies off too, they were quite bright for their age, what had she done?

They looked across the lagoon then and saw the swans, black and shining, as if the visiting dark tiring of its form, had changed to birds, hundreds of them resting and moving softly about on the water. Why the lagoon was filled with swans, like secret sad ships, secret and quiet. Hush-sh the water said, rush-hush, the wind passed over the top of the water, no other sound but the shaking of rushes and far away now it seemed the roar of the sea like a secret sea that had crept inside your head for ever. And the swans, they were there too, inside you, peaceful and quiet watching and sleeping and watching, there was nothing but peace and warmth and calm, everything found, train and sea and mother and father and earwig and slater and spider.

And Gypsy?

But when they got home Gypsy was dead.

ALONG RIDEOUT ROAD
THAT SUMMER

Maurice Duggan

I'd walked the length of Rideout Road the night before, following the noise of the river in the darkness, tumbling over ruts and stones, my progress, if you'd call it that, challenged by farmers' dogs and observed by the faintly luminous eyes of wandering stock, steers, cows, stud-bulls or milk-white unicorns or, better, a full quartet of apocalyptic horses browsing the marge. In time and darkness I found Puti Hohepa's farmhouse and lugged my fibre suitcase up to the verandah, after nearly breaking my leg in a cattle-stop. A journey fruitful of one decision – to flog a torch from somewhere. And of course I didn't. And now my feet hurt; but it was daylight and, from memory, I'd say I was almost happy. Almost. Fortunately I am endowed both by nature and later conditioning with a highly developed sense of the absurd; knowing that you can imagine the pleasure I took in this abrupt translation from shop-counter to tractor seat, from town pavements to back-country farm, with all those miles of river-bottom darkness to mark the transition. In fact, and unfortunately there have to be some facts, even fictional ones, I'd removed myself a mere dozen miles from the parental home. In darkness, as I've said, and with a certain stealth. I didn't consult dad about it, and, needless to say, I didn't tell mum. The moment wasn't propitious; dad was asleep with the *Financial Gazette* threatening to suffocate him and mum was off somewhere moving, as she so often did, that this meeting make public its whole-hearted support for the introduction of flogging and public castration for all sex offenders and hanging, drawing and quartering, for almost everyone else, and as for delinquents (my boy!). . . . Well, put yourself in my shoes, there's no need to go on. Yes, almost happy, though my feet were so tender I winced every time I tripped the clutch.

Almost happy, shouting Kubla Khan, a bookish lad, from the seat of the clattering old Ferguson tractor, doing a steady five miles an hour in a cloud of seagulls, getting to the bit about the damsel with the dulcimer and looking up to see the reputedly wild Hohepa girl perched on the gate, feet hooked in the bars, ribbons fluttering from her ukulele. A perfect moment of recognition, daring rider, in spite of the belch of carbon monoxide from the tin-can exhaust up front on the bonnet. Don't, however, misunderstand me: I'd not have you think we are here embarked on the trashy clamour of boy meeting girl. No, the problem, you are to understand, was one of connexion. How connect the dulcimer with the ukulele, if you follow. For a boy of my bents this problem of how to cope with the shock of the recognition of a certain discrepancy between the real and the written was rather like watching mum with a shoehorn wedging nines into sevens and suffering merry hell. I'm not blaming old STC for everything, of course. After all, some other imports went wild too; and I've spent too long at the handle of a mattock, a critical function, not to know that. The stench of the exhaust, that's to say, held no redolence of that old hophead's pipe. Let us then be clear and don't for a moment, gentlemen, imagine that I venture the gross unfairness, the patent absurdity, the rank injustice (your turn) of blaming him for spoiling the pasture or fouling the native air. It's just that there was this problem in my mind, this profound, cultural problem affecting dramatically the very nature of my inheritance, nines into sevens in this lovely smiling land. His was the genius as his was the expression which the vast educational brouhaha invited me to praise and emulate, tranquillisers ingested in maturity, the voice of the ring-dove, look up though your feet be in the clay. And read on.

Of course I understood immediately that these were not matters I was destined to debate with Fanny Hohepa. Frankly, I could see that she didn't give a damn; it was part of her attraction. She thought I was singing. She smiled and waved, I waved and smiled, turned, ploughed back through gull-white and coffee loam and fell into a train of thought not entirely free of Fanny and her instrument, pausing to wonder, now and then, what might be the symptoms, the early symptoms, of carbon monoxide poisoning. Drowsiness? Check. Dilation of the pupils? Can't check. Extra cutaneous sensation? My feet. Trembling hands? Vibrato. Down and back, down and back, turning again, Dick and his Ferguson, Fanny from her perch seeming to gather about her the background of green paternal acres, fold on fold. I bore down upon her in all the eager erubescence of youth, with my hair slicked back. She trembled, wavered, fragmented and re-formed in the pungent vapour through which I viewed her. (Oh for an open-air job, eh mate?) She plucked, very picture in jeans and summer shirt of youth and suspicion, and seemed to sing. I couldn't of course hear a note. Behind me the dog-leg furrows and the bright ploughshares.

Certainly she looked at her ease and, even through the gassed-up atmosphere between us, too deliciously substantial to be creature down on a visit from Mount Abora. I was glad I'd combed my hair. Back, down and back. Considering the size of the paddock this could have gone on for a week. I promptly admitted to myself that her present position, disposition or posture, involving as it did some provocative tautness of cloth, suited me right down to the ground. I mean to hell with the idea of having her stand knee-deep in the thistle thwanging her dulcimer and plaintively chirruping about a pipedream mountain. In fact she was natively engaged in expressing the most profound distillations of her local experience, the gleanings of a life lived in rich contact with a richly understood and native environment: A Slow Boat To China, if memory serves. While I, racked and shaken, composed words for the plaque which would one day stand here to commemorate our deep rapport: *Here played the black lady her dulcimer. Here wept she full miseries. Here rode the knight Fergus' son to her deliverance. Here put he about her ebon and naked shoulders his courtly garment of leather, black, full curiously emblazoned – Hell's Angel.*

When she looked as though my looking were about to make her leave I stopped the machine and pulled out the old tobacco and rolled a smoke, holding the steering wheel in my teeth, though on a good day I could roll with one hand, twist and lick, draw, shoot the head off a pin at a mile and a half, spin, blow down the barrel before you could say:

Gooday. How are yuh?

All right.

I'm Buster O'Leary.

I'm Fanny Hohepa.

Yair, I know.

It's hot.

It's hot right enough.

You can have a swim when you're through.

Mightn't be a bad idea at that.

Over there by the trees.

Yair, I seen it. Like, why don't you join me, eh?

I might.

Go on, you'd love it.

I might.

Goodoh then, see yuh.

A genuine crumpy conversation if ever I heard one, darkly reflective of the Socratic method, rich with echoes of the Kantian imperative, its universal mate, summoning sharply to the minds of each the history of the first trystings of all immortal lovers, the tragic and tangled tale, indeed, of all star-crossed moonings, mum and dad, mister and missus unotoo and all. Enough? I should bloody well hope so.

Of course nothing came of it. Romantic love was surely the invention of a wedded onanist with seven kids. And I don't mean dad. Nothing? Really and truly nothing? Well, I treasure the under-statement; though why I should take such pleasure in maligning the ploughing summer white on loam, river flats, the frivolous ribbons and all the strumming, why I don't know. Xanadu and the jazzy furrows, the wall-eyed bitch packing the cows through the yardgate, the smell of river water . . . Why go on? So few variations to an old, old story. No. But on the jolting tractor I received that extra jolt I mentioned and am actually now making rather too much of, gentlemen: relate Fanny Hohepa and her uke to that mountain thrush singing her black mountain blues.

But of course now, in our decent years, we know such clay questions long broken open or we wouldn't be here, old and somewhat sour, wading up to our battered thighs (forgive me, madam) at the confluence of the great waters, paddling in perfect confidence in the double debouchment of universal river and regional stream, the shallow fast fan of water spreading over the delta, Abyssinia come to Egypt in the rain . . . ah, my country! I speak of cultural problems, in riddles and literary puddles, perform this act of divination with my own entrails: Fanny's dark delta; the nubile and Nubian sheila with her portable piano anticipating the transistor-set; all gathered into single demesne, O'Leary's orchard. Even this wooden bowl, plucked from the flood, lost from the hand of some anonymous herdsman as he stopped to cup a drink at the river's source. Ah, Buster. Ah, Buster. Buster. Ah, darling. Darling! Love. You recognise it? Could you strum to that? Suppose you gag a little at the sugar coating, it's the same old fundamental toffee, underneath.

No mere cheap cyn . . . sm intended. She took me down to her darkling avid as any college girl for the fruits and sweets of my flowering talents, taking me as I wasn't but might hope one day to be, honest, simple and broke to the wide. The half-baked verbosity and the conceit she must have ignored, or how else could she have borne me? It pains me, gentlemen, to confess that she was too good for me by far. Far. Anything so spontaneous and natural could be guaranteed to be beyond me: granted, I mean, my impeccable upbringing under the white-hot lash of respectability, take that, security, take that, hypocrisy, take that, cant, take that where, does it seem curious?, mum did all the beating flushed pink in ecstasy and righteousness, and that and that and THAT. Darling! How then could I deem Fanny's conduct proper when I carried such weals and scars, top-marks in the lesson on the wickedness of following the heart. Fortunately such a question would not have occurred to Fanny: she was remarkably free from queries of any kind. She would walk past the Home Furnishing Emporium without a glance.

She is too good for you.

It was said clearly enough, offered without threat and as just comment, while I was bent double stripping old Daisy or Pride of the Plains or Rose of Sharon after the cups came off. I stopped what I was doing, looked sideways until I could see the tops of his gumboots, gazed on *Marathon*, and then turned back, dried off all four tits and let the cow out into the race where, taking the legrope with her, she squittered off wild in the eyes.

She is too good for you.

So I looked at him and he looked back. I lost that game of stare-you-down, too. He walked off. Not a warning, not even a reproach, just something it was as well I should know if I was to have the responsibility of acting in full knowledge – and who the hell wants that? And two stalls down Fanny spanked a cow out through the flaps and looked at me, and giggled. The summer thickened and blazed.

The first response on the part of my parents was silence; which can only be thought of as response in a very general sense. I could say, indeed I will say, stony silence; after all they were my parents. But I knew the silence wouldn't last long. I was an only child (darling, you never guessed?) and that load of woodchopping, lawnmowing, hedgeclipping, dishwashing, carwashing, errandrunning, garden-choring and the rest of it was going to hit them like a folding mortgage pretty soon. I'd like to have been there, to have seen the lank grass grown beyond window height and the uncut hedges shutting out the sun: perpetual night and perpetual mould on Rose Street West. After a few weeks the notes and letters began. The whole gamut, gentlemen, from sweet and sickly to downright abusive. Mostly in mum's masculine hand. A unique set of documents reeking of blood and tripes. I treasured every word, reading between the lines the record of an undying, all-sacrificing love, weeping tears for the idyllic childhood they could not in grief venture to touch upon, the care lavished, the love squandered upon me. The darlings. Of course I didn't reply. I didn't even wave when they drove past Fanny and me as we were breasting out of the scrub back on to the main road, dishevelled and, yes, almost happy in the daze of summer and Sunday afternoon. I didn't wave. I grinned as brazenly as I could manage with a jaw full of hard boiled egg and took Fanny's arm, brazen, her shirt only casually resumed, while they went by like burnished doom.

Fanny's reaction to all this? An expression of indifference, a downcurving of that bright and wilful mouth, a flirt of her head. So much fuss over so many fossilised ideas, if I may so translate her expression which was, in fact, gentlemen, somewhat more direct and not in any sense exhibiting what mum would have called a due respect for elders and betters. Pouf! Not contempt, no; not disagreement; simply an impatience with what she, Fanny, deemed the irrelevance of so many many words for so light and tumbling a matter. And, for the season at least, I shared the mood, her demon lover in glossy brilliantine.

But as the days ran down the showdown came nearer and finally the stage was set. Low-keyed and sombre notes in the sunlight, the four of us variously disposed on the unpainted Hohepa verandah, Hohepa and O'Leary, the male seniors, and Hohepa and O'Leary, junior representatives, male seventeen, female ready to swear, you understand, that she was sixteen, turning.

Upon the statement that Fanny was too good for me my pappy didn't comment. No one asked him to: no one faced him with the opinion. Wise reticence, mere oversight or a sense of the shrieking irrelevance of such a statement, I don't know. Maori girls, Maori farms, Maori housing: you'd only to hear my father put tongue to any or all of that to know where he stood, solid for intolerance, mac, but solid. Of course, gentlemen, it was phrased differently on his lips, gradual absorption, hmm, perhaps, after, say, a phase of disinfecting. A pillar of our decent, law-abiding community, masonic in his methodism, brother, total abstainer, rotarian and non-smoker, addicted to long volleys of handball, I mean pocket billards cue and all. Mere nervousness, of course, a subconscious habit. Mum would cough and glance down and dad would spring to attention hands behind his back. Such moments of tender rapport are sweet to return to, memories any child might treasure. Then he'd forget again. Straight mate, there were days, especially Sundays, when mum would be hacking away like an advanced case of t.b. Well, you can picture it, there on the verandah. With the finely turned Fanny under his morose eye, you know how it is, hemline hiked and this and that visible from odd angles, he made a straight break of two hundred without one miscue, Daddy! I came in for a couple of remand home stares myself, bread and water and solitary and take that writ on his eyeballs in backhand black while his mouth served out its lying old hohums and there's no reason why matters shouldn't be resolved amicably, etc, black hanging-cap snug over his tonsure and tongue moistening his droopy lip, ready, set, drop. And Puti Hohepa leaving him to it. A dignified dark prince on his ruined acres, old man Hohepa, gravely attending to dad's mumbled slush, winning hands down just by being there and saying nothing, nothing, while Fanny with her fatal incapacity for standing upright unsupported for more than fifteen seconds, we all had a disease of the spine that year, pouted at me as though it were all my fault over the back of the chair (sic). All my fault being just the pater's monologue, the remarkably imprecise grip of his subject with consequent proliferation of the bromides so typical of all his ilk of elk, all the diversely identical representatives of decency, caution and the colour bar. Of course daddy didn't there and then refer to race, colour creed or uno who. Indeed he firmly believed he believed, if I may recapitulate, gentlemen, that this blessed land was free from such taint, a unique social experiment, two races living happily side by side, respecting each others etc and etc. As a banker he knew the value of discretion, though what was home if not a place to hang up your reticence along with your hat and get stuck into all the hate that was inside you, in the name of justice? Daddy Hohepa said nothing, expressed nothing, may even have been unconscious of the great destinies being played out on his sunlit verandah, or of what fundamental principles of democracy and the freedom of the individual were being here so brilliantly exercised; may have been, in fact, indifferent to daddy's free granting tautologies now, of the need for circumspection in all matters of national moment, all such questions as what shall be done for our dark brothers and sisters, outside the jails? I hope so. After a few minutes Hohepa rangatira trod the boards thoughtfully and with the slowness of a winter bather lowered himself into a pool of sunlight on the wide steps, there to lift his face broad and grave in full dominion of his inheritance and even, perhaps, so little did his expression reveal of his inward reflection, full consciousness of his dispossessions.

What, you may ask, was my daddy saying? Somewhere among the circumlocutions, these habits are catching among the words and sentiments designed to express his grave ponderings on the state of the nation and so elicit from his auditors (not me, I wasn't listening) admission, tacit though it may be, of his tutored opinion, there was centred the suggestion that old man Hohepa and daughter were holding me against my will, ensnaring me with flesh and farm. He had difficulty in getting it out in plain words; some lingering cowardice, perhaps. Which was why daddy Hohepa missed it, perhaps. Or did the view command all his attention?

111

Rideout Mountain far and purple in the afternoon sun; the jersey cows beginning to move, intermittent and indirect, towards the shed; the dog jangling its chain as it scratched; Fanny falling in slow movement across the end of the old cane lounge chair to lie, an interesting composition of curves and angles, with the air of a junior and rural odalisque. Me? I stood straight, of course, rigid, thumbs along the seams of my jeans, hair at the regulation distance two inches above the right eye, heels together and bare feet at ten to two, or ten past ten, belly flat and chest inflated, chin in, heart out. I mean, can you see me, mac? Dad's grave-suit so richly absorbed the sun that he was forced to retreat into the shadows where his crafty jailer's look was decently camouflaged, blending white with purple blotched with silver wall. Not a bad heart, surely?

As his audience we each displayed differing emotions. Fanny, boredom that visibly bordered on sleep: Puti Hohepa, an inattention expressed in his long examination of the natural scene: Buster O'Leary, a sense of complete bewilderment over what it was the old man thought he could achieve by his harangue and, further, a failure to grasp the relevance of it all for the Hohepas. My reaction, let me say, was mixed with irritation at certain of father's habits. (Described.) With his pockets filled with small change he sounded like the original gypsy orchestra, cymbals and all. I actually tried mum's old trick of the glance and the cough. No luck. And he went on talking, at me now, going so wide of the mark, for example, as to mention some inconceivable, undocumented and undemonstrated condition, some truly monstrous condition, called your-mother's-love. Plain evidence of his distress, I took it to be, this obscenity uttered in mixed company. I turned my head the better to hear, when it came, the squelchy explosion of his heart. And I rolled a smoke and threw Fanny the packet. It landed neatly on her stomach. She sat up and made herself a smoke then crossed to her old man and, perching beside him in the brilliant pool of light, fire of skin and gleam of hair bronze and blue-black, neatly extracted from his pocket his battered flint lighter. She snorted smoke and passed the leaf to her old man.

Some things, gentlemen, still amaze. To my dying day I have treasured that scene and all its rich implications. In a situation so pregnant of difficulties, in the midst of a debate so fraught with undertones, an exchange (quiet there, at the back) so bitterly fulsome on the one hand and so reserved on the other. I ask you to take special note of this observance of the ritual of the makings, remembering, for the fullest savouring of the nuance, my father's abstention. As those brown fingers moved on the white cylinder, or cone, I was moved almost, to tears, almost, by this companionable and wordless recognition of our common human frailty, father and dark child in silent communion and I too, in some manner not to be explained because inexplicable, sharing their hearts. I mean the insanity, pal. Puti Hohepa and his lass in sunlight on the steps, smoking together, untroubled, natural and patient; and me and daddy glaring at each other in the shades like a couple of evangelists at cross pitch. Love, thy silver coatings and castings. And thy neighbours! So I went and sat by Fanny and put an arm through hers.

The sun gathered me up, warmed and consoled; the bitter view assumed deeper purples and darker rose; a long way off a shield flashed, the sun striking silver from a water trough. At that moment I didn't care what mad armies marched in my father's voice nor what the clarion was he was trying so strenuously to sound. I didn't care that the fire in his heart was fed by such rank fuel, skeezing envy, malice, revenge, hate and parental power. I sat and smoked and was warm; and the girl's calm flank was against me, her arm through mine. Nothing was so natural as to turn through the little distance between us and kiss her smoky mouth. Ah yes, I could feel, I confess, through my shoulder blades as it were and the back of my head, the crazed rapacity and outrage of my daddy's Irish stare, the blackness and the cold glitter of knives. (Father!) While Puti Hohepa sat on as though turned to glowing stone by the golden light, faced outward to the violet mystery of the natural hour, monumentally content and still.

You will have seen it, known it, guessed that there was between this wild, loamy daughter and me, sunburnt scion of an ignorant, insensitive, puritan and therefore prurient, Irishman (I can't stop) no more than a summer's dalliance, a season's thoughtless sweetness, a boy and a girl and the makings.

In your wisdom, gentlemen, you will doubtless have sensed that something is lacking in this lullaby, some element missing for the articulation of this ranting tale. Right. The key to daddy's impassioned outburst, no less. Not lost in this verbose review, but so far unstated. Point is he'd come to seek his little son (someone must have been dying because he'd never have come for the opposite reason) and, not being one to baulk at closed doors and drawn shades, wait for it, he'd walked straight in on what he'd always somewhat feverishly imagined and hoped he feared. Fanny took it calmly: I was, naturally, more agitated. Both of us ballocky in the umber light, of course. Still, even though he stayed only long enough to let his eyes adjust and his straining mind take in this historic disposition of flesh, those mantis angles in which for all our

horror we must posit our conceivings, it wasn't the greeting he'd
expected. It wasn't quite the same, either, between Fanny and me,
after he'd backed out, somewhat huffily, on to the verandah. Ah,
filthy beasts! He must have been roaring some such expression as
that inside his head because his eyeballs were rattling, the very
picture of a broken doll, and his face was liver-coloured. I felt sorry
for him, for a second, easing backward from the love-starred couch
and the moving lovers with his heel hooked through the loop of
Fanny's bra, kicking it free like a football hero punting for touch,
his dream of reconciliation in ruins.

It wasn't the same. Some rhythms are slow to re-form. And once
the old man actually made the sanctuary of the verandah he just had
to bawl his loudest for old man Hohepa, Mr Ho-he-pa, Mr
Ho-he-pa. It got us into our clothes anyway. Fanny giggling and
getting a sneezing fit at the same time, bending forward into the
hoof-marked brassiere and blasting off every ten seconds like a
burst air hose until I quite lost count on the one-for-sorrow
two-for-joy scale and crammed myself sulkily into my jocks.

Meantime dad's labouring to explain certain natural facts and
common occurrences to Puti Hohepa, just as though he'd made an
original discovery; as perhaps he had considering what he probably
thought of as natural. Puti Hohepa listened, I thought that
ominous, then silently deprecated, in a single slow movement of
his hand, the wholly inappropriate expression of shock and rage, all
the sizzle of my daddy's oratory.

Thus the tableau. We did the only possible thing, ignored him
and let him run down, get it off his chest, come to his five battered
senses, if he had so many, and get his breath. Brother, how he
spilled darkness and sin upon that floor, wilting collar and boiling
eyes, the sweat running from his face and, Fanny, shameless,
languorous and drowsy, provoking him to further flights. She was
young, gentlemen: I have not concealed it. She was too young to
have had time to accumulate the history he ascribed to her. She was
too tender to endure for long the muscular lash of his tongue and
the rake of his eyes. She went over to her dad, as heretofore
described, and when my sweet sire, orator general to the dying
afternoon, had made his pitch about matters observed and
inferences drawn, I went to join her. I sat with my back to him. All
our backs were to him, including his own. He emptied himself of
wrath and for a moment, a wild and wonderful moment, I thought
he was going to join us, bathers in the pool of sun. But no.

Silence. Light lovely and fannygold over the pasture; shreds of
mist by the river deepening to rose. My father's hard leather soles
rattled harshly on the bare boards like rim-shots. The mad figure of

him went black as bug out over the lawn, out over the loamy furrows where the tongue of ploughed field invaded the home paddock, all my doing, spurning in his violence anything less than this direct and abrupt charge towards the waiting car. Fanny's hand touched my arm again and for a moment I was caught in a passion of sympathy for him, something as solid as grief and love, an impossible pairing of devotion and despair. The landscape flooded with sadness as I watched the scuttling, black, ignominious figure hurdling the fresh earth, the waving arms, seemingly scattering broadcast the white and shying gulls, his head bobbing on his shoulders, as he narrowed into distance.

I wished, gentlemen, with a fervour foreign to my young life, that it had been in company other than that of Puti Hohepa and his brat that we had made our necessary parting. I wished we had been alone. I did not want to see him diminished, made ridiculous and pathetic among strangers, while I so brashly joined the mockers. (Were they mocking?) Impossible notions; for what was there to offer and how could he receive? Nothing. I stroked Fanny's arm. Old man Hohepa got up and unchained the dog and went off to get the cows in. He didn't speak; maybe the chocolate old bastard was dumb, eh? In a minute I would have to go down and start the engine and put the separator together. I stayed to stare at Fanny, thinking of undone things in a naughty world. She giggled, thinking, for all I know, of the same, or of nothing. Love, thy sunny trystings and nocturnal daggers. For the first time I admitted my irritation at that girlish, hiccoughing, tenor giggle. But we touched, held, got up and with our arms linked went down the long paddock through the infestation of buttercup, our feet bruising stalk and flower. Suddenly all I wanted and at whatever price was to be able, sometime, somewhere, to make it up to my primitive, violent, ignorant and crazy old man. And I knew I never would. Ah, what a bloody fool. And then the next thing I wanted, a thing far more feasible, was to be back in that room with its shade and smell of hay-dust and warm flesh, taking up the classic story just where we'd been so rudely forced to discontinue it. Old man Hohepa was bellowing at the dog; the cows rocked up through the paddock gate and into the yard: the air smelled of night. I stopped; and holding Fanny's arm suggested we might run back. Her eyes went wide: she giggled and broke away and I stood there and watched her flying down the paddock, bare feet and a flouncing skirt, her hair shaken loose.

Next afternoon I finished ploughing the river paddock, the nature of Puti Hohepa's husbandry as much a mystery as ever, and ran the old Ferguson into the lean-to shelter behind the cow shed. It was far too late for ploughing: the upper paddocks were hard and dry. But Puti hoped to get a crop of late lettuce off the river flat; just in time, no doubt, for a glutted market, brown rot, wilt and total failure of the heart. He'd have to harrow it first, too; and on his own. Anyway, none of my worry. I walked into the shed. Fanny and her daddy were deep in conversation. She was leaning against the flank of a cow, a picture of rustic grace, a rural study of charmed solemnity. Christ knows what they were saying to each other. For one thing they were speaking in their own language: for another I couldn't hear anything, even that, above the blather and splatter of the bloody cows and the racket of the single cylinder diesel, brand-name Onan out of Edinburgh so help me. They looked up. I grabbed a stool and got on with it, head down to the bore of it all. I'd have preferred to be up on the tractor, poisoning myself straight out, bellowing this and that and the other looney thing to the cynical gulls. Ah, my mountain princess of the golden chords, something was changing. I stripped on, sullenly: I hoped it was me.

We were silent through dinner: we were always silent, through all meals. It made a change from home where all hell lay between soup and sweet, everyone taking advantage of the twenty minutes of enforced attendance to shoot the bile, bicker and accuse, rant and wrangle through the grey disgusting mutton and the two veg. Fanny never chattered much and less than ever in the presence of her pappy: giggled maybe but never said much. Then out of the blue father Hohepa opened up. Buster, you should make peace with your father. I considered it. I tried to touch Fanny's foot under the table and I considered it. A boy shouldn't hate his father: a boy should respect his father. I thought about that too. Then I asked should fathers hate their sons; but I knew the answer. Puti Hohepa didn't say anything, just sat blowing into his tea, looking at his reputedly wild daughter who might have been a beauty for all I could tell, content to be delivered of the truth and so fulfilled. You should do this: a boy shouldn't do that – tune into that, mac. And me thinking proscription and prescription differently ordered in this farm world of crummy acres. I mean I thought I'd left all that crap behind the night I stumbled along Rideout Road following, maybe, the river Alph. I thought old man Hohepa, having been silent for so long, would know better than to pull, of a sudden, all those generalisations with which for seventeen years I'd been beaten dizzy – but not so dizzy as not to be able to look back of the billboards and see the stack of rotting bibles. Gentlemen, I was, even noticeably, subdued. Puti Hohepa clearly didn't intend to add anything more just then. I was too tired to make him an answer. I think I was too tired even for hate; and what better indication of the extent of my exhaustion than that? It had been a long summer; how long I was only beginning to discover. It was cold in the kitchen. Puti Hohepa got up. From the doorway, huge and merging into the night, he spoke again: You must make up your own mind. He went away, leaving behind him the vibration of a gentle sagacity, tolerance, a sense of duty (mine, as usual) pondered over and pronounced upon. The bastard. You must make up your own mind. And for the first time you did that mum had hysterics and dad popped his gut. About what? Made up my mind about what? My black daddy? Fanny? Myself? Life? A country career and agricultural hell? Death? Money? Fornication? (I'd always liked that.) What the hell was he trying to say? What doing but abdicating the soiled throne at the first challenge? Did he think fathers shouldn't hate their sons, or could help it, or would if they could? Am I clear? No matter. He didn't have one of the four he'd sired at home so what the hell sort of story was he trying to peddle? Father with the soft centre. You should, you shouldn't, make up your own mind. Mac, my head was going round. But it was brilliant, I conceded, when I'd given it a bit of thought. My livid daddy himself would have applauded the perfect ambiguity. What a bunch: they keep a dog on a chain for years and years and then let it free on some purely personal impulse and when it goes wild and chases its tail round and round, pissing here and sniffing there in an ecstasy of liberty, a freedom for which it has been denied all training, they shoot it down because it won't come running when they hold up the leash and whistle. (I didn't think you'd go that way, son.) Well, my own green liberty didn't look like so much at that moment; for the first time I got an inkling that life was going to be simply a matter of out of one jail and into another. Oh, they had a lot in common, her dad and mine. I sat there, mildly stupefied, drinking my tea. Then I looked up at Fanny; or, rather, down on Fanny. I've never known such a collapsible sheila in my life. She was stretched on the kitchen couch, every vertebra having turned to juice in the last minute and a half. I thought maybe she'd have the answer, some comment to offer on the state of disunion. Hell. I was the very last person to let my brew go cold while I pondered the nuance of the incomprehensible, picked at the dubious unsubtlety of thought of a man thirty years my senior who had never, until then, said more than ten words to me. She is too good for you: only six words after all and soon forgotten. Better, yes, if he'd stayed mum, leaving me to deduce from his silence whatever I could, Abora Mountain and the milk of paradise, consent in things natural and a willingness to let simple matters take their simple course.

I was wrong: Fanny offered no interpretation of her father's thought. Exegesis to his cryptic utterance was the one thing she couldn't supply. She lay with her feet up on the end of the couch, brown thighs charmingly bared, mouth open and eyes closed in balmy sleep, displaying in this posture various things but mainly her large unconcern not only for this tragedy of filial responsibility and the parental role but, too, for the diurnal problem of the numerous kitchen articles, pots, pans, plates, the lot. I gazed on her, frowning on her bloom of sleep, the slow inhalation and exhalation accompanied by a gentle flare of nostril, and considered the strength and weakness of our attachment. Helpmeet she was not, thus to leave her lover to his dark ponderings and the chores.

Puti Hohepa sat on the verandah in the dark, hacking over his bowl of shag. One by one, over my second cup of tea, I assessed my feelings, balanced all my futures in the palm of my hand. I crossed to Fanny, crouched beside her, kissed her. I felt embarrassed and, gentlemen, foolish. Her eyes opened wide; then they shut and she turned over.

The dishes engaged my attention not at all, except to remind me, here we go, of my father in apron and rubber gloves at the sink, pearl-diving while mum was off somewhere at a lynching. Poor bastard. Mum had the natural squeeze for the world; they should have changed places. (It's for your own good! Ah, the joyous peal of that as the razor strop came whistling down like tartars blade.) I joined daddy Hohepa on the verandah. For a moment we shared the crescent moon and the smell of earth damp under dew, Rideout Mountain massed to the west.

I've finished the river paddock.

Yes.

The tractor's going to need a de-coke before long.

Yes.

I guess that about cuts it out.

Yes.

I may as well shoot through.

Buster, is Fanny pregnant?

I don't know. She hasn't said anything to me so I suppose she can't be.

You are going home?

No. Not home. There's work down south. I'd like to have a look down there.

There's work going here if you want it. But you have made up your mind?

I suppose I may as well shoot through.

Yes.

After milking tomorrow if that's okay with you.

Yes.

He hacked on over his pipe. Yes, yes, yes, yes, yes is Fanny pregnant? What if I'd said yes? I didn't know one way or the other. I only hoped, and left the rest to her. Maybe he'd ask her; and what if she said yes? What then, eh Buster? Maybe I should have said why don't you ask her. A demonstrative, volatile, loquacious old person: a tangible symbol of impartiality, reason unclouded by emotion, his eyes frank in the murk of night and his pipe going bright, dim, bright as he calmly considered the lovely flank of the moon. I was hoping she wasn't, after all. Hoping; it gets to be a habit, a bad habit that does you no good, stunts your growth, sends you insane and makes you, demonstrably, blind. Hope, for Fanny Hohepa.

Later, along the riverbank, Fanny and I groped, gentlemen, for the lost rapport and the parking sign. We were separated by just a little more than an arm's reach. I made note then of the natural scene. Dark water, certainly; dark lush grass underfoot; dark girl; the drifting smell of loam in the night: grant me again as much. Then, by one of those fortuitous accidents not infrequent in our national prosings, our hands met, held, fell away. Darkness. My feet stumbling by the river and my heart going like a tango. Blood pulsed upon blood, undenied and unyoked, as we busied ourselves tenderly at our ancient greetings and farewells. And in the end, beginning my sentence with a happy conjunction, I held her indistinct, dark head. We stayed so for a minute, together and parting as always, with me tumbling down upon her the mute dilemma my mind then pretended to resolve and she offering no restraint, no argument better than the dark oblivion of her face.

Unrecorded the words between us: there can't have been more than six, anyway, it was our fated number. None referred to my departure or to the future or to maculate conceptions. Yet her last touch spoke volumes. (Unsubsidised, gentlemen, without dedication or preamble.) River-damp softened her hair: her skin smelled of soap: Pan pricking forward to drink at the stream, crushing fennel, exquisitely stooping, bending . . .

And, later again, silent, groping, we ascended in sequence to the paternal porch.

Buster?

Yair?

Goodnight, Buster.

'Night, Fanny. Be seein' yuh.

. . .

Fourteen minute specks of radioactive phosphorus brightened by weak starlight pricked out the hour: one.

119

In the end I left old STC in the tractor tool box along with the spanner that wouldn't fit any nut I'd ever tried it on and the grease gun without grease and the last letter from mum, hot as radium. I didn't wait for milking. I was packed and gone at the first trembling of light. It was cold along the river-bottom, cold and still. Eels rose to feed: the water was like pewter; old pewter. I felt sick, abandoned, full of self-pity. Everything washed through me, the light, the cold, a sense of what lay behind me and might not lie before, a feeling of exhaustion when I thought of home, a feeling of despair when I thought of Fanny still curled in sleep. Dark. She hadn't giggled: so what? I changed my fibre suitcase to the other hand and trudged along Rideout Road. The light increased; quail with tufted crests crossed the road: I began to feel better. I sat on the suitcase and rolled a smoke. Then the sun caught a high scarp of Rideout Mountain and began to finger down slow and gold. I was so full of relief, suddenly, that I grabbed my bag and ran. Impetuous. I was lucky not to break my ankle. White gulls, loam flesh, dark water, damsel and dome; where would it take you? Where was there to go, anyway? It just didn't matter; that was the point. I stopped worrying that minute and sat by the cream stand out on the main road. After a while a truck stopped to my thumb and I got in. If I'd waited for the cream truck I'd have had to face old brownstone Hohepa and I wasn't very eager for that. I'd had a fill of piety, of various brands. And I was paid up to date.

I looked back. Rideout Mountain and the peak of ochre red roof, Maori red. That's all it was. I wondered what Fanny and her pappy might be saying at this moment, across the clothes-hanger rumps of cows. The rush of relief went through me again. I looked at the gloomy bastard driving: he had a cigarette stuck to his lip like a growth. I felt almost happy. Almost. I might have hugged him as he drove his hearse through the tail-end of summer.

THE SILK

Joy Cowley

When Mr Blackie took bad again that autumn both he and Mrs Blackie knew that it was for the last time. For many weeks neither spoke of it; but the understanding was in their eyes as they watched each other through the days and nights. It was a look, not of sadness or despair, but of quiet resignation tempered with something else, an unnamed expression that is seen only in the old and the very young.

Their acceptance was apparent in other ways, too. Mrs Blackie no longer complained to the neighbours that the old lazy-bones was running her off her feet. Instead she waited on him tirelessly, stretching their pension over chicken and out-of-season fruits to tempt his appetite; and she guarded him so possessively that she even resented the twice-weekly visits from the District Nurse. Mr Blackie, on the other hand, settled into bed as gently as dust. He had never been a man to dwell in the past, but now he spoke a great deal of their earlier days and surprised Mrs Blackie by recalling things which she, who claimed the better memory, had forgotten. Seldom did he talk of the present, and never in these weeks did he mention the future.

Then, on the morning of the first frost of winter, while Mrs Blackie was filling his hot water bottle, he sat up in bed, unaided, to see out of the window. The inside of the glass was streaked with tears of condensation. Outside, the frost had made an oval frame of crystals through which he could see a row of houses and lawns laid out in front of them, like white carpets.

'The ground will be hard,' he said at last. 'Hard as nails.'

Mrs Blackie looked up quickly. 'Not yet,' she said.

'Pretty soon, I think.' His smile was apologetic.

She slapped the hot water bottle into its cover and tested it against her cheek. 'Lie down or you'll get a chill,' she said.

Obediently, he dropped back against the pillow, but as she moved about him, putting the hot water bottle at his feet, straightening the quilt, he stared at the frozen patch of window.

'Amy, you'll get a double plot, won't you?' he said. 'I wouldn't rest easy thinking you were going to sleep by someone else.'

'What a thing to say!' The corner of her mouth twitched. 'As if I would.'

'It was your idea to buy single beds,' he said accusingly.

'Oh Herb – ' She looked at the window, away again. 'We'll have a double plot,' she said. For a second or two she hesitated by his bed, then she sat beside his feet, her hands placed one on top of the other in her lap, in a pose that she always adopted when she had something important to say. She cleared her throat.

'You know, I've been thinking on and off about the silk.'

'The silk?' He turned his head towards her.

'I want to use it for your laying-out pyjamas.'

'No Amy,' he said. 'Not the silk. That was your wedding present, the only thing I brought back with me.'

'What would I do with it now?' she said. When he didn't answer, she got up, opened the wardrobe door and took the camphorwood box from the shelf where she kept her hats. 'All these years and us not daring to take a scissors to it. We should use it sometime.'

'Not on me,' he said.

'I've been thinking about your pyjamas.' She fitted a key into the brass box. 'It'd be just right.'

'A right waste, you mean,' he said. But there was no protest in his voice. In fact, it had lifted with a childish eagerness. He watched her hands as she opened the box and folded back layers of white tissue paper. Beneath them lay the blue of the silk. There was a reverent silence as she took it out and spread it under the light.

'Makes the whole room look different, doesn't it?' he said. 'I nearly forgot it looked like this.' His hands struggled free of the sheet and moved across the quilt. Gently, she picked up the blue material and poured it over his fingers.

'Aah,' he breathed, bringing it closer to his eyes. 'All the way from China.' He smiled. 'Not once did I let it out of me sight. You know that, Amy? There were those on board as would have pinched it quick as that. I kept it pinned round me middle.'

'You told me,' she said.

He rubbed the silk against the stubble of his chin. 'It's the birds that take your eye,' he said.

'At first,' said Mrs Blackie. She ran her finger over one of the peacocks that strutted in the foreground of a continuous landscape. They were proud birds, iridescent blue, with silver threads in their tails. 'I used to like them best, but after a while you see much more, just as fine only smaller.' She pushed her glasses on to the bridge of her nose and leaned over the silk, her finger guiding her eyes over islands where waterfalls hung, eternally suspended, between pagodas and dark blue conifers, over flat lakes and tiny fishing boats, over mountains where the mists never lifted, and back again to a haughty peacock caught with one foot suspended over a rock. 'It's a work of art like you never see in this country,' she said.

Mr Blackie inhaled the scent of camphorwood. 'Don't cut it, Amy. It's too good for an old blighter like me.' He was begging her to contradict him.

'I'll get the pattern tomorrow,' she said.

The next day, while the District Nurse was giving him his injection, she went down to the store and looked through a pile of pattern books. Appropriately, she chose a mandarin style with a high collar and piped cuffs and pockets. But Mr Blackie, who had all his life worn striped flannel in the conventional design, looked with suspicion at the pyjama pattern and the young man who posed so easily and shamelessly on the front of the packet.

'It's the sort them teddy bear boys have,' he said.

'Nonsense,' said Mrs Blackie.

'That's exactly what they are,' he growled. 'You're not laying me out in a lot of new-fangled nonsense.'

Mrs Blackie put her hands on her hips. 'You'll not have any say in the matter,' she said.

'Won't I just? I'll get up and fight – see if I don't.'

The muscles at the corner of her mouth twitched uncontrollably. 'All right, Herb, if you're so set against it – '

But now, having won the argument, he was happy. 'Get away with you, Amy. I'll get used to the idea.' He threw his lips back against his gums. 'Matter of fact, I like them fine. It's that nurse that done it. Blunt needle again.' He looked at the pattern. 'When d'you start?'

'Well – '

'This afternoon?'

'I suppose I could pin the pattern out after lunch.'

'Do it in here,' he said. 'Bring in your machine and pins and things and set them up so I can watch.'

She stood taller and tucked in her chin. 'I'm not using the machine,' she said with pride. 'Every stitch is going to be done by hand. My eyes mightn't be as good as they were once, mark you, but there's not a person on this earth can say I've lost my touch with a needle.'

His eyes closed in thought. 'How long?'

'Eh?'

'Till it's finished.'

She turned the pattern over in her hands. 'Oh – about three or four weeks. That is – if I keep at it.'

'No,' he said. 'Too long.'

'Oh Herb, you'd want a good job done, wouldn't you?' she pleaded.

'Amy –' Almost imperceptibly, he shook his head on the pillow.

'I can do the main seams on the machine,' she said, lowering her voice.

'How long?'

'A week,' she whispered.

When she took down the silk that afternoon, he insisted on an extra pillow in spite of the warning he'd had from the doctor about lying flat with his legs propped higher than his head and shoulders.

She plumped up the pillow from her own bed and put it behind his neck; then she unrolled her tape measure along his body, legs, arms, around his chest.

'I'll have to take them in a bit,' she said, making inch-high black figures on a piece of cardboard. She took the tissue-paper pattern into the kitchen to iron it flat. When she came back, he was waiting, wide-eyed with anticipation and brighter, she thought, than he'd been for many weeks.

As she laid the silk out on her bed and started pinning down the first of the pattern pieces, he described, with painstaking attempts at accuracy, the boat trip home, the stop at Hong Kong, and the merchant who had sold him the silk. 'Most of his stuff was rubbish,' he said. 'You wouldn't look twice at it. This was the only decent thing he had and even then he done me. You got to argue with these devils. Beat him down, they told me. But there was others as wanted that silk and if I hadn't made up me mind there and then I'd have lost it.' He squinted at her hands. 'What are you doing now? You just put that bit down.'

'It wasn't right,' she said, through lips closed on pins. 'I have to match it – like wallpaper.'

She lifted the pattern pieces many times before she was satisfied. Then it was evening and he was so tired that his breathing had become laboured. He no longer talked. His eyes were watering from hours of concentration; the drops spilled over his red lids and soaked into the pillow.

'Go to sleep,' she said. 'Enough's enough for one day.'

'I'll see you cut it out first,' he said.

'Let's leave it till the morning,' she said, and they both sensed her reluctance to put the scissors to the silk.

'Tonight,' he said.

'I'll make the tea first.'

'After,' he said.

She took the scissors from her sewing drawer and wiped them on her apron. Together they felt the pain as the blades met cleanly, almost without resistance, in that first cut. The silk would never again be the same. They were changing it, rearranging the pattern of fifty-odd years to form something new and unfamiliar. When she had cut out the first piece, she held it up, still pinned to the paper, and said, 'The back of the top.' Then she laid it on the dressing table and went on as quickly as she dared, for she knew that he would not rest until she had finished.

One by one the garment pieces left the body of silk. With each touch of the blades, threads sprang apart; mountains were divided, peacocks split from head to tail; waterfalls fell on either side of fraying edges. Eventually, there was nothing on the bed but a few shining snippets. Mrs Blackie picked them up and put them back in the camphorwood box, and covered the pyjama pieces on the dressing table with a cloth. Then she removed the extra pillow from Mr Blackie's bed and laid his head back in a comfortable position before she went into the kitchen to make the tea.

He was very tired the next morning but refused to sleep while she was working with the silk. She invented a number of excuses for putting it aside and leaving the room. He would sleep then, but never for long. No more than half an hour would pass and he would be calling her. She would find him lying awake and impatient for her to resume sewing.

In that day and the next, she did all the machine work. It was a tedious task, for first she tacked each seam by hand, matching the patterns in the weave so that the join was barely noticeable. Mr Blackie silently supervised every stitch. At times she would see him studying the silk with an expression that she still held in her memory. It was the look he'd given her in their courting days. She felt a prick of jealousy, not because she thought that he cared more for the silk than he did for her, but because he saw something in it that she didn't share. She never asked him what it was. At her age a body did not question these things or demand explanations. She would bend her head lower and concentrate her energy and attention into the narrow seam beneath the needle.

On the Friday afternoon, four days after she'd started the pyjamas, she finished the buttonholes and sewed on the buttons. She'd deliberately hurried the last of the hand sewing. In the four days, Mr Blackie had become weaker, and she knew that the sooner the pyjamas were completed and put back in the camphorwood box out of sight, the sooner he would take an interest in food and have the rest he needed.

She snipped the last thread and put the needle in its case.

'That's it, Herb,' she said, showing him her work.

He tried to raise his head. 'Bring them over here,' he said.

'Well – what do you think?' As she brought the pyjamas closer, his eyes relaxed and he smiled.

'Try them on?' he said.

She shook her head. 'I got the measurements,' she said. 'They'll be the right fit.'

'Better make sure,' he said.

She hesitated but could find no reason for her reluctance. 'All right,' she said, switching on both bars of the electric heater and drawing it closer to his bed. 'Just to make sure I've got the buttons right.'

She peeled back the bedclothes, took off his thick pyjamas and put on the silk. She stepped back to look at him.

'Well, even if I do say so myself, there's no one could have done a better job. I could move the top button over a fraction, but apart from that they're a perfect fit.'

He grinned. 'Light, aren't they?' He looked down the length of his body and wriggled his toes. 'All the way from China. Never let it out of me sight. Know that, Amy?'

'Do you like them?' she said.

He sucked his lips in over his gums to hide his pleasure. 'All right. A bit on the tight side.'

'They are not, and you know it,' Mrs Blackie snapped. 'Never give a body a bit of credit, would you? Here, put your hands down and I'll change you before you get a chill.'

He tightened his arms across his chest. 'You made a right good job, Amy. Think I'll keep them on a bit.'

'No.' She picked up his thick pyjamas.

'Why not?'

'Because you can't,' she said. 'It's – it's disrespectful. And the nurse will be here soon.'

'Oh, get away with you, Amy.' He was too weak to resist further but as she changed him, he still possessed the silk with his eyes. 'Wonder who made it?'

Although she shrugged his question away, it brought to her a definite picture of a Chinese woman seated in front of a loom surrounded by blue and silver silkworms. The woman was dressed from a page in a geographic magazine, and except for the Oriental line of her eyelids, she looked like Mrs Blackie.

'D'you suppose there's places like that?' Mr Blackie asked.

She snatched up the pyjamas and put them in the box. 'You're the one that's been there,' she said briskly. 'Now settle down and rest or you'll be bad when the nurse arrives.'

The District Nurse did not come that afternoon. Nor in the evening. It was at half-past three the following morning that her footsteps, echoed by the doctor's sounded along the gravel path.

Mrs Blackie was in the kitchen, waiting. She sat straight-backed and dry-eyed, her hands placed one on top of the other in the lap of her dressing gown.

'Mrs Blackie. I'm sorry – '

She ignored the nurse and turned to the doctor. 'He didn't say goodbye,' she said with an accusing look. 'Just before I phoned. His hand was over the side of the bed. I touched it. It was cold.'

The doctor nodded.

'No sound of any kind,' she said. 'He was good as gold last night.'

Again, the doctor nodded. He put his hand, briefly, on her shoulder, then went into the bedroom. Within a minute he returned, fastening his leather bag and murmuring sympathy.

Mrs Blackie sat still, catching isolated words. Expected. Peacefully. Brave. They dropped upon her – neat, geometrical shapes that had no meaning.

'He didn't say goodbye.' She shook her head. 'Not a word.'

'But look, Mrs Blackie,' soothed the nurse. 'It was inevitable. You knew that. He couldn't have gone on – '

'I know. I know.' She turned away, irritated by their lack of understanding. 'He just might have said goodbye. That's all.'

The doctor took a white tablet from a phial and tried to persuade her to swallow it. She pushed it away; refused, too, the cup of tea that the district nurse poured and set in front of her. When they picked up their bags and went towards the bedroom, she followed them.

'In a few minutes,' the doctor said. 'If you'll leave us – '

'I'm getting his pyjamas,' she said. 'There's a button needs changing. I can do it now.'

As soon as she entered the room, she glanced at Mr Blackie's bed and noted that the doctor had pulled up the sheet. Quickly, she lifted the camphorwood box, took a needle, cotton, scissors, her spectacle case, and went back to the kitchen. Through the half-closed door she heard the nurse's voice, 'Poor old thing,' and she knew, instinctively, that they were not talking about her.

She sat down at the table to thread the needle. Her eyes were clear but her hands were so numb that for a long time they refused to work together. At last, the thread knotted, she opened the camphorwood box. The beauty of the silk was always unexpected. As she spread the pyjamas out on the table, it warmed her, caught her up and comforted her with the first positive feeling she'd had that morning. The silk was real. It was brought to life by the electric light above the table, so that every fold of the woven landscape moved. Trees swayed towards rippling water and peacocks danced with white fire in their tails. Even the tiny bridges –

Mrs Blackie took off her glasses, wiped them, put them on again. She leaned forward and traced her thumbnail over one bridge, then another. And another. She turned over the pyjama coat and closely examined the back. It was there, on every bridge; something she hadn't noticed before. She got up, and from the drawer where she kept her tablecloths, she took out a magnifying glass.

As the bridge in the pattern of the silk grew, the figure which had been no larger than an ant, became a man.

Mrs Blackie forgot about the button and the murmur of voices in the bedroom. She brought the magnifying glass nearer her eyes.

It was a man and he was standing with one arm outstretched, on the highest span between two islands. Mrs Blackie studied him for a long time, then she straightened up and smiled. Yes, he was waving. Or perhaps, she thought, he was beckoning to her.

A FITTING TRIBUTE

C. K. Stead

I don't ask you to believe me when I say I knew Julian Harp, but I ask you to give me a hearing because in every detail the story I'm going to tell is gospel true. I've tried to tell it before. After Julian's flight I even got a reporter along to the house and he wrote me up as 'just another hysterical young woman claiming to have known the National Hero'. That was a year or more ago and I haven't mentioned Julian Harp since.

What reason can a person have for telling a story that she knows won't be believed? I have two: a cross-grained magistrate and a statue. You might have heard about the case in Auckland in which a woman, a shopkeeper in court for trading without a licence, happened to say in evidence that Julian Harp had once come into her shop and bought one of those periscopes short people use for seeing over the heads of a crowd. The magistrate asked her to please keep calm and stick to the truth. Then he called for a psychiatrist's report because he said she was obviously a born liar. Next day, which happened to be the anniversary of Julian's flight, he sentenced her to a month in jail and the *Herald* published an editorial saying No one knew Julian Harp. Julian Harp knew no one. A privileged few watched his moment of glory; but he died as he had lived, a Man Alone. . . .

Of course if the woman hadn't mentioned Julian Harp she might have got away with a fine. But she insisted she remembered his name because he asked her to keep the periscope aside until he had money to pay for it. And she said he wore his hair down around his shoulders. That was unthinkable!

When I read about that case I knew what no one else could know, that the woman was telling the truth. But it was the statue that really persuaded me it was time I tried to write down the facts. I was walking in the Domain pushing my baby Christopher in his pram. Some workmen were digging on the slope among those trees between the main gates and the pavilion and what pulled me up was that they were working right on the spot where Julian first got the idea for his wings. Then a truck arrived with a winch and a great slab of polished granite and in no time all the workmen were round it swearing at one another and pulling and pushing at the chains until the stone was lowered into the hole. I thought why do they want a great ugly slab of graveyard stone there of all places? I didn't know I had asked it aloud, but one of the workmen turned and said it was for the new statue. The statue was to go on top of it. What new statue? The statue of Julian Harp of course. The one donated by the Bank of New Zealand. *The statue of Julian Harp*! You can imagine how I felt. I sat down on a bench and took Christopher out of his pram and rocked him backwards and forwards and thought how extraordinary! Miraculous! That after all the arguments in the newspapers about a site, not to mention the wrangling about whether the statue should be modern or old fashioned, they had at last landed it by accident plonk on the spot where Julian thought of his solution to the problem of engineless flight.

I sat there rocking my baby while he held on to my nose with one hand and hit me around the head with the other, and all the time I was thinking. I might even have been saying it aloud, what have I got to lose? I must tell someone. If they laugh at me, too bad. At least I will have tried. And besides, I owe it to Christopher to let everyone know the solemn truth that he is the son of Julian Harp. By the time I had wheeled the pram back through the Domain I was ready to start by telling Vega but when I saw her there in the kitchen cutting up beans for dinner and looking all straggly and cross I knew I oughtn't to tell anyone until I had the whole story sorted out in my head and perhaps written down.

I should explain before I go any further that Vega is a sort of awful necessity in my life. Before Christopher was born I had to give up work and I didn't know how I was going to pay the rent. I wanted to stay on in the house I lived in with Julian, because although everyone says he is dead no one knows for certain that he is. I wasn't planning to sit around expecting him, but I had to keep in mind that if he did come back the house would be the only place he would know to look for me. The house and Gomeo's coffee bar. So when someone advertised in the *Auckland Star* that she was a respectable middle-aged female clerk wanting board, I took her in; and now there are the three of us, Christopher and Vega and me, sharing the little two-storeyed wooden house with three rooms upstairs and two down that sits a yard from the footpath in Kendall Road on the eastern edge of the Domain. Vega isn't a great companion or anything. She hasn't much to say – except in her sleep; and then although she goes on for hours at a time it isn't in English or any other language. But when I was ready to start work again at Gomeo's I discovered I had been lucky to find her. I needed someone in the house at night to watch over Christopher, and when I mentioned it to Vega she said in her flat voice I could stop worrying about it because hadn't I noticed she never went out at night. She was afraid of the dark! Then she told me she was named after a star we don't often see in the Southern Hemisphere; and she made a noise that sounded like a laugh and said had I ever heard of a star going out at night.

All the time I was feeding Christopher that evening after seeing the workmen in the Domain I kept thinking about the statue and how wrong it would be if no one ever knew that Julian had a son. So when Christopher was asleep and I was helping Vega serve the dinner I asked her whether she thought Julian Harp might have had a family. She said no. I asked her what she thought would happen if someone claimed to be the mother of Julian's child. She said she didn't know, but she did know there was a good deal too much money being spent on a statue that made him look like nothing she'd ever seen and that kind of sculpture was a pretty disgusting way to honour a man who had given his life. I said but leaving aside the statue what would she think if a girl in Auckland claimed to be the mother of his child? Vega said she thought some of the little minxes had claimed that already, out for all they could get, but she didn't think Julian Harp would have been the marrying kind. She said she imagined him like Lawrence of Arabia, married to an idea. When I said I hadn't mentioned marriage but only paternity she said there was no need to be obscene.

I gave up at that and I didn't have time to think about Julian for the rest of the evening until it was quite late and something happened at the coffee bar that made me remember my first meeting with him. I was bending over one of the tables when Gomeo came out of the kitchen and put his hand on my buttocks and said in a sort of stage whisper you could hear all over the shop that tonight he'd gotta have me or that's the end. The sack. Finish. I said nothing and went to wipe down another table but he followed me and said in the same whisper well was it yes or no. So I swung round and said no, no, no – and each time I said it I pushed the wet cloth in his face until he had backed all the way into the kitchen. By now the people in the shop were waiting to hear me get the sack but Gomeo only said one day I would really make him mad and my God that would be the finish of us both.

You might wonder why that should remind me of Julian. It's because Gomeo threatens to sack me and for the same reason nearly every time there's a full moon and it was after one of his more spectacular performances I first talked to Julian. Julian was in the shop and like everyone else he took it all seriously and thought I had lost my job. So when I had finished pushing Gomeo back into

131

the kitchen where he belongs Julian asked could he help me find a new job and he said he would even be willing to hit Gomeo for me if I thought it would help. I had to explain that Gomeo isn't quite one hundred per cent and he doesn't mean what he says. But you have to pretend he means it and fight him off. If you just laughed at him, or if you said yes you'd like to go to bed with him, you would be out on the pavement in five minutes, because Gomeo only wants the big drama, nothing real. I explained all this to Julian and he looked relieved but then he said he was sorry because now there wasn't any excuse to invite me to his bed-sitter after I finished work. When I looked at his face I could see he meant just what he said so I asked him did he have to have an excuse.

And thinking of Julian's face reminds me I ought to say something about his appearance because reading about him in the papers will have given you a wrong picture of him. It's well known there's only one photograph of Julian, the one taken by a schoolgirl with a box camera just before he took off. His face is slightly obscured by the crash helmet he's just going to put on and the camera hasn't been properly focused. So all the local Annigonis have got to work and done what they call impressions of him and I can tell you quite honestly the more praise the picture gets the less it looks like Julian. They all dress him up in tidy clothes and cut his hair short and some of them have even put him in a suit and tie and stuck his hair down with Brylcreem. Well if it's important to you that your local hero should look like a young army officer I'm sorry but the fact is when I first knew Julian he was one of the most disreputable looking men I had seen. His clothes never seemed to fit or match and he never went near a barber. Every now and then he would reach round to the back and sides of his head and snip off bits of hair with a pair of scissors but that was all. I think he had given up shaving altogether at the time but he didn't have the kind of growth to make a beard so he was what you might call half way between clean-shaven and bearded. He wore a rather tattered raincoat done right up to the neck, and at midnight when I finished work and he took me to a teen club under the street where you could twist and stomp he kept it on and buttoned up until I began to wonder whether he had a shirt underneath.

I hadn't turned eighteen then but I was older than most of the others in the teen club and Julian was probably twenty-two or three so I felt embarrassed especially because Julian looked such a clown. When we arrived we sat at a table and didn't dance until one of the kids called out Hey Jesus can't you dance? and several others laughed and jeered. Julian laughed too and clapped in a spastic kind of way and looked all round like a maniac as if he couldn't see who they were jeering at and then he got up without me and drifted backwards into the middle of the dancers and began to jerk and twist and stamp and roll in time to the music. Julian could certainly dance and in no time they had all stopped and made a circle round him clapping and shouting and urging him on until the sweat was pouring off him. He had to break out of the circle and make his way back to our table waving one hand behind him while they all shouted for more.

After that we drank coffee and danced and talked but you couldn't have much of a conversation above the noise of electric guitars and when we came out at 2 a.m. I felt wide awake and not very keen to go back to my bed-sitter. Julian said I should come to his and I went. We walked up Grey's Avenue under the trees and then between two buildings and through an alley that came out at the back of the house where Julian had a room. I followed him up a narrow outside stairway right to the top of the building and through French doors off a creaky verandah. He threw up a sash window and we sat getting our breath back looking out over a cluster of old wooden houses like the one we were in and the new modern buildings beyond and the harbour and the bridge. Julian said the nice thing about coming back to Auckland after being away was the old wooden houses. I had thought that was what people coming back complained about, a town where nothing looked solid, but Julian said it was as if people lived in lanterns. He liked the harbour too and the bridge and everything he looked at and I found that unusual because the people who came into Gomeo's were forever arguing about which buildings in Auckland were any good and which were not and nobody was ever enthusiastic about anything, least of all those like Julian who had been away overseas.

Julian said he liked living right in the busy part of the city and he liked to be up high. He had worked as a window cleaner on the A.M.P. building in Sydney and as a waiter in the Penn Top of the Statler Hilton in New York. And before coming back to Auckland he had driven a glass elevator that ran up and down the face of a hotel at the top of Nob Hill in San Francisco looking out over the harbour and the Golden Gate Bridge and the Bay. He said that was the best job he had ever had and he was willing to make a career of it but they made the elevator automatic to save the expense of an operator. Julian offered to run it for nothing and live off whatever tips he could get from sightseers, and when the hotel managers refused he still spent hours of every day going up and down as a member of the public until it was decided he was making a nuisance of himself and he was told not to come into the building again. A week or so later when he tried to slip in wearing dark glasses someone called the police and Julian decided it was time to leave San Francisco.

We sat without any light drinking and talking or rather Julian talking and me listening and I remember being surprised when I noticed the wine bottle was half empty and I could see the colour of the heavy velvet cloth it stood on was not black but dark red. It had got light and still I didn't feel tired. Julian said he would make us some breakfast and while he cut bread and toasted it I had a chance to look around at his things, and especially at a big old desk that had taken my eye. It was half way down the room facing one wall and it was covered with a strange collection of letters, newspaper clippings, stationery, bottles of ink of all different colours and makes, every kind of pen from a quill to a Parker, and three typewriters. Pinned to the wall above the desk there was a huge chart, but before I could begin to read it Julian saw me looking at it and called me over to help him make the breakfast.

I got to know that chart well later on because it was the nerve centre of what Julian called his Subvert the Press Campaign. On it were the names and addresses of all the people Julian had invented to write letters to the editor, then a series of numbers which showed the colour of ink each one used, the type of notepaper, and the kind of pen – or t^1, t^2, or t^3 if one of the typewriters was used; then examples of their scripts and signatures and details about their opinions and prejudices. Each name had stars beside it to show the number of letters published, and the letters themselves hung in bulldog clips at the end of each horizontal section. It had come to Julian that a newspaper really prefers letters signed with pseudonyms because it can pick and choose among them and print the opinions it likes but within reason it has to print all the signed letters that come in. So the idea of his Subvert the Press Campaign was very very gradually to introduce a whole new group of letter writers who all signed their names. They had to be all different types and live in different parts of town so the paper wouldn't suspect what was going on; but as Julian explained to me later, once he had established his group he could concentrate them suddenly on one issue and create a controversy. He called them his Secret Weapon because he said only a small group of people reads the editorials but everyone reads the correspondence columns.

But when it was put to the test and Julian decided to bring the Government down (I think it was over the cancellation of the Lyttelton scaffolding factory and the issue of extra import licences) the Secret Weapon misfired. He sent letter after letter, not only to the *Herald* and the *Star* but all over the country and soon there was a raging controversy. But he wrote his letters in a sort of daze, almost as if voices were telling him what to write, and what each letter said seemed to depend on the person supposed to be writing it instead of depending on what Julian himself really wanted to say. In the end his letter writers said as many different things as it was possible to say about the cancellation of the contract and when Parliament assembled for the special debate not only the Opposition members but the Government ones as well were armed with clippings of letters Julian had written. That was a great disappointment for Julian. He lost faith in his Secret Weapon and when I tried to get him going again he said what was the use of secretly taking over the correspondence column of a newspaper if when you succeeded it looked exactly the same as it looked before.

But it wasn't until I knew Julian well that he let me into the secret about his letters. That first morning he called me away to help with the breakfast before I had got more than a quick glance over the desk and when I thought about the chart afterwards all I could guess was that he might be the ringleader of a secret society of anarchists, or even a criminal.

We sat at the big sash window eating breakfast and watching the sun hitting off the water on to the white weatherboards and listening to pop songs and the ads on 1ZB. Julian sang some of the hits and we did some twisting and while the ads were on we finished off the wine. Julian told me the Seraphs were his favourite pop singers and that was weeks before anyone else was talking about them or voting them on to the Top Twenty. I often thought about that when Julian got to be famous and the Seraphs were at the top of the Hit Parade with 'Harp's in Heaven Now'. And when the N.Z.B.C. banned the song because they said it wasn't a fitting tribute to the national hero I felt like writing some letters to the editor myself.

It must have been eleven o'clock before I left to go home that morning and I left in a bad temper partly because I hadn't had any sleep I suppose but partly because Julian had stretched out on his divan and gone to sleep and left me to find my own way out. He hadn't said goodbye or anything about seeing me again and when I thought about it I didn't even know his second name and he didn't know mine.

I slept all that afternoon and had a ravioli at Gomeo's before starting work and I spent a miserable evening watching out for Julian to come in. It wasn't that I had any romantic feelings about him, the sort I might have had in those days about one of those good looking boys in elastic sided boots and tapered trousers. But I had a picture fixed in my head of Julian with his straggly hair and mottled blue eyes going up and up in that glass elevator like a saint on a cloud, and I kept looking for him to come into Gomeo's as if it would be almost a relief to see just the ordinary Julian instead of the Julian in my head.

He didn't come of course because he was busy writing his letters to the newspapers, but I wasn't to know that. The next day was Sunday and I spent the afternoon wandering around the lower slopes of the Domain among the trees – in fact it must have been somewhere near where they've built the Interdenominational Harp Memorial Chapel. I was feeling angry with Julian and I started to think I might get back at him by ringing the police and telling them he was a dangerous communist. I probably would have done it too but I didn't know his address exactly and I only knew his Christian name.

I still go for walks down there, with Christopher in the pram, and sometimes I sit inside the chapel and look out at the trees through all that tinted glass. People who come into Gomeo's say it's bad architecture but I like it whatever kind of architecture it is and sometimes I think I can get some idea in there of how Julian felt in the glass elevator. I've had a special interest in the chapel right from the start because Vega belongs to the Open Pentecostal Baptists and her church contributed a lot of money to the building. She told me about all the fighting that went on at first and how the Anglicans tried to get the Catholics in because of the Ecumenical thing. She said they nearly succeeded but then a Catholic priest testified to having seen Julian cross himself shortly before he put on his wings and the Catholics decided to put up a memorial of their own. Vega said it was nonsense, Julian Harp couldn't have been a Catholic, and I agreed with her because I know he wasn't anything except that he used to call himself a High Church Agnostic and an occasional Zen Buddy. Of course Vega was really pleased to have the Catholics out of the scheme and so were a lot of other people even though it meant raising a lot more money. Vega said it was better raising extra money than having the Catholics smelling out the place with incense.

It must have been nearly a week went by before Julian came into Gomeo's again and when I saw what a scraggy looking thing he was I wondered why I had given him a second thought. I ignored him quite successfully for half an hour but when he asked me to come to his bed-sitter after I finished work I went and the next night he came to mine and before long it seemed uneconomical paying two rents. We more or less agreed we would take a flat together but weeks passed and Julian did nothing about it. By now he had told me about his Subvert the Press Campaign and I knew how busy he was so I decided to find us a flat myself and surprise him with it. I answered probably twenty ads before I got one at Herne Bay at a good rent with a fridge and the bathroom shared with only one other couple. I paid a week's rent in advance and when Julian came into Gomeo's and asked for a spaghetti I brought him a clean plate with the key on it wrapped in a note giving the address of the flat and saying if Mr Julian Harp would go to the above address he would find his new home and in the fridge a special shrimp salad all for him. I watched him from behind the espresso machine. Instead of looking pleased he frowned and screwed up the note and called me over and said he wanted a spaghetti. I didn't know what to do so I brought him what he asked for and he ate it and went out. When I finished work I went to his bed-sitter to explain about the flat. He wouldn't even go with me to look at it because he said anywhere you had to take a bus to get to was the suburbs and he wasn't going to live in the suburbs.

I decided I wouldn't have anything more to do with him. I knew he was friendly with a Rarotongan girl who was a stripper in a place in Karangahape Road and I thought he was possibly just amusing himself with me while she did a three-month sentence she had got for obscene exposure. A few days later when he came into Gomeo's and said he had found a flat in Grafton for us I brought him a plate of spaghetti he hadn't asked for and when I finished work I went out by the back door of the shop and left him waiting for me at the front. The next evening and the next I refused even to talk to him. I was quite determined. But then he stopped coming to Gomeo's and began to send me letters, not letters from him but from his people who wrote to the newspapers. Every letter looked different from the one before and told me something different. Some told me Julian Harp ought to be hanged or flogged and I was right to have nothing to do with him. Others said he was basically good but he needed my help if he was going to be reformed. One said there was nothing wrong with him, it was only his mind that was disordered. One told me in strictest confidence that J. Harp was too good for this world and would shortly depart for another. They were really quite funny in a way that made it silly to stay angry about the flat, so when he had run through his whole list of letter writers I went round to his place and knocked and when he came to the door I said I had come to sing the Candy Roll Blues with him. It wasn't long after that we took the little two-storeyed house in Kendall Road, the one I'm in now with Christopher and Vega.

The first few months we spent there Julian wasn't easy to live with. He liked the house well enough and especially the look of it from the outside. He used to cross the street sometimes early in the morning and sit on a little canvas stool and stare at the house. He said if you looked long enough you would see all the dead people who had once lived there going about doing the things they had always done. But I soon discovered he was missing the view he had from his bed-sitter of the city and the harbour, and if I woke and he wasn't down in the street he was most likely getting the view from the steps in front of the museum. I used to walk up there often to call him for breakfast or lunch and I would find him standing on the steps above the cenotaph staring down at the ships and the cranes or more often straight out across the water beyond the North Shore and the Gulf and Rangitoto.

We had lots of arguments during those first couple of months. I used to lose my temper and walk up and down the kitchen shouting every mean thing I could think of until I ran out of breath and if I was still angry I would throw things at him. Julian couldn't talk nearly as fast but he didn't waste words like I did, every one was barbed, so we came out pretty nearly even. But Julian caused most of the fights and I used to make him admit that. It was because he didn't have anything better to do. His Subvert the Press Campaign had ended in a way he hadn't meant it should and now there didn't seem to be anything especially needing to be done. He took a job for a while as an orderly in the hospital because the money he had brought back from America was beginning to run out but when they put him on duty in the morgue he left because he said he didn't like seeing the soles of people's feet.

It was Anzac Day the year before his flight that Julian first thought of making himself a set of wings. In the morning there were the usual parades, and the servicemen and bands marched up Kendall Road on their way to the cenotaph. Julian wasn't patriotic. He couldn't remember any more about the war than I can. But he liked crowds and noise so he tied our tablecloth to the broom handle and waved it out of the upstairs window over the marchers until a man with shiny black shoes and a lot of medals on a square suit stopped and shouted what did he think he was up to waving a red flag over the Anzac parade. Julian said it wasn't a red flag it was a tablecloth and that made the man angrier. He shouted and shook his fist and a crowd gathered. When the Governor-General's car arrived on its way to the cenotaph it was held up at the corner. By this time Julian was making a speech from the window. He was leaning out so far I could only see the bottom half of him and I couldn't hear much of what he was saying but I did hear him shout:

> Shoot if you must this old grey head
> But spare my tablecloth she said.

Then the police arrived and began clearing a path for the

Governor-General's Rolls and I persuaded Julian to come in and close the window.

By now he was in a mood for Anzac celebrations and we followed the crowd up to the cenotaph and listened to the speeches and sang the hymns. After the service we wandered about in the Domain. Julian kept chanting Gallipoli, El Alamein, Minqar Qaim, Tobruk, Cassino and all the other places the Governor-General had talked about in his speech until I got sick of hearing them and I turned up my transistor to drown him out. He wandered away from me across the football fields and kept frightening a flock of seagulls into the air every time they came down. When he came back to where I was sitting he was quiet and rather solemn. We walked on and it was then we came to the place where the workmen are putting in the statue and right on that spot Julian stopped and stared in front of him and began slowly waving one arm up and down at his side. I asked him what was the matter and he said quick come and have a look at this and he ran down the slope and lay flat on his stomach on one of those park benches that have no backs and began flapping his arms. When I got down to the bench he asked me did his arms look anything like a bird's wings. I said no but when he asked me why I couldn't think of the answer. Then he turned over on his back and began flapping his arms again and asked me did they look anything like a bird's wings now. At first I said no but when I looked properly I had to admit they did. His forearms were moving up and down almost parallel with his body and the part of his arms from the shoulders to the elbows stayed out at right angles from him. So I said yes they did look more like a bird's wings now because a bird's wings bent forward to the elbows and then back along the body and that was why his arms hadn't looked like wings when he lay on his stomach. As soon as I said that he jumped up and kissed me on both cheeks and said I was a bright girl, I had seen the point, he would have to fly upside down.

It wasn't long before I began to notice sketches of wings lying about the house and soon there were little models in balsa wood and paper. One of the things that annoy me every time I read about Julian's flight is that it's not treated as a proper scientific achievement. People talk as if he flew by magic or just willed himself to stay in the air. They seem to think if no one in human history, not even Leonardo da Vinci, could make wings that would carry a man, Julian Harp can't have been human or his flight must have been a miracle. And now Vega tells me there's a new sect called the Harpists and they believe Julian wasn't a man but an angel sent down as a sign that God has chosen New Zealand for the

139

C. K. Stead

Second Coming. I've even wondered whether Vega doesn't half believe what the Harpists say and it won't surprise me at all if she leaves the Open Pentecostals and joins them.

Gradually I learned a lot about the wings because designing them and building the six or seven sets he did before he got what he wanted spread over all that winter and most of the following summer, and once Julian had admitted what he was doing he was willing to explain all the stages to me. I don't suppose I understood properly very much of what he told me because I haven't a scientific sort of brain but I do remember the number 1.17 which had something to do with the amount of extra energy you needed to get a heavier weight into the air. And also .75 which I think proved that animals as big as man could fly if they used their energy properly but animals that weighed more than 350 pounds, like cows and horses, couldn't, not even in theory. But the main thing I remember, because Julian said it so often, was that everyone who had tried to fly, including Leonardo da Vinci, had made problems instead of solving them by adding unnecessarily to the weight they had to get into the air. The solution to the problem Julian used to say was not to build yourself a machine. It was simply to make yourself wings and use them like a bird. But you could only do that by making your arm approximate to the structure of a bird's wing – that was what he said – and that meant flying upside down. Once you imagined yourself flying upside down it became obvious your legs were no longer legs but the bird's tail, and that meant the gap between the legs had to be filled in by a triangle of fabric. In theory your legs ought then to grow out of the middle of your back, about where your kidneys are, and that of course was one of Julian's biggest problems – how he was to take off lying flat on his back.

But his first problem and it was the one that nearly made him give up the whole project was finding the right materials for the framework. He must have experimented with twenty different kinds of wood and I was for ever cleaning up shavings off the floor, but they were all either too brittle or too heavy or too inflexible. Then I think he got interested in a composition that was used to make frames for people's glasses but you would have needed to be a millionaire to pay for it in large amounts. It was the same with half a dozen other materials, they were light enough and strong enough but too expensive.

By the middle of that winter Julian was ready to give up and go to work. It was certainly difficult the two of us living off what I earned at Gomeo's and paying the rent but Julian was so happy working on his wings even when he was in despair about them I said he must keep going at least until he had given his theory a

140

proper trial. It was about this time he decided nothing but the most expensive materials would do and he wasted weeks thinking up schemes to make money instead of thinking how to make his wings.

It must have been June or early July he hit on a solution. He had gone to Sir Robert Kerridge's office, the millionaire who has a big new building in Queen Street, and offered to take off from the building as a publicity stunt if K.O. would put up the money for making the wings, but he hadn't got very far because the typists and clerks mistook him for a student and he was shown out of the building without seeing Sir Robert. It had begun to rain heavily and Julian had no coat and no bus fare and he walked all the way back to Kendall Road that day with nothing to keep him dry but a battered old umbrella with a broken catch and a match stick wedged in it to keep it open. When he got home he couldn't get the match out and he had to leave the umbrella outside in our little concrete yard. He was standing at the kitchen window staring out and I didn't ask him about his idea of taking off from the Kerridge building because I could see it hadn't been a success when suddenly the match must have come out and the umbrella sprang shut so fast it took off and landed on the other side of our six-foot paling fence. I could se Julian was very angry by now because he walked slowly into the neighbour's yard and back with the umbrella and slowly into the shed and out again with the axe and quite deliberately with the rain pouring down on his back he chopped the umbrella to pieces. I went into the other room to give him time to cool off and when I came back ten minutes or so later he was sitting quite still on one of our kitchen chairs with the water running off him into pools on the floor and held up in front of him between the thumb and the forefinger of his right hand was a single steel strut from the framework of the umbrella. He seemed to be smiling at it and talking to it and even I could see what a perfect answer it was, light, thin, strong, flexible, with even an extra strut hinged to the main one.

Julian was impatient now to get on but he needed a lot of umbrellas because his wings were to be large and working by trial and error a lot of struts would be wasted. We couldn't afford to buy umbrellas and in two days searching around rubbish tips he found only three, all of them damaged by rust. The next morning he was gone when I woke and when I walked up to the museum steps where he was standing staring out across the harbour he said we would have to steal every umbrella we could lay our hands on. So that afternoon and every afternoon it rained during the next few weeks I left Julian at home working and I went to some place like the post office or the museum or the art gallery and came away with somebody's umbrella. It was easy enough when Julian wanted women's umbrellas but when he wanted the heavier struts I always felt nervous walking away with a man's. Occasionally there were umbrellas left at Gomeo's in the evenings and I took these home as well. Soon the spare room upstairs, the one Vega sleeps in now, was crammed with all kinds and I got expert at following a person carrying the particular make Julian needed and waiting until a chance came to steal it. I still have a special feeling about umbrellas and sometimes even now I steal one just because it reminds me of how exciting it was when Julian was getting near to finishing his final set of wings. I even stole one at the town hall on the night of the National Orchestra concert when that poet read the ode the Government commissioned him to write about Julian and the Orchestra played a piece called 'Tone Poem: J . . . H . . .' by a local composer.

I should mention that all the time this was going on Julian was in strict training for his flight. I used to tell him he was overdoing it and that he didn't need to train so hard, because to be honest I always felt embarrassed in the afternoons sitting on the bank watching him panting around the Domain track in sandshoes and baggy white shorts while Halberg and Snell and all those other Auckland Olympic champions went flying past him. But Julian insisted that success didn't only depend on making a set of wings that would work. It depended on having enough stamina left to keep using them after the first big effort of getting into the air. The flight he said would be like running a mile straight after a 220 yard sprint and that was what he used to do during his track training. He had put himself on a modified Lydiard schedule and apart from the sharpening-up work on the track he kept up a steady fifty miles jogging a week. There were also special arm exercises for strength and co-ordination and he spent at least ten minutes morning and evening lying flat on his back on the ironing board flapping his arms and holding a ten-ounce sinker in each hand. Julian was no athlete but he was determined and after six months in training he began to get the scrawny haggard look Lydiard world champions get when they reach a peak. It wasn't any surprise to me when he timed himself over the half mile and found he was running within a second of the New Zealand women's record.

By now the framework for the final set of wings was built and ready to be covered with fabric and there were only a few struts still to be welded in to the back and leg supports. Julian had bought a periscope too and attached it to the crash helmet so he could hold his position steady, flat on his back, and still see ahead in the direction of his flight. Everything seemed to be accounted for except there was still no answer to the problem of how he was to take off lying on his back. He needed a run to get started but he could hardly run backwards and jump into the air. He considered jumping off something but that seemed unnecessarily dangerous and besides he thought it would be important to hold his horizontal position right from the start and that meant a smooth take-off not a wild jump.

I suppose I won't be believed when I say this but if it hadn't been for an idea that came to me one morning while I was watching Julian lying on his back flapping on the ironing board he would probably have had to risk jumping off a building. It came to me right out of the blue that if the ironing board had wheels and Julian was wearing his wings he would shoot along the ground faster and faster until he took off and left the ironing board behind. I don't think I realised what a good idea it was until I said it aloud and Julian stopped flapping and stared at me for I don't know how many seconds with his arms out wide still holding the ten-ounce sinkers and then he said very loudly my God why didn't I think of that. The next moment he was gone, clattering up the stairs, and then he was down again kissing me and saying I was the brightest little bugger this side of Bethlehem and for the rest of the day he got nothing done or nothing that had anything to do with his flight. Of course Julian dropped the idea of actually putting wheels on the ironing board, and the take-off vehicle he did use is the only publicly owned relic of his flight. I find it strange when I go to the museum sometimes and see a group of people standing behind a velvet cord staring at it and reading a notice saying this tubular-steel chromium-plated folding vehicle on six-inch wheels was constructed by the late Julian Harp and used during the commencement of his historic flight. It puzzles me why no one ever says good heavens that's one of those things undertakers use to wheel coffins on, because that's what it is. Julian had seen undertakers using them – church trucks they call them – when he was working in the hospital morgue, and when I suggested putting wheels on the ironing board he immediately thought how much better a church truck would be. I don't know where he got the one he used but I think he must have raided the morgue or an undertaker's chapel at night because one morning I came down to breakfast and there it was gleaming in the middle of the kitchen like a Christmas present.

If I'm going to tell the whole story of the flight and tell it truthfully I might as well come straight out with it and say Julian didn't get any help or encouragement from the organisers of that day's gymkhana. It makes me very angry the way it's always written about as if the whole programme was built around Julian's flight, and the way everyone who was there, Vega for example, talks as if she went only to see that part of the programme and even tells you she had a feeling Julian Harp would succeed. Up in the museum under glass that's supposed to be protected by the most efficient burglar alarm system in the Southern Hemisphere they show you the form Julian had to fill in when he asked the gymkhana organisers to put him on the programme. They don't tell you he had to call on them six or seven times before he got them to agree. Even then I don't think he would have succeeded if he hadn't revived two of his letter writers and had them send letters to the *Herald*, one saying he had seen an albatross flying in the Domain and another, a woman, saying she didn't think it was an albatross, it looked remarkably like a man.

Then you find there's a lot of fuss made by some people about the fact the Governor-General was there and how wonderful it is that the Queen's representative went in person to see Julian Harp try his wings. The truth is the Governor-General was there because the gymkhana was sponsored jointly by the fund-raising committees of the Blind Institute and the Crippled Children's Society and he agreed as their patron to present the prizes for the main event of the day. And in case like everyone else I talk to you have forgotten what the main event was and allowed yourself to think it was Julian Harp's flight, let me just add that it was an attempt on the unofficial world record for the one thousand yards on grass. In fact Julian had to sit round while the mayor made his speech, a pole-sitting contest was officially started, twelve teams of marching girls representing all the grades competed, the brass and Highland bands held their march past, and the police motor cycle division put on a display of trick riding. And when he did try to begin his event at the time given on the programme he was stopped because the long jump was in progress.

Of course now it's different. It's different partly because Julian succeeded, partly because he's supposed to be dead and everyone likes a dead hero better than a live one, but mostly because he made us famous overseas, and when all those reporters came pouring into the country panting to know about the man who had succeeded where men throughout history had failed – that was what they said – everyone began to pretend New Zealand had been behind him on the day. People started to talk about him in the same breath as Snell and Hillary and Don Clark, and then in no time he was up with Lord Rutherford and Katherine Mansfield and now he seems to be ahead of them and there's a sort of religious feeling starts up every time his name is mentioned.

There's nothing to get heated about, I know, but when I hear the Prime Minister (Our Beloved Leader, Julian used to call him) on the radio urging the youth of the nation to aim high like Harp I can't help remembering Julian so nervous that morning about appearing in public he even cleaned his shoes and with me just as nervous the only person there to give him any help or encouragement. And then when we got to the Domain Julian was told he couldn't have an assistant with him because the field was already too cluttered with officials and sportsmen, so there he was crouching down in front of the pavilion with his shiny coffin carrier and his scarlet wings for hour after hour waiting his turn while I sat on the far bank knowing there wasn't a thing more I could do for him. We were nervous partly because he hadn't given the wings a full test and partly because he had tested them enough to know they would carry him. They couldn't be tested in broad daylight and remain a secret, so Julian had to be satisfied with a trial late one night. I remember it almost as clearly as the day of the flight, Julian's church truck speeding across the grass getting faster and faster until I could just see the wings, black they looked in the dark, lift him clear of it. Each time he was airborne he let himself drop back on to the truck because he didn't trust his vision through the periscope at night and he was afraid of colliding with overhead wires. But there was enough for us both to know what he could do and to put me in a terrible state of nerves that afternoon watching the marching girls and the bands and waiting for Julian to get his chance.

Everyone knows what happened when that chance came. I don't think many people saw him climb on to his truck and lie down and the few around me who were watching were saying look at this madman, he thinks he's Yuri Gagarin. But by the time the little truck and the scarlet wings were shooting full speed across the grass everyone was looking, and when somebody shouted over the loud speakers look at the wheels and the whole crowd saw the truck was rolling free there was a tremendous cheer. There was a gasp when he cleared the trees at the far end of the ground and then as he veered away towards the museum with those scarlet wings beating and beating perfectly evenly something got into the crowd and it forgot all about the athletic events and surged over the track and up the slope through the grove of trees by the cricket scoreboard, then down into the hollow of the playing fields and up again towards the museum. I would have followed Julian of course but I didn't have to make up my mind to follow. I was one of the crowd now and I was swept along with it running and tripping with my eyes all the time on Julian like a vision of a heavenly angel rising on those wings made out of hundreds of stolen bits and pieces. He rose a little higher with each stroke of his wings and even when he seemed to try for a moment to come down and almost went into a spin I didn't understand what was happening. I didn't think about whether he intended to go on climbing like that I was so completely absorbed in the look of it, the wings opening and the sunlight striking through the fabric showing the pattern of the struts, and then closing and lifting the tiny figure of Julian another wing-beat up and out and away from us. I had stopped with the crowd on the slopes in front of the museum and Julian must have crossed the harbour and crossed the North Shore between Mt Victoria and North Head and got well out over the Hauraki Gulf towards Rangitoto before it came to me and it came quite calmly as if someone outside me was explaining to me that I was seeing the last of him. I don't know any more than anyone else whether it was a fault in the wings or whether flying put Julian into some kind of trance he couldn't break or whether he just had somewhere to go, but it seemed as you watched him that once he began to climb there was no way to go but higher and further until his energy was used up. I stood there with everyone else watching him get smaller and smaller until we were only catching flashes of colour and losing them again and finally there was nothing to see and we all went on standing there for I don't know how long, until tea time anyway.

After that I was ill and I lay in a bed in hospital for ten days without saying a word seeing Julian's wings opening and closing above me until I was sick of the sight of them and all through the day hearing people talking about him and reading bits out of the newspapers about him. By the time I began to feel better he was famous and I remember when a doctor came to see me and explained I was pregnant and asked who the father was I said Julian Harp and I heard him say to the sister she needs rest and quiet. Soon I learned to say nothing about Julian. He belongs to the public and the public makes what it likes of him. But if you ever came out of a building and found your umbrella missing you might like to believe my story because it may mean you contributed a strut to the wings that carried him aloft.

THE LONERS

O. E. Middleton

As long as he had been working, all had been well. The other men in the timber-yard had been friendly enough once he had got to know them. They had taught him all the gauges, shown him how to tell rimu from matai, totara from kauri and white pine. Once he had grown used to their rough teasing ways, he had come to like working in the timber-yard.

The day the foreman had told him he was to 'finish-up' he had not at first understood.

'Bad luck, Luke!' one of the gang had growled, clapping him on the shoulder. 'There's seven of us been given our walking-tickets today.'

' . . . You too?'

'Yes. Me, my mate Bill here, young Jimmy from the joinery shop and three from one of the other gangs.'

'B-b-but, why?' he had managed to bring out, his eyes searching the man's weathered, unsmiling face.

'Not enough orders. That's why! The country's in a bad way at the moment. The building industry's one of the hardest hit. I've seen it happen before and it'll happen again!' The man had drawn a hand across the grey stubble on his chin, stared past the even stacks of timber at the gleam of sea.

All the next, workless morning, he had sat about, not knowing what to do. There were no labourers' jobs in the paper.

'Why don't you sit on the verandah?' Pine had suggested.

He had gone there meekly enough, glad to be out of the way while the two women made beds and cleaned the house. After a while, though, he had grown uneasy. It seemed to him that the people who strolled past, especially the stiff-faced women with their trundlers and shopping baskets, looked at him disdainfully, as if he had no right to be there. As soon as he had gone back inside, his brother's wife, Rebecca, had begun to scold him.

'Aw, Luke! Can't you give us a chance to get the house straight!'

Ashamed, ill-at-ease, he had gone out again, wandered off alone, not thinking or caring where he went, yet always making for the sea. He had sauntered moodily past the other old wooden houses, all like the one he shared with his brother Matthew, had become aware all at once that this was his first *free* day, his first day to himself since they had got off the ship. From then on, he had wandered through the town, glancing almost furtively into shop-windows. In the window of a fish-shop, something had caught his eye. For some moments he had stared intently, almost affectionately, through the streaming glass at the object; a sizeable squid on a large dish. . . .

He had been on the point of going in to ask the price of the succulent thing, but just in time, realised that he did not know its English name. Besides, he had given Pine all his money the day before, so his pockets were empty.

Moodily, he had turned away. It did not do to go anywhere without money in *this* country. With money in the pocket, there was always something to buy.

At home, he had always gone fishing with friends: either in a boat on the lagoon, or, at night, with torches and spears on the reef. Whatever the catch, there had always been plenty of fun, the warmth of talk and laughter. . . .

Here, everything was different. The people went about singly, many of them with grim, stony faces. Often they passed one another in the street without so much as a greeting.

At last, hardly knowing where he was, he had reached the harbour, walked the length of the old wharf. A solitary fisherman squinting down at a dancing float had glanced at him briefly. In that instant, the two halves of his longing had come together. He would ask Pine for enough to buy a couple of lines and some hooks.

Ever since, he had hardly missed a day. Once he had scanned the job columns, been to see about any work that was offering, his thoughts would turn to the hours stretching ahead. With his gear and a morsel of food in an old basket, he would set out for the wharf.

Though he no longer followed that first, roundabout route, wasted no time gazing into shop-windows, it was still a long way. Sometimes, another man, or even two, were there before him. One day, when he had been to see about a job, he found four of them perched, intent as gulls, at the end of the wharf.

At the weekends and late in the afternoons, small boys sometimes drifted down in twos and threes to fish for sprats.

The old man he had seen that first day came down on his bicycle two or three times a week. He used a homemade rod that he carried tied to the bar of his bicycle, rarely stayed beyond midday and usually went home with a fish. He wore spectacles, moved stiffly and sometimes had trouble taking off and putting on the clips he wore around the bottoms of his trousers. He seldom smiled, spoke little, but usually greeted the other regulars with a nod. Once or twice, Luke thought he saw a gleam, like the sudden sparkle of sun on sea, light up the old man's eyes.

Jock, as the others called him, kept all his tackle in a wooden box strapped to the carrier of his bicycle. Nestling in a honeycomb of small cells were hooks and sinkers, swivels, rod-rings, spare coils of fine wire and nylon, spinners and oddments of all kinds. Once, the old fellow had gone to the box, rummaged a while, and handed Luke a sharp new hook to replace one lost on a snag. He had shown him how to tie a stop-knot, how to 'kinch' it tight so that it would never slip. Another time, Jock had tossed him a piece of fresh mullet, signing to him to exchange it for the bait he had been using without success.

Three other men came down to the wharf almost every day. One rode a motor-bike, another drove a battered car, while a third came on foot. All were married men in their late twenties or early thirties. From the few words they exchanged, Luke guessed that all were out of work and came to the wharf as much to get away from their wives, as in the hope of taking something home for the pot. He would have liked to ask them what work they did; to have told them how strange he found everything after the life he had been used to. But the chance never came.

If one of them spoke to him, it was teasingly, as though he were a child. His halting replies usually brought only shakes of the head, pitying smiles. Their eyes would return to their fishing-lines that seemed to transfix the water like fine spears. He guessed that the three had all been born in the town, had grown up there at about the same time. Yet they were not *real* friends. Perhaps they had gone to different schools, belonged to different churches, worked at different jobs? Often, as he sat brooding on these things, Luke's thoughts would return to his wife. He would stare past the breakwater at the great rock thrusting up through the pale sea like a huge, blunt tooth, his heart swelling with love.

It was natural that she should feel anxious, now that she was again with child. At least Matthew still went to his job at the freezing works every morning. When the wind blew from that quarter, the wail of the works siren would come clearly over the intervening sea. Luke would cock his head, stare uneasily across the water.

There had been a hooter at the timber-yard. The first new words he had learned had been *smoko, knock-off, pay-day*: his workmates had seen to that. Each time he heard the siren, it reminded him of the men he had worked with in the timber-yard, the things they had said. The sound seemed to stir some chord in the others too.

They would get up, stretch their limbs, swallow mouthfuls of tea from their flasks, light a cigarette or fill a pipe when the smoko hooter went. Whenever the noon whistle blew, old Jock would get up stiffly, begin reeling-in. Although the old man lived on a pension and none of the others had regular jobs, the mournful call of the hooter seemed to tug at them all, as the sun and moon affect the tide.

Since they were fond of eating their fish raw, Pine had tried to buy limes at the greengrocer's. But even the shops that sold taro had only lemons to offer.

Luke was still out of work in May when the mackerel began to come in. He caught a few of the smaller type known locally as 'English mackerel', found them good bait for larger fish and fine to eat raw when there were enough for a meal.

One day, the other man who also came down on foot hauled in a fine 'horse-mackerel'. 'Don't often get them like that in the daytime,' he said, holding it up to take out the hook. Shy of the light, the fish quivered and fought, its scutes and nacreous sides catching fire. Adroitly, unmoved by its frenzy, the man held the fish, slipped out the hook. He slid the mackerel into a sack where it went on shivering and vibrating.

There were only the two of them on the wharf that morning and it was the first time the man had ever spoken to Luke. The 'horse mackerel' reminded him of a type of small tuna much prized in the islands for its fine flavour.

'What is the *best* time?' he brought out slowly at last.

'Night-time is best,' the other answered briefly. 'Use a small hook – a treble is best – and no sinker.'

' . . . I used to come down after mackerel a lot at one time,' he went on after a pause. 'It's different now though. My wife doesn't like me coming down here after dark. Says it's too risky for a married man. . . .' He gave a short, scornful laugh, spat between his dangling legs into the sea. 'They're beautiful eating, too,' he finished wistfully.

Luke said nothing and the other soon fell silent. Not long afterwards, he rolled up his lines, slung the sugar-bag over his shoulder. 'So long!' he threw out as he set off home.

As he watched him swing away down the wharf, Luke wondered what Pine would say when he told her he wanted to fish at night.

In the paper next morning, there was an advertisement for men to fill and sew sacks of wheat in a grain store. He was one of the early ones, was given three days' work with some other men in a cold, dimly-lit warehouse.

After that, he came down to the wharf at night two or three

times a week, took home several fine horse-mackerel. Even after dark, quite a few people came down to the old wharf to fish. They were mostly men in steady jobs with a sprinkling of boys from the High School. The only daytime fishermen Luke recognised among them was the man who drove the battered car. He offered Luke a lift home one night, on the way, told him that he was an out-of-work carpenter.

Late one night, after he had got back from the wharf, a strong wind sprang up. As he cleaned his fish, the old house started to creak and sigh. Matthew's youngest child began to cry and woke the others. By the time Pine had got their own small daughter back to sleep, he was in bed. When at last she slipped in beside him, hugging his back for warmth, they lay awake for a long time, talking in whispers, awed by the strange howling of the wind.

In the morning, the wind still blew from the mountains. Matthew went off to work swathed like an Eskimo in the warm gear he usually wore only in the freezing-chambers. The wind still prowled about the house, fumbling with a loose sheet of iron on the roof, making the branch of an old tree scrape mournfully against the weatherboards. When the children had been wrapped up and sent off to school, Luke went onto the verandah. The sea was an uneven strip of frosty green under scudding clouds. There would be no fishing that day.

Pine pounced on him the moment he went inside again.

'You can do the shopping for us today, man! Too cold for Rebecca and me to go out . . . !' She handed him a kit, a list and her purse, helped him on with the army greatcoat he had bought at the surplus stores.

At the fruiterer's, he saw two women who came from the same village as his wife. They were buying taro, weighing the tubers expertly in their hands, searching for blemishes. They gave the customary polite greetings, which he returned. Yet he was glad when they were gone. It seemed to him that there had been something mocking, sly, in the looks they had darted at the kit. When you did not have a job to go to, everyone, even your own countrymen, began to look at you askance. At home, if a man chose to be idle, no one frowned.

At the butcher's and the baker's, he felt awkward, out of place. In the grocer's shop, he gave up trying to stumble through the list, handed it to the young assistant.

When he came out at last, the kit was bulging. A bell began to clang from a doorway further down the street over which a banner flapped. People came hurrying, jostling one another to get in. Guessing that it must be some kind of entertainment, he went in

151

too. A man with a face as red as the banner outside and a pencil behind his ear, mounted a platform, began to harangue the crowd in a loud, sing-song voice. Two other men in long aprons hunted among piles of furniture, old radios, crockery, lawn-mowers, clothes-wringers, books, peering at labels, turning or holding up the goods for the crowd to see.

Although at first, Luke did not follow all that was said, he soon saw that the things were being sold. How stupid he was! Was not this the very place where Pine and Rebecca had bought most of the things for the house?

The kit was heavy. He put it down, could not help smiling at the antics of the red-faced auctioneer. The man grinned at him, caught his eye; Luke gave an answering nod. Only when a chorus of other bids followed and the auctioneer looked at him again, did he realise that he had very nearly bought a large iron double bedstead with brass knobs. Hastily, he gathered up the basket, hurried out, his face burning. How the women would laugh if they knew!

As he came out onto the footpath, he bumped into someone, almost knocking him over. 'Sorry!' he said, putting out his free hand to steady the man who seemed dazed by the blow.

'So you should be!' the man answered unexpectedly. 'Do you always treat your old mates so rough?'

Luke stared at him, saw with surprise that it was one of the men from the timber-yard – the one who had spoken kindly to him that last day. 'I didn't see you,' he said smiling.

'How are things, Luke? Got a job yet?'

'No,' he said. 'Not yet.'

'Nor me either,' said the man. Their eyes met, held.

The same greying stubble stood out on the man's furrowed cheeks and bony jaws. His breath carried a sweetish reek of alcohol and his pale, blue-grey eyes held a misty, far-off look. 'All on your own?' he asked: then, without waiting for an answer, 'Come and have a drink!'

Luke had been into a pub a couple of times with his brother. Once or twice, he and Matthew had cracked a bottle of beer in the house in the weekend. At home, people had often brewed their own from bananas, oranges, all kinds of things. He had once got very drunk on the stuff when he was still in his teens.

After their third beer, Jack said, 'Oh it's good to have someone to talk to. You get fed-up with your own company and the sight of four walls! . . . I had a missus too, once; and a kiddie. Little girl. I made good wages in those days. Putting up houses for a big builder . . . . ' He paused, stared into his glass for a moment before going on. 'Then the Slump came. The builder went broke and for months I was on relief. I started to hit the booze . . . . My wife left me and took the kid. I've never seen them since. I guess the girl will have a family of her own by now.' He raised his glass, tilted his head, closed his eyes as the beer went down.

By the time Luke had swallowed his own drink, much of his shyness had gone and he had forgotten his blunder at the auction. He might have forgotten the shopping too, if Jack had not said to him: 'Now, whatever you do, don't leave that basket behind – or your wife will use you for a chopping-block!'

He wanted to bring Jack home, introduce him to Matthew and their wives, give him a meal. But Jack would not hear of it, kept shaking his head. ' . . . I'll have a bite to eat somewhere after,' he said vaguely. 'There's a place I know . . . . '

While he was speaking, he must have made a sign to the barman and before Luke could say anything, two more beers had been bought.

Outside, the wind still blew with the same force, plastering the thick stuff of the greatcoat against him, making him lean forward to keep his feet. Where did the others spend their days? he wondered. Some, he knew, came to the pub. Jack had introduced him to a few of them. He was glad he had met Jack. Another time, when it was too rough to fish, he might look in at the pub. It was good for a man to make friends outside his own countrymen, his own family. Pine would understand.

He was smiling when he reached their gate. Pine, a blanket about her shoulders, looked anxiously out from the verandah. Her face melted into a smile the instant she saw him, but clouded as he stumbled, almost fell, on his way up the steps.

'Luke! Where have you been?'

'Doing your shopping . . . . ' Why was she looking so solemn?

'Man, you've been drinking!'

'I – I met a friend. A man I used to work with. I wanted him to come and eat with us. He's out of work too . . . . We went to a pub, had a few beers.'

'Did you do all the shopping?'

'Yes. See, it's here!' He held out the bulging kit, was astonished at the ease with which she took it from him.

'Where's the purse?'

He began to fumble for it in his pants, fished it out at last from one of the deep pockets in the greatcoat.

'Here it is!' he said cheerfully.

Pine opened the purse, counted out what was left. 'Where is the milk-money?' she asked at length.

'What do you mean?'

'There should have been more than a dollar left after you did the shopping. That money was for our next week's milk!'

He stared into her hot, troubled face and the full import of it smote him, left him aghast. 'It's gone,' he mumbled, hanging his head. 'I used it for beer.'

He stood waiting for an outburst from her. It did not come. She simply stood there, looking at him, her eyes wide, the tears close. Then, without a word, she turned, opened the door and went in.

Dumbly, he followed her, his face burning, his limbs beginning to feel numb.

In the morning, while everyone was still asleep, he slipped out of bed, crept onto the verandah. It was still too dark to make out the sea. The wind had shifted but it was still cold.

Silently, he gathered his gear together, shrugged on the greatcoat and went out. A solitary vehicle bumbled about the street. He heard the merry, jingling rattle of bottles in metal crates, hurried his steps as though pursued. Light gleamed from only one or two houses. As though weary from their night-long vigil, even the street lamps seemed to burn with a subdued, worn-out glow.

It was still early when he reached the wharf. The wind was coming straight off the ocean and every so often, breakers boomed against the seaward edge of the breakwater. He baited his small line, turned up the collar of his coat, settled down to wait.

It was the first time he had been out so early. Maybe he should have told Pine? Matthew would not yet be setting out for work. It was a fine place to live, in spite of everything. When you grew used to it, even the cold had something fine about it. Matthew said it helped you work better. The colder water certainly seemed to make the fish taste sweet.

When the sun began to peer over the ridge of hills beyond the town, the air seemed at first to grow colder. He shrugged deeper into his collar, stared out through slitted eyes at the glittering, grey-green sea.

Footsteps sounded at the far end of the wharf. He turned to see who it was, could not at first recognise the man because of his parka and woollen head-gear.

'You're early!' the newcomer said. 'Any luck?'

Luke shook his head.

'Cunt of a day, yesterday!' the other remarked when he had set his lines.

'No good for fishing!' Luke agreed.

They fell silent. Under them, the sea sucked and gurgled around the piles. Every so often, a comber smashed itself against the breakwater, sending up a smother of white. All at once, the man in

154

the parka got to his feet, began to haul in one of his lines. Luke could tell from the run of the line, the man's movements, that it was something big. He secured his own lines, went to see if he could help.

'Just as well he grabbed my new line!' the other muttered. As he spoke, the water churned and boiled some way out. A red-gold mass flashed for a moment, then beat back out of sight.

'Big snapper!' grunted the man, paying out line.

Luke said nothing. He slipped off his coat, lowered himself over the end of the wharf, began to climb down. By the time the fish came up again, it was close under him. Its great, humped, red-gold back heaved up, glittered an instant, then was gone. Luke glanced up, met the blue eyes staring uneasily down.

'Don't know how long I can hold him!' the man called, gingerly hauling in again.

As the snapper swam up, Luke bent down, steadying the line with his free hand. With a deft movement, he slipped his fingers into the gills, felt the nails rasp the harsh lining of the gullet. As he inched back over the cross-ties, the kicking and jumping of the heavy fish made his arm ache. At last he felt the rough timber of the combing, a hand gripped his shoulder. With a final heave, he swung the heavy fish onto the decking.

They stood for a long while looking down at the snapper as it flapped and gasped at their feet. 'What a beaut!' crowed the man in the parka for the third time. 'He must be all of twenty pounds!'

Luke smiled, flexing his aching muscles.

The man turned to him. 'You don't often get them like that. He's a moocher. A loner.' His plain, colourless face had come to life. His frosty, blue-grey eyes shone with a pale lustre. 'They say they're the survivors of old shoals . . . .'

Luke nodded, went on smiling, though he understood only part of what the man said. He began to shiver, turned away and put on his coat.

The other man pushed back the hood of his parka. Tufts of fair hair stuck out from under his woollen cap.

Luke felt rapid, sharp bites on his small line. He pulled it up, unhooked a plump little fish spotted brown and yellow.

'Do you want him?' the other man called, his eyes on the small fish.

'No! You take him!' Luke got up, glad to have something to give.

The man in the parka stuck one prong of a treble hook through the body of the little fish just below the dorsal fin, carefully lowered it into the water. Just then, the wail of the starting-whistle at the works came faintly to them during a lull in the wind.

They fished in silence for the best part of an hour. All at once, the other man got up, began to haul in the line baited with the live fish. This time he did not pause, kept bringing in the line hand-over-hand, until an ugly greyish fish with a dark blotch on each side lay gasping on the wharf.

Luke went to look at it. 'What do you call that one?' he asked. He had seen a few of these fish caught, had even watched a man casting a murderous-looking weighted jag at one of the slow-swimming creatures on a still day, but had not liked to ask the name.

'Oh that's a johnny: a john-dory. Best eating fish in the sea! My missus will be pleased! Loves them, she does . . . . Only fish she's keen on.' He began to whistle under his breath, rebaited the line with a dead sprat, lapsed into silence once more. Before long, the men's solitary figures became as still as two bollards. The sun slid over the faces of the rocky islands beyond the breakwater, caught the occasional flash of a diving gannet. The wind never ceased to worry at the grey-green sea, making the white under-fur bristle, plucking at the men's lines until they danced and sang.

The sad, peremptory wail of a hooter came faintly again across the water. The man in the parka lifted his hand, looked puzzled. 'It's not smoko yet,' he muttered. He glanced uneasily at the tide, which had begun to drop, got up and began to haul in his lines. As he wound them onto their sticks, his elbows wagged in a comical rhythm and he stared fixedly towards the town.

When he was ready to go, he took the snapper from the sack, put it down beside Luke's basket. 'Better take that home with you,' he said.

Luke glanced up with a smile, made a ritual gesture of refusal.

'Look there's only the two of us. We've got any amount with the johnny. You take the snapper – it's a family-sized feed!' He turned away, his boots thudding dully on the wooden decking, his cowled head turned against the wind.

When the man's footfalls had died away, Luke bent over the fish. The huge tail was dry and stiff where it had stuck out in the wind. But where the sack had covered it, the snapper had kept its moist bloom under the scales, was dappled red-gold, blue-green.

He took out his knife, began to clean the fish. As if by magic, red-legged gulls sprang into the air, began to squall and bicker around him.

Before he set out for home, he slipped a length of cord through the fish's gills, climbed down over the cross-ties once more, rinsed the fish in the sea. All the way back, he had to keep shifting the dead weight from one side to the other, to rest his arm.

As he crossed the railway-tracks near the freezing works, knots of men carrying lunch-cases passed him in twos and threes. One of them chivvied him, asked if the fish were for sale. Grinning, he shook his head, kept on walking.

He felt suddenly hungry, tried to remember what Jack had said about the place where the out-of-work could get bread and hot soup. Anyway, he was almost home. Yesterday, Pine had been angry, but by now she would be glad to see him. Pine was like that. Still, now that he knew that other world, he could always return there when he felt the need . . . .

He climbed the steps to the verandah, opened the front door and went in. For a moment, he thought he had heard Matthew's voice: then Pine ran to him, threw her arms about his neck.

Next moment, he was in the kitchen. They were all there, talking, admiring the fish.

Soon, it was Matthew's turn. Smiling, he spread his knees, cleared his throat, began once more to explain about the strike. They all listened, watching his face. A couple of times, Rebecca asked him to repeat things she had not understood. When he had finished, everyone began to talk at once.

The brothers looked at one another and laughed. 'Might as well make it a *real* holiday,' Matthew said. 'Let's go into the other room.'

As he watched his brother bring in the bottles, take off the caps, pour out the beer, Luke could not help thinking: 'It's all right now. This is only the first day. Wait till the women begin to scold at him. . . .' Matthew was fond of fish but did not have the patience to sit hour after hour, waiting for bites. Since he had come here, he had learned to play snooker, though, and kelly pool. Perhaps he would fill in the time with some of his mates in one of the billiard saloons in the town. As long as he had something in his pocket, Matthew would be happy. If the strike dragged on and he ran out of money, he would soon grow fretful . . . .

But why worry? The beer warmed him, reminded him he had eaten nothing so far that day. Pine came in, offered him some slices of cold taro, drank a little from his glass.

'Such a fish will need careful cooking,' she remarked.

'We will have it this evening, when the children are here and we are all together.'

'How long will the strike last?' Luke asked when the women had gone back to the kitchen.

'Maybe a week, maybe a month. Some of the men say it may last even longer.'

From the kitchen came the sounds of running water and of Pine's singing. It was some new song she had heard on the radio, but her

157

voice had all its old warmth, as though she were helping prepare one of the family feasts back home.

Luke remembered the way the snapper had flashed in the early light as it came up out of the sea, its bony gill-plates gleaming. He saw again the look in the frosty blue eyes of the fair-haired man.

'If the wind is not too strong, I will go down again tomorrow,' he decided. 'As long as things are like this, I might as well be the fisherman of the family.'

A GAME OF CARDS

Witi Ihimaera

The train pulled into the station. For a moment there was confusion: a voice blaring over the loudspeaker system, people getting off the train, the bustling and shoving of the crowd on the platform.

And there was Dad, waiting for me. We hugged each other. We hadn't seen each other for a long time. Then we kissed. But I could tell something was wrong.

– Your Nanny Miro, he said. She's very sick.

Nanny Miro . . . among all my nannies, she was the one I loved most. Everybody used to say I was her favourite mokopuna, and that she loved me more than her own children who'd grown up and had kids of their own.

She lived down the road from us, right next to the meeting house in the big old homestead which everybody in the village called 'The Museum' because it housed the prized possessions of the whanau, the village family. Because she was rich and had a lot of land, we all used to wonder why Nanny Miro didn't buy a newer, more modern house. But Nanny didn't want to move. She liked her own house just as it was.

– Anyway, she used to say, what with all my haddit kids and their haddit kids and all this haddit whanau being broke all the time and coming to ask me for some money, how can I afford to buy a new house?

Nanny didn't really care about money though. Who needs it? she used to say. What you think I had all these kids for, ay? To look after me, I'm not dumb!

Then she would cackle to herself. But it wasn't true really, because her family would send all their kids to her place when they were broke and she looked after them! She liked her mokopunas, but not for too long. She'd ring up their parents and say:

– Hey! When you coming to pick up your hoha kids! They're wrecking the place!

Yet, always, when they left, she would have a little weep, and give them some money . . . .

I used to like going to Nanny's place. For me it was a big treasure house, glistening with sports trophies and photographs, pieces of

159

carvings and greenstone, and feather cloaks hanging from the walls.

Most times, a lot of women would be there playing cards with Nanny. Nanny loved all card games – five hundred, poker, canasta, pontoon, whist, euchre – you name it, she could play it.

The sitting room would be crowded with the kuias, all puffing clouds of smoke, dressed in their old clothes, laughing and cackling and gossiping about who was pregnant – and relishing all the juicy bits too!

I liked sitting and watching them. Mrs Heta would always be there, and when it came to cards she was both Nanny's best friend and worst enemy. And the two of them were the biggest cheats I ever saw.

Mrs Heta would cough and reach for a hanky while slyly slipping a card from beneath her dress. And she was always reneging in five hundred! But her greatest asset was her eyes, which were big and googly. One eye would look straight ahead, while the other swivelled around, having a look at the cards in the hands of the women sitting next to her.

– Eeee! You cheat! Nanny would say. You just keep your eyes to yourself, Maka tiko bum!

Mrs Heta would look at Nanny as if she were offended. Then she would sniff and say:

– You the cheat yourself, Miro Mananui. I saw you sneaking that ace from the bottom of the pack.

– How do you know I got an ace Maka? Nanny would say. I know you! You dealt this hand, and you stuck that ace down there for yourself, you cheat! Well, ana! I got it now! So take that!

And she would slap down her hand.

– Sweet, ay? she would laugh. Good? Kapai lalelale? And she would sometimes wiggle her hips, making her victory sweeter.

– Eeee! Miro! Mrs Heta would say. Well, I got a good hand too!

And she would slap her hand down and bellow with laughter.

– Take that!

And always, they would squabble. I often wondered how they ever remained friends. The names they called each other!

Sometimes, I would go and see Nanny and she would be all alone, playing patience. If there was nobody to play with her, she'd always play patience. And still she cheated! I'd see her hands fumbling across the cards, turning up a jack or queen she needed, and then she'd laugh and say:

– I'm too good for this game!

She used to try to teach me some of the games, but I wasn't very interested, and I didn't yell and shout at her like the women did. She liked the bickering.

160

– Aue . . . she would sigh. Then she'd look at me and begin dealing out the cards in the only game I ever knew how to play.

And we would yell snap! all the afternoon . . . .

Now, Nanny was sick.

I went to see her that afternoon after I'd dropped my suitcases at home. Nanny Tama, her husband, opened the door. We embraced and he began to weep on my shoulder.

– Your Nanny Miro, he whispered. She's . . . she's . . . .

He couldn't say the words. He motioned me to her bedroom.

Nanny Miro was lying in bed. And she was so old looking. Her face was very grey, and she looked like a tiny wrinkled doll in that big bed. She was so thin now, and seemed all bones.

I walked into the room. She was asleep. I sat down on the bed beside her, and looked at her lovingly.

Even when I was a child, she must have been old. But I'd never realised it. She must have been over seventy now. Why do people you love grow old so suddenly?

The room had a strange, antiseptic smell. Underneath the bed was a big chamber pot, yellow with urine . . . And the pillow was flecked with small spots of blood where she had been coughing.

I shook her gently.

– Nanny . . . Nanny, wake up.

She moaned. A long, hoarse sigh grew on her lips. Her eyelids fluttered, and she looked at me with blank eyes . . . and then tears began to roll down her cheeks.

– Don't cry, Nanny, I said. Don't cry. I'm here.

But she wouldn't stop.

So I sat beside her on the bed and she lifted her hands to me.

– Haere mai, mokopuna. Haere mai. Mmm. Mmm.

And I bent within her arms and we pressed noses.

After a while, she calmed down. She seemed to be her own self.

– What a haddit mokopuna you are, she wept. It's only when I'm just about in my grave that you come to see me.

– I couldn't see you last time I was home, I explained. I was too busy.

– Yes, I know you fullas, she grumbled. It's only when I'm almost dead that you come for some money.

– I don't want your money, Nanny.

– What's wrong with my money! she said. Nothing's wrong with it! Don't you want any?

– Of course I do, I laughed. But I know you! I bet you lost it all on poker!

She giggled. Then she was my Nanny again. The Nanny I knew.

We talked for a long time. I told her about what I was doing in Wellington and all the neat girls who were after me.

– You teka! she giggled. Who'd want to have you!

And she showed me all her injection needles and pills and told me how she'd wanted to come from the hospital, so they'd let her.

– You know why I wanted to come home? she asked. I didn't like all those strange nurses looking at my bum when they gave me those injections. I was so sick, mokopuna, I couldn't even go to the lav, and I'd rather wet my own bed not their neat bed. That's why I come home.

Afterwards, I played the piano for Nanny. She used to like *Me He Manurere* so I played it for her, and I could hear her quavering voice singing in her room.

Me he manurere aue . . . .

When I finally left Nanny I told her I would come back in the morning.

But that night, Nanny Tama rang up.

– Your Nanny Miro, she's dying.

We all rushed to Nanny's house. It was already crowded. All the old women were there. Nanny was lying very still. Then she looked up and whispered to Mrs Heta:

– Maka . . . Maka tiko bum . . . I want a game of cards . . . .

A pack of cards was found. The old ladies sat around the bed, playing. Everybody else decided to play cards too, to keep Nanny company. The men played poker in the kitchen and sitting room. The kids played snap in the other bedrooms. The house overflowed with card players, even onto the lawn outside Nanny's window, where she could see . . . .

The women laid the cards out on the bed. They dealt the first hand. They cackled and joked with Nanny, trying not to cry. And Mrs Heta kept saying to Nanny:

– Eee! You cheat Miro. You cheat! And she made her googly eye reach far over to see Nanny's cards.

– You think you can see, ay, Maka tiko bum? Nanny coughed. You think you're going to win this hand, ay? Well, take that!

She slammed down a full house.

The other women goggled at the cards. Mrs Heta looked at her own cards. Then she smiled through her tears and yelled:

– Eee! You cheat Miro! I got two aces in my hand already! Only four in the pack. So how come you got three aces in your hand?

Everybody laughed. Nanny and Mrs Heta started squabbling as they always did, pointing at each other and saying: You cheat, not me! And Nanny Miro said: I saw you, Maka tiko bum, I saw you sneaking that card from under the blanket.

She began to laugh. Quietly. Her eyes streaming with tears.

162

And while she was laughing, she died.

Everybody was silent. Then Mrs Heta took the cards from Nanny's hands and kissed her.

– You the cheat, Miro, she whispered. You the cheat yourself. . . .

We buried Nanny on the hill with the rest of her family. During her tangi, Mrs Heta played patience with Nanny, spreading the cards across the casket.

Later in the year, Mrs Heta, she died too. She was buried right next to Nanny, so that they could keep on playing cards . . . .

And I bet you they're still squabbling up there . . . .

– Eee! You cheat Miro . . .

– You the cheat, Maka tiko bum. You, you the cheat . . . .

A GLORIOUS MORNING,
COMRADE

Maurice Gee

Mercy tied her father's scarf in a mean granny knot.

'Now remember, darling, if you want the little house just bang on the wall. We don't want any wets with the girls all here.' And Barbie, gentler, but not to be outdone, knelt and zipped up his slippers. 'You'll be lovely and warm in the sun, won't you? Just bang on the wall. No little accidents please. 'Bye daddums.'

They left him in his rocking chair on the verandah and he rocked a little, pitying their innocence. He did not mean to pee in his pants today. He had other plans.

Presently the 'girls' came, driving their little cars, and they walked up the path in twos and threes, dumpy women or stringy, the lot, in Saturday clothes and coloured hair. They stopped for a little chat of course, politely, and sniffed behind their hands to see if he had behaved himself today. They were good-hearted women. Mercy and Barbie attracted such.

'Lucky you, Mr Pitt-Rimmer. Just loafing in the sun.'

He counted them. Ten. Three tables. There was Madge Ogden, a daughter of divorcees; and Pearl Edwards who taught mathematics at the Girls' High School; and Mary Rendt who had wanted to be a nun but had lost her faith and married a German Christian Scientist and lost that faith and her husband too; and the three Bailey girls, with not a husband amongst them, whose mother had broken their hearts by choosing to live in an old people's home; and Christine Hunt who had been caught shoplifting when she was a girl and lived it down and married the son of the mayor; and Jean Murray-Briggs, whose name annoyed him; and last the lesbians, though none of the others knew – Phyllis Wedderburn and Margaret Way. Charles Pitt-Rimmer, he knew. He winked at them and they blushed, but seemed a little pleased.

'Such lovely sun. We've only got old bridge.'

He gave them time to get warmed up. Mercy looked out once and wagged her finger, and Barbie once and kissed him on the cheek.

They would forget him when they were well ahead. His daughters were the top pair in the district and he wished he could feel more pleased with them for it.

When the time came he stood up and walked along the verandah. He went down the path, down the steps, along the footpath to the park, and into the trees. It was twenty–nine minutes past two. He had run away twice before. Today he would outfox them. He would keep away from roads and butcher shops, where he had been caught twice before looking at roasts of beef. They would not think of searching on the hill.

Girls, he wrote in his mind, *There are other things than meat. Your father played chess.*

At nineteen minutes to three he reached the dairy. 'Here you children out of my way,' he said, and they stood aside with a quickness that pleased him. He did not mind that they giggled. That was proper in children.

'A bag of Turkish delight,' he said. He had planned it all morning and it came out with an English sound. 'And a packet of cigarettes.'

The woman behind the counter had a half-witted face, a nose that seemed to snuffle for scent like a dog's. She gave a smile and said. 'It's Mr Pitt-Rimmer, isn't it?'

'My name is not your concern. Turkish delight. And a packet of cigarettes.'

'Sit down, Mr Pitt-Rimmer. There's a chair right there. As soon as I've served these kiddies I'll ring Mrs Parsloe.'

'You will not ring Mrs Parsley. I wish to be served. Am I a customer or am I not? And are you in business? Answer me that.'

He was pleased to see confusion in her eyes. 'I'll have de Reszke.'
'Whosie?'

'De Reszke. You don't seem to know your business, madam. Do you make a living? I wonder at it.'

'There's nothing here called de Reszke.'

'Cigarettes. Cigarettes. Named after a great operatic tenor. Before your time, of course. I understand. It's all Bing Crosby today.'

The woman went suddenly to the telephone. 'You kiddies wait.' She started to dial.

'Very well,' cried Charles Pitt-Rimmer. 'You may ring Mrs Parsley. Tell her I'm striking out. I have my life. Tell her I'm smoking again. De Reszke. And eating Turkish delight.' He stopped at the door. 'And if she wishes to know where I am you may say that I've gone to the butcher's for a piece of German sausage.'

165

'Mrs Parsloe?' the woman said. 'It's the Regal dairy. Your father's here.'

He was very pleased with himself as he turned up the hill. Capablanca would have been proud of that move.

Girls, bridge is for simple folk. You must think ahead. I've never cared for German sausage.

He looked at his watch. It was thirteen minutes to three. Already he had beaten his old record. He pictured the little cars scuttling about Hardinge, driven in a dangerous manner by women with blue and pink hair. Barbie would be crying – he was sorry about that – and Mercy with her eye like a hanging judge's.

Girls; a man's a man for a' that.

He followed a path into the trees and climbed until he stood on the edge of the cliff with the wharves below him. Three minutes past three. He would have liked some Turkish delight. He had not had any since his last day in court, which was twenty-two years ago. His secretary used to bring in a paper bag full with his lunch. The gob-stopper he'd taken from the Regal dairy's counter would be no substitute. But he found that he enjoyed it once he'd torn the paper off. It tasted of raspberry, a flavour he'd forgotten.

He went to the safety fence and looked down. A girl had jumped down there on Boxing Day because her employer, a well-known man in Hardinge, had put her in the family way. She had lived for two hours but not said a word. He had heard Mercy and Barbie discussing it, in voices hushed but full of glee and dread. The man, Barbie said, was 'a weed in the garden of life' – which she'd pinched from her mother, who had also believed that such men should be hanged. Women had a poor understanding of certain needs.

The gob-stopper made him feel bilious. He put it in his pocket. Below him ships were tied up at the wharves, all piddling water out of their sides. One of them was a phosphate tub, moored at a wharf that he remembered now was Pitt-Rimmer Wharf. There had been those years on the Harbour Board – a tedious business. Jack Hunt had picked his nose behind the agenda. The Hunts had never been up to much though they liked to believe that they were the bosses of Hardinge. He walked on and the cape came into sight, standing up like Chunuk Bair. He had no wish to be reminded of that. That had been a very great piece of nonsense.

Girls, you persist in reminding me. . . .

A woman came towards him leading a tiny black dog in a tartan jacket.

'I don't care for dogs, madam. Keep him off.'

'Mr Pitt-Rimmer. Don't you remember me?'

'I've met many people. Fifteen thousand is my calculation.'

'But I'm Maisie Transome. Maisie Jack that was. You used to give me lollies.'

'Your mother was an excellent secretary. And a kindly soul. She had extraordinary bosoms.'

'Ooh, Mr Pitt-Rimmer, you're a rogue.'

'I don't care for animals sniffing about my feet.'

'Come here, Bruce. Where are your manners, darling? Mr Pitt-Rimmer, can I walk home with you? You shouldn't be out you know, dressed like that. Barbie told me you're being very naughty.'

'My daughter has more kindness than sense. She's a good woman but she's had a tragic life.'

'Who? Barbie?'

'She fell in love with a young man in my office. Parsley was his name. Mercy stole him away. "Mercy" was not my choice. I want that understood. My wife had a poor grip on reality. But Parsley – she married him and broke her sister's heart. Barbie never married. Parsley was not a good catch, mind you. She was well out of it. He played around as they say. There was a woman in my office called Rona Jack. Her marriage was unsatisfactory. Parsley used to visit there.'

'Oh Mr Pitt-Rimmer – '

'He died of course. They nursed him. My daughters are good girls.'

'But my parents had an ideal marriage. They were in love till the day they died.'

'Indeed. I congratulate them. You should not speak with strangers. The risks are very great. Good day to you.'

'But I'm taking you home, remember?'

'I wish to relieve myself.'

She did not follow him though her dog yapped in an impertinent way. The path led downhill and had many troublesome curves. His legs began to be sore. But a bank of nasurtiums pleased him and a smell of fennel. Fennel made him think of aniseed balls. He stopped at the memory. When sucked an aniseed ball turned white. And Turkish delight left sugar round the mouth.

Girls, when you were children I bought you sweets. Straps of licorice. Be fair. Bags of sherbet. Bags of chocolate fudge.

The path ended by the Salvation Army Eventide Home. Two old men were sitting on a bench. 'A glorious morning, comrade,' one of them said.

'Glorious,' Charles Pitt-Rimmer agreed, smiling at his better knowledge. It was twenty-nine minutes past three in the afternoon and his daughters were thoroughly bamboozled. He stopped by the

167

reservoir and sat down on a bank. A boy was walking along a pipe, and a smaller boy rode up on a tricycle.

'Why are you wearing your dressing-gown?'

'Old men are allowed to.'

'Mummy makes me get dressed. Have you wet your pants?'

'I believe I have.'

'Couldn't you find a toilet? You could use ours.'

'The word is lavatory. You should not be frightened of calling things by their names.'

'Mummy said lavatory's not nice.'

'And you should not pay too much attention to women.'

Charles Pitt-Rimmer dozed for a moment. 'Poor Parsley. They made him eat his vegetables. Curly kale. A weed.'

'Mummy makes me eat my vegetables.'

'What do you have for pudding?'

His mind was lucid about food but cloudy about everything else. He was not quite sure where he was. 'My favourite is lemon meringue pie.' He felt in his pocket for the gob-stopper and gave it to the child who put it in his mouth at once, leaving only the stick poking out.

'You speak too much of your mother. The conspiracy starts at the cradle.'

The boy who had been walking on the pipe ran up to join them.

'Give us a lick, Tony. Come on.'

Charles Pitt-Rimmer went to sleep. He believed he was in a bath of luke-warm water that was turning cold about his legs. Soon he was wakened by a woman's voice.

'Let me see that. Give it to me at once. It's filthy. It's got a hair on it.'

She moved her arm violently and the boy on the tricycle cried. Charles did not know what was happening, but he saw that the woman was looking at him with hatred and was astonished at the ease with which people felt this emotion. Forty years of court work had not got him used to it.

'Beware, madam. It can get to be a habit.'

'You ought to be ashamed of yourself. And you' – she rounded on the older boy – 'I told you to look after him. Why can't you listen for once? Get into the wash-house and wait till your father comes home.'

Now the older boy cried. They were an emotional family and seemed to be without reason, Charles decided. They vanished and he was relieved. He lay on the bank and tried to sleep, curled into a ball to defeat the cold. Where were his daughters? Where were the wretched women?'

168

Girls, you're selfish creatures . . .

Again a woman woke him. This time it was Christine Hunt, with her hair like candy floss. He reached out for some.

'What are you doing? Oh! Mr Pitt-Rimmer. Let go.'

'Christine Perkins, you were lucky to get off with a fine. If you hadn't had me to conduct your defence you would have gone to prison.'

'Oh! Oh! My hair. You've ruined it.'

'Why did you choose such frilly things, Christine? If you remember, I told the court they were for your glory box? A clever touch. But you can tell me. I can be discreet.'

'You're a horrible man. Oh, look, you've wet your pyjamas. This is dreadful.'

'I understand, Christine. It's difficult to be poor. No nice frillies, eh? A girl likes frillies. But I always believed you married beneath you. Your father-in-law picks his nose.'

'My father-in-law has been dead for twenty years. And you've ruined our afternoon. You know that, don't you? It's a wonder to me how Mercy and Barbie keep going. They must be saints.'

'They're vegetarians. They struggle to ward off despair. I do my best.'

'Mr Pitt-Rimmer, I'm going to take you home. I am. Now come with me. Come on.'

She put out her hand and he was appalled at the size of it. It went right round his wrist, and her silver nails poked up from the underside. She was appalled too. She jerked away.

'Barbie will be the invalid when I'm dead,' said Charles Pitt-Rimmer.

Christine Hunt went away. 'I'm going to get your daughters. Don't you move.' Her little car scuttled off, and Charles lay curled up tightly.

Girls, it's time for my nap. You're selfish creatures . . .

'Oh daddums, daddums, why do you do these things?'

'Put down the rubber sheet, Barbie. No, spread it out, you ninny.'

They put him in the back seat and Barbie sat with him, rubbing his hands.

'You're so naughty, so naughty – '

'I've had enough,' Mercy cried. 'I'm going to put you in a home. You've made a fool of me for the last time. Wipe his mouth Barbie, can't you see?'

'You make it so hard for us, daddums. Oh, your hands are so cold.'

'I walked on the pipe, Mercy. If I'd fallen off you would never have been born.'

They washed him and put him to bed. He slept smiling for two hours, then rang his bell for tea. They propped him up with pillows, and Barbie sat with him while he ate.

'It's a special salad, daddums. One Mercy found. It's got avocados in it. Now drink your apple juice.'

She took away the tray and came back with his library book.

'Promise me you won't be naughty again. It makes us so sad.'

'What was the time when you caught me?'

'Four o'clock. You were gone for two hours. 'Oh daddums – '

'An hour and thirty-one minutes.' He grinned at her.

When she had gone he finished his book. He corrected one split infinitive and underlined two mentions of female breasts. Then he made his secret sign on page eighty-eight.

Barbie was doing the dishes and Mercy watching a television show full of American voices. On the final page, below a scene of love, Charles wrote a message:

My daughters are keeping me prisoner. Help! I have not had a piece of meat for twenty years . . .

BETWEEN EARTH AND SKY

Patricia Grace

I walked out of the house this morning and stretched my arms out wide. Look, I said to myself. Because I was alone except for you. I don't think you heard me.

Look at the sky, I said.

Look at the green earth.

How could it be that I felt so good? So free? So full of the sort of day it was? How?

And at that moment, when I stepped from my house, there was no sound. No sound at all. No bird call, or tractor grind. No fire crackle or twig snap. As though the moment had been held quiet, for me only, as I stepped out into the morning. Why the good feeling, with a lightness in me causing my arms to stretch out and out? How blue, how green, I said into the quiet of the moment. But why, with the sharp nick of bone deep in my back and the band of flesh tightening across my belly?

All alone. Julie and Tamati behind me in the house, asleep, and the others over at the swamp catching eels. Riki two paddocks away cutting up a tree he'd felled last autumn.

I started over the paddocks towards him then, slowly, on these heavy knotted legs. Hugely across the paddocks I went almost singing. Not singing because of needing every breath, but with the feeling of singing. Why, with the deep twist and pull far down in my back and cramping between the legs? Why the feeling of singing?

How strong and well he looked. How alive and strong, stooping over the trunk steadying the saw. I'd hated him for days, and now suddenly I loved him again but didn't know why. The saw cracked through the tree setting little splinters of warm wood hopping. Balls of mauve smoke lifted into the air. When he looked up I put my hands to my back and saw him understand me over the skirl of the saw. He switched off, the sound fluttered away.

I'll get them, he said.

We could see them from there, leaning into the swamp, feeling for eel holes. Three long whistles and they looked up and started towards us, wondering why, walking reluctantly.

Mummy's going, he said.

171

We nearly got one, Turei said. Ay Jimmy, ay Patsy, ay Reuben?

Yes, they said.

Where? said Danny.

I began to tell him again, but he skipped away after the others. It was good to watch them running and shouting through the grass. Yesterday their activity and noise had angered me, but today I was happy to see them leaping and shouting through the long grass with the swamp mud drying and caking on their legs and arms.

Let Dad get it out, Reuben turned, was calling. He can get the lambs out. Bang! Ay Mum, ay?

Julie and Tamati had woken. They were coming to meet us, dragging a rug.

Not you again, they said taking my bag from his hand.

Not you two again, I said. Rawhiti and Jones.

Don't you have it at two o'clock.

We go off at two.

Your boyfriends can wait.

Our sleep can't.

I put my cheek to his and felt his arm about my shoulders.

Look after my wife, he was grinning at them.

Course, what else.

Go on. Get home and milk your cows, next time you see her she'll be in two pieces.

I kissed all the faces poking from the car windows then stood back on the step waving. Waving till they'd gone. Then turning felt the rush of water.

Quick, I said. The water.

Water my foot; that's piddle.

What you want to piddle in our neat corridor for? Sit down. Have a ride.

Helped into a wheelchair and away, careering over the brown lino.

Stop. I'll be good. Stop I'll tell Sister.

Sister's busy.

No wonder you two are getting smart. Stop. . . .

That's it missus, you'll be back in your bikini by summer. Dr McIndoe.

And we'll go water-skiing together. Me.

Right you are. Well, see you both in the morning.

The doors bump and swing.

Sister follows.

Finish off girls. Maitland'll be over soon.

All right Sister.

Yes Sister. Reverently.

The doors bump and swing.

You are at the end of the table, wet and grey. Blood stains your pulsing head. Your arms flail in these new dimensions and your mouth is a circle that opens and closes as you scream for air. All head and shoulders and wide mouth screaming. They have clamped the few inches of cord which is all that is left of your old life now. They draw mucous and bathe your head.

Leave it alone and give it here, I say.

What for? Haven't you got enough kids already?

Course. Doesn't mean you can boss that one around.

We should let you clean your own kid up?

Think she'd be pleased after that neat ride we gave her. Look at the little hoha. God he can scream.

They wrap you in linen and put you here with me.

Well anyway, here you are. He's all fixed, you're all done. We'll blow. And we'll get them to bring you a cuppa. Be good.

The doors swing open.

She's ready for a cuppa Freeman.

The doors bump shut.

Now. You and I. I'll tell you. I went out this morning. Look, I said, but didn't know why. Why the good feeling. Why, with the nick and press of bone deep inside. But now I know. Now I'll tell you and I don't think you'll mind. It wasn't the thought of knowing you, and having you here close to me that gave me this glad feeling, that made me look upwards and all about as I stepped out this morning. The gladness was because at last I was to be free. Free from that great hump that was you, free from the aching limbs and swelling that was you. That was why this morning each stretching of flesh made me glad.

And freedom from the envy I'd felt, watching him these past days, stepping over the paddocks whole and strong. Unable to match his step. Envying his bright striding. But I could love him again this morning.

These were the reasons each gnarling of flesh made me glad as I came out into that cradled moment. Look at the sky, look at the earth, I said. See how blue, how green. But I gave no thought to you.

And now. You sleep. How quickly you have learned this quiet and rhythmic breathing. Soon they'll come and put a cup in my hand and take you away.

You sleep, and I too am tired, after our work. We worked hard you and I and now we'll sleep. Be close. We'll sleep a little while ay, you and I.

173

PARADISE

Ian Wedde

It was winter. The wind blasted from the south-west, straight off the pack ice, he imagined. The rain, with a rattle of hail in it, had soaked through his parka to his skin. Water was roaring in the storm drains. The fingers with which he held the mail felt like parsnips. He kept his head down and thought of double whiskeys and saunas. The addresses on the envelopes blurred and ran with wet. His trousers were plastered to his legs. He turned corners and shoved letters into boxes by memory and instinct, pausing from time to time to pick up rocks in anticipation of certain dogs: just let any mutt try him today. Wait till they think they've got you then let them have it, yiiii yi yi.

The corgi was worrying at his trousers and had got a few nips into his ankle as well. He marched up the garden path with the dog hanging on and snarling. Dingaling, knock knock. Blast of warm as the door opens. Is this your dog madam? Yes. . . . He let poochie have the rock then booted the animal into the shrubbery. Let's call it quits now lady, I won't claim for the trousers. Back up the path, shreds of pant leg flapping. That made it even colder. Fuck them. Why all the mail, it wasn't Mother's Day. Half was Tisco Television Repairs accounts, the rest was Readers' Digest bullshit. The energy chocolate was so hard with cold he almost broke his teeth. Below him the city was invisible. Because he was so wet the walking no longer kept him warm. Sickie time tomorrow. It would take at least two days to thaw. Have a steam bath, lie in bed dreaming Gauguin, move the TV in, smoke dope.

He turned a corner watching for Honey, a killer Alsatian who hunted silently. The top letter in his bundle was for Taimaile, ha ha . . . the envelope plasted with gorgeous Samoan stamps, *tropique sensuel*: fish, butterflies, lagoons, all that. Handsful of hail struck him in the face and froze on to the surface of his parka. Fuck, *oneone, one . . . one . . . oneone. . . .* The litany had a certain rhythm to it. Homage to J. J. Rousseau. He flapped on. Then it began to snow. Dear Oates, we miss you.

Peeking out at six the next morning before deciding whether to ring the post office, he saw the stars burning with cold fire in the firmament. The air was as still as ice. Moonlight lit snowy pine trees on the far side of the valley. Frost had set on the surface of snow in the yard. The crystals glittered in light from the kitchen door. His breath smoked out through the crack. Wow. Shut the door, turn on the heater, make coffee. He drank it listening to silly patter on the pre-breakfast programme, then slewed and crawled in the car to town. Along the roadside were abandoned vehicles 'of various denominations'. He pondered this phrase which had come so glibly to mind. From the left hand window of the car he could see the empty harbour, very still and moonlit, with channel beacons flashing green and red. Navigational aids for Li Po. Beyond the fluorescent pallor of the water was the peninsula wrapped in snow. It looked to him like an immense old samurai lizard crouched in patience until dinosaurs should once again rule the world, when man with his silly services would have bred himself out of survival. Gone out, and been some time, and not been missed. With avalanches of loose shale the ridges and peninsulas would rise on short legs, open ancient eyes, and taste the foul air with forked tongues.

Or, he now thought, as the car minced across icy satin, the peninsula was like a lady's thigh, very white. Next he saw a lizard crouched on a lady's thigh. Then *he* was there. Lady, lady, fold your thighs upon my ears. The water turns like a limb and the dry land rustles its claws. I'm ascetic at heart. Near town they'd dumped grit on the road. The car gripped and sped. Reality equals velocity as a function of direction. Inspiration: whatever comes out eventually and needs to be purified again. Why so luxurious then. Easy: the true voluptuary needs to be able to draw a clear bead on the target. There has to be a bare firepath. The metaphor's formally not factually violent. Oh darling you're killing me. Summer pleasures are blurry and fun but their peaks lack piquancy.

Next question.

If survival's not enough, what is?

Oates, can you hear me?

What an immense relief to get out of the mailroom after sorting. He slipped on his dark glasses. The cold air poured down his throat. The light had a musical quality: it rang like burnished metal. The dark latticework of twigs of the Chinese poplars was in perfect focus. He felt extra sharp. There was a nice power in selection and discrimination: a buoyancy. Cleaning the teeth of your senses, keeping them brighteyed. Then wallow and don't miss a thing. Oboy!

To Taimaile he delivered letters smeared with *fauve* extravagance. It left him cold. He was digging the Pacific horizon from his high vantage point. Cortez: 'So that's what it's called.' Here and there the snow had melted, but mostly it was still thick with a frosted crust. Schools were closed. The dogs were playing with kids and mostly ignored him. He whistled and slid. The Four Square grocer gave him a cup of tea. The Catholic Bishop's sister gave him a whiskey and a slice of plumcake. He accepted a chocolate fish from a little boy, and a free packet of chips from the fish and chip shop. Everyone felt magnanimous and cheerful. Everywhere people were playing in the snow. A few businessmen with pissedoff expressions trudged to work. So their Ford Falcons wouldn't start. Let them hike off their flatulence, their greasy breakfasts.

Oh yes he was 'in a crowing temper', to borrow the phrase from a dear friend who'd recently used it with some bitterness. A few weeks ago he'd been toe-springing up the hill under crisp autumn skies when she'd whizzed past in her little car. He'd seen her hand make a brief vicious signal at the window. It had spoiled his day. He'd realised that his limber pleasure was solitary. Putting letters in boxes. Her car had disappeared downhill taking his joy with it like a little fluttering trophy.

But today sparrows scuffled shrilly where horse turds unfroze in sunlight. Below him the city glittered under a thin veil of coppery fumes. He was satisfied.

But he needed a leak . . . fortunately his route reached the limits of the city's outer suburbs. For some of it he actually walked beside fields of cows. The children in this fringe neighbourhood kept ponies. There was a long lane, petering out into an unsealed track, which ran steeply up a hillside among stands of large oak trees. He had to go some distance up this to serve a house situated back from the road in a spacious well-planted garden. With relief and pleasure he stood staling loudly into a frosty patch of snow, attempting to write his initials, or 'Oates': this obsession. . . . Above the small port where he lived was a monument to Scott of the Antarctic. The expedition had sailed from there. Well, you needed signals like that. He was going to be a poet. That was *his* raise on survival. There was this soft whine as though some bowel was about to barf loudly. He was just nine years old. He found himself thinking of Scott of the Antarctic of whom his dad had been telling him and of brave Oates. He imagined Oates going out and taking his pants down. It all came out in riming couplets like someone was making his finger crawl like Oates over white. How long does it take to take a shit in Antarctica, how long to write riming couplets at nine? Oh Oates was dead, frozen, and he was a boy poet, frozen also, aghast, the feat accomplished. 'Brave Oates' he called it and showed it to his dad who beat him with the back of a hairbrush. It was necessary to survive, he decided, remembering the lines that had been destroyed, tracks leading out somewhere he would return from soon. It was a fiction he clung to. Meanwhile steam rose through the crisp air to the branches of the oaks above which he could see the faultless blue of the winter sky. Everything was fresh and lovely after the rain and the gales. He whistled between his teeth, craning his neck to look up through the branches.

'Aie!'

Today's bringdown.

She was standing by the gate with a hand to her mouth, a Chinese lady in her late thirties.

Chinese?

Someone had moved and he hadn't even noticed. The last lady hadn't been Chinese, what's more she'd never come to the gate.

'What you-do, what you-do!'

'Excuse me,' turning away and swinging his stream with him. Behind him he heard the gritting of gravel under her heels. Reality. Looking back he saw that she was still there, in fact she'd moved closer. The last of his steam drifted away into the cerulean. The air, calm and cold, was filled with birdsong. There they stood. Between them the immaculate surface of the snow was spoiled by strafings of sour yellow. She pointed at this, mutely aghast, stamping forward on small feet, her body held rigid as though in formal preparation for some martial ballet. She was right, of course (he sensed that her outrage was aesthetic rather than scatalogical): he *had* ruined it, a crude barbarian squirting urine around the immaculate interior of this winter morning. He noticed how the blood had risen under the clear surface of her skin, a kind of emotional haemophilia, passionate vulnerability. Her aristocratic nostrils were pinched whitely together with rage or disgust.

She turned and marched back towards her gate. It was not a retreat. Her back was stiff with the pride of a formal victor.

'I'm sorry,' he said after her. Bugger it, good pissing spots were scarce. This one had been idyllic. Birds in the branches, a paddock on the other side where in summer the ragwort was a sullen blaze of flower heads. Worth the steep fifty yards grunt to the single letter box there, to stand pissing in sunlight as John Clare might have done in 1860 in Epping Forest

> I found the poems in the fields
> And only wrote them down

or Li Po in the courtyard of the Empress, leaning a dipsomaniacal elbow against exquisite marble, or more likely splashing his rice wine into the pond housing ornamental carp. These thoughts improved his spirits.

All the same, next day, he approached the lane without joy. The name he was delivering was Ngaei, a doctor. So he'd met Madame Ngaei, the wife of a Chinese doctor. It occurred to him that it was a good name for an acupuncturist:

'Ngaaeeeeiiii!!'

Ha ha. It was another pristine day. Shoving the doctor's drug company handouts into the letterbox he cast a glance up the driveway to the house. There in sunshine he saw Madame Ngaei standing with the flaccid hose of a vacuum cleaner in one hand. She was singing

> Takem han
> Ahm stlanga in paladeye

It was poignant enough to make him squawk with laughter. The door slammed. He felt ashamed and barbaric. He really liked her. The style and economy with which she'd registered her complaint had been lovely. He admired her sense of form. Also, an admission he suppressed, he was flattered that she'd seen his cock. He trudged down the hill with a sense of failure worrying at his trouser leg, which he longed to lug to her front door and confront her with:

'This your poochie (succubus) lady?'

Bam!

And facing her, his grossness annulled by this immaculate gesture.

He'd recaptured his pissing spot but he wouldn't crow again for a while, no, nor throw his head back! Oh, his self-esteem had been badly punctured! He was in love. What a lousy trade. In return for being allowed (by default) to piss, he was a victim of that 'formal violence' . . . ah fuckwit! . . . his morning monologues were now from the heart, as his car veered on the black asphalt, as he contemplated the moon's pale carpet rolled out upon the water.

Daily he trudged up the steep lane, shoved glossy pharmaceutical advertising material into the letterbox of Doctor Ngaei, and pee'd just down from the gate, sometimes into mud, sometimes into an ochre rivulet which coursed down the slope from a ditch further up the road, sometimes into snow, sometimes on to the loamy surface of the verge.

Inspiration! Purify me. . . . Always he experienced a nagging sense of desecration. The muddy rivulet was beautiful before he augmented it. Seeds germinated in the rich loam. Frost crystals on fallen twigs were blasted by his stream. He observed the seasons with uncharacteristic attention. Within the small enclosure of his woody urinal he watched the light grow softer and dimmer as the oaks put out leaves. Along the verge a variety of tiny flowers appeared, minute blue or pink corollas turning their faces upward. With shame and despair he pissed on them. He couldn't help it. The moment he'd put the doctor's garish rubbish in the letterbox, his bladder ached with tension. Soon even spring had passed and the lane was filled with the honeysweet scent of gorseflower. To this he added his own bitter fragrance. Bees and flies buzzed and hummed in the dense growth of the oaks whose leaves broadcast a constant spray of sticky sap. As summer advanced this secretion stopped and the flies turned their attentions to his staling ground. They were transformed from summer musicians into gutter communicators of pestilence. Again and again he imagined the blood rising under her perfect skin. He could no longer distinguish between her real outrage in the face of his barbaric intrusion last winter, and the passion with which, in his imagination, he saw her responding to his presence this summer. His daily desecrations were painfully fraught with hope. Burning flowers with his hot urine, he felt 'love's tender shoot cracking the cold clod of his heart'. Ashamed, he continued to be flattered. His atavistic id continued to regard this daily ritual as a ceremonial of display. He imagined that the exquisite Madame Ngaei watched it from behind the trees.

His daydreams, fed by his own memories of travel, were filled with fantasies of her past life. He saw her as a young secretary with the Esso company in Hong Kong, riding the morning ferry from Kowloon across to Victoria Island, perfect in a cheongsam, turning the heads of clumsy tourists. Sometimes he saw her as a nurse on the floating clinic in the Aberdeen inlet, surrounded by a chaos of sampans . . . or having dinner with a young doctor, probably Swiss, in the Tai Pak restaurant. Stimulated by images of food, his fantasies took on a sexual colouration. He saw her clitoris as a delicate morsel in a bowl of soup.

At night he awoke yelling from a dream of a lizard scrabbling on dry claws up her white thigh.

When, now, he went to piss on the verge just down from her gate, he experienced a painful moment of paralysis before his stream consented to flow.

He trembled at the prospect of having to deliver a registered letter to her door.

He caught glimpses of her. Once she was in the greengrocer's when he delivered mail there. Her perfume was subtle and subdued. His senses culled it from the dying breaths of cabbages and mushrooms. He banged into the door going out.

179

He asked for, and got, a transfer. It was late summer. The verge was beginning to be covered by a mantle of dry oak leaves. He pissed for the last time. His water splashed where gallons had gone before. He knew this spot more intimately than any on earth. He'd observed how it was never the same from one day to the next. Madame Ngaei had taught him something.

'I may be some time.'

With relief and despair he walked off down the hill, into exile.

From the autumn garden the beautiful Madame Ngaei noted, in due course, his absence. She sighed with regret. It had become an amusement. The clumsy boy had been fetching and arrogant. From time to time she'd imagined his crude embraces. She'd occasionally enjoyed watching him pee. She'd stood in her hiding place in the garden with a hand over her mouth while she giggled. Now she stood in the front door of her house, in the late summer sunshine. She was vacuuming. Under her breath she sang

> Takem han
> Ahm stlanga in paladeye

On the far side of the lane, beyond the oaks which she could once again begin to see through as their leaves fell, the hill paddock was filled with a urinous frenzy of yellow ragwort. How barbaric nature could be. How she longed to be educated in its gross intrusions. How she hated winter which was coming fast.

HOOKS AND FEELERS

Keri Hulme

On the morning before it happened, her fingers were covered with grey, soft clay.

'Charleston.' she says. 'It comes from Charleston. It's really a modeller's clay, but it'll make nice cups. I envisage,' gesturing in the air, 'tall fluted goblets. I'll glaze them sea blue and we'll drink wine together, all of us.'

I went out to the shed and knocked on the door. There's no word of welcome, but the kerosene lamp is burning brightly, so I push on in.

She's pumping the treadle potter's wheel with a terrible urgency, but she's not making pots. Just tall, wavery cones. I don't know what they are. I've never seen her make them before. The floor, the shelves, the bench – the place is spikey with them.

'They've rung,' I say.

She doesn't look up.

'They said he'll be home tomorrow.'

The wheel slowed, stopped.

'So?'

'Well, will you get him?'

'No.'

The wheel starts purring. Another cone begins to grow under her fingers.

'What are you making those for?'

She still won't look at me.

'You go,' she says, and the wheel begins to hum.

Well, you can't win.

I go and get him and come home, chattering brightly all the way. He is silent.

I carry him inside, pointing out that I've repainted everywhere, that we've got a new stove and did you like your present? And he ignores it all.

But he says, very quietly, to his ma, 'Hello.' Very cool.

She looks at him, over him, round him, eyes going up and down but always avoiding the one place where she should be looking. She says, 'Hello,' back.

181

'Put me down please,' he says to me then.

No 'Thanks for getting me.' Not a word of appreciation for the new clothes. Just that polite, expressionless, 'Put me down please.'

Not another word.

He went into his bedroom and shut the door.

'Well, it's just the shock of being back home, eh?'

I look at her, and she looks at me. I go across and slide my hands around her shoulders, draw her close to me, nuzzle her ear, and for a moment it's peace.

Then she draws away.

'Make a coffee,' she says brusquely. 'I'm tired.'

I don't take offence. After grinding the beans, I ask, 'What are you making the cones for?'

She shrugs.

'It's just an idea.'

The smell from the crushed coffee beans is rich and heavy, almost sickening.

His door opens.

He has his doll in his hand. Or rather, parts of his doll. He's torn the head off, the arms and legs apart.

'I don't want this anymore,' he says into the silence.

He goes to the fire, and flings the parts in. And then he reaches in among the burning coals and plucks out the head, which is melted and smoking. He says, 'On second thoughts, I'll keep this.'

The smoke curls round the steel and lingers, acridly.

Soon after, she went back to the shed.

I went down to the pub.

'Hey!' yells Mata, 'c'mon over here!'

'Look at that,' he says, grinning hugely, waving a crumpled bit of paper. It's a Golden Kiwi ticket. 'Bugger's won me four hundred dollars.' He sways. 'Whatta yer drinking?'

I never have won anything. I reach across, grab his hand, shake it. It's warm and calloused, hard and real.

'Bloody oath, Mat what good luck!'

He smiles more widely still, his eyes crinkling almost shut. 'Shout you eh?'

'Too right you can. Double whisky.'

And I get that from him and a jug and another couple of doubles and another jug. I am warm and happy until someone turns the radio up.

'Hands across the water, hands across the sea . . . ' the voices thunder and beat by my ears, and pianos and violins wail and wind round the words.

The shed's in darkness.

I push the door open, gingerly.

'Are you there?'

I hear her move.

'Yes.'

'How about a little light on the subject?' I'm trying to sound happily drunk, but the words have a nasty callous ring to them.

'The lamp is on the bench beside you.'

I reach for it and encounter a soft, still wet, cone of clay. I snatch my fingers away hurriedly.

'Are you revealing to the world what the cones are for yet?'

I've found the lamp, fumble for my matches. My fingers are clumsy, but at last the wick catches a light, glows and grows.

She sniffs.

'Give me the matches please.'

I throw the box across and she snatches them from the air.

She touches a match to a cigarette, the match shows blue and then flares bright, steady, gold. The cigarette pulses redly. The lamp isn't trimmed very well.

She sighs and the smoke flows thickly out of her mouth and nose.

'I put nearly all of them back in the stodge-box today.'

What? Oh yes, the cones. The stodge-box is her special term for the pile of clay that gets reworked.

'Oh.' I add after a moment, apologetically, 'I sort of squashed one reaching for the lamp.'

'It doesn't matter,' she says, blowing out another stream of smoke.

'I was going to kill that one too.'

I take my battered, old, guitar and begin to play. I play badly. I've never learned to play properly.

He says, out of the dark, 'Why are you sad?'

'What makes you think I am?'

'Because you're playing without the lights on.'

I sigh. 'A man can play in the dark if he wants.'

'Besides I heard you crying.'

My dear cool son.

' . . . so I cry sometimes . . . '

'Why are you sad?' he asks again.

Everlasting questions ever since he began to talk.

'Shut up.'

'Because of me?' he persists. He pauses, long enough to check whether I'm going to move.

'Or because of her?'

'Because of me, now get out of here,' I answer roughly, and bang the guitar down. It groans. The strings shiver.

He doesn't move.

'You've been to the pub?'

I prop the guitar against the wall and get up.

'You've been to the pub,' he states, and drifts back into his room.

My mother came to visit the next day, all agog to see the wreckage. She has a nice instinct for disasters. She used to be a strong little woman but she's run to frailty and brittle bones now. Alas; all small and powdery, with a thick fine down over her face that manages, somehow, to protrude through her make-up. It'd look so much better if she didn't pile powder and stuff on, but I can't imagine her face without pink gunk clogging the pores. That much has never changed.

She brought a bag of blackballs for him. When he accepts them, reluctantly, she coos and pats him and strokes his hair. He has always hated that.

'Oh dear,' she says, 'your poor careless mother,' and 'You poor little man' and (aside to me) 'It's just as well you didn't have a daughter, it'd be so much worse for a girl.' (He heard that, and smiled blandly.)

She asks him, 'However are you going to manage now? Your guitar and football and all? Hmmm?'

He says, steadily, 'It's very awkward to wipe my arse now. That's all.'

For a moment I like him very much.

My mother flutters and tchs, 'Oh, goodness me, dear, you mustn't say . . .'

He's already turned away.

As soon as my mother left, I went out to the shed.

'You could have come in and said hello,' I say reproachfully.

'It would have only led to a fight.' She sits hunched up on the floor. Her face is in shadow.

I look round. The shed's been tidied up. All the stray bits and pieces are hidden away. There's an innovation, however, an ominous one. The crucifix she keeps on the wall opposite her wheel has been covered with black cloth. The only part that shows is a hand, nailed to the wooden cross.

'Is that a reminder for penitence? Or are you mourning?'
She doesn't reply.

Early in the morning, while it's still quite dark, I awake to hear him
sobbing. I lift the bedclothes gently – she didn't stir, drowned in
sleep, her black hair wreathed about her body like seaweed – and
creep away to his room.

The sobbing is part stifled, a rhythmic choking and gasping,
rough with misery.

'Hello?'

'E pa . . . ' he turns over and round from his pillow and reaches
out his arms. He doesn't do that. He hasn't done that since he was a
baby.

I pick him up, cradling him, cuddling him.

'I can still feel it pa. I can feel it still.' He is desperate in his
insistence and wild with crying. But he is also coldly angry at
himself.

'I know it's not there anymore,' he struck himself a blow, 'but I
can *feel* it still . . . '

I kiss and soothe and bring a tranquilliser that the people at the
hospital gave me. He sobs himself back to sleep, leaning, in the
end, away from me. And I go back to bed.

Her ocean, her ocean, te moananui a Kiwa, drowns me. Far away
on the beach I can hear him calling, but I must keep on going down
into the greeny deeps, down to where her face is, to where the soft
anemone tentacles of her fingers beckon and sway and sweep me
onward to the weeping heart of the world.

He stays home from school for another week. It's probably just as
well, for once, the first time he ventured outside the house, the next
door neighbour's kids shouted crudities at him.

I watched him walk over to them, talk, and gesture, the hook
flashing bravely in the sun. The next door neighbour's kids fell
silent, drew together in a scared huddled group.

'What did you do to stop that?' I ask, after he has stalked proudly
back inside.

He shook his head.

'Tell me.'

'I didn't have to do anything.' He smiles.

'Oh?'

'I don't imagine,' he says it so coolly, 'that anyone wants this in
their eyes.'

The hair on the back of my neck bristles with shock.

185

'Don't you dare threaten anybody like that! No matter what they say!' I shout at him in rage, in horror. 'I'll beat you silly if you do that again.'

He shrugs. 'Okay, if you say so pa.'

(Imagine that cruel, steel curve reaching for your eyes. That pincer of unfeeling metal gouging in.) The steel hook glints as he moves away.

How can he be my son and have so little of me in him? Oh, he has my colouring, fair hair and steelgrey eyes, just as he has her colour and bone structure; a brown thickset chunk of a boy.

But his strange cold nature comes from neither of us. Well, it certainly doesn't come from me.

Later on that day – we are reading in front of the fire – a coal falls out. He reaches for it.

'Careful, it's hot,' I warn.

'I don't care how hot it is,' he says, grinning.

The two steel fingers pick up the piece of coal and slowly crush the fire out of it.

It hasn't taken long for him to get very deft with those pincers. He can pluck up minute things, like pins, or the smallest of buttons. I suspect he practises doing so, in the secrecy of his bedroom. He can handle almost anything as skilfully as he could before.

At night, after he's had a shower, I ask, 'Let me look?'

'No.'

'Ahh, come on.'

He holds it out, silently.

All his wrist bones are gone. There remains a scarred purplish area with two smooth, rounded knubs on either side. In the centre is a small socket. The hook, which is mounted on a kind of swivel, slots into there. I don't understand how it works, but it looks like a nice practical piece of machinery.

He is looking away.

'You don't like it?'

'It's all right . . . will you string my guitar backwards? I tried, and I can't do it.'

'Of course.'

I fetch his guitar and begin immediately.

'There is something quite new we can do, you know.' The specialist draws a deep breath of smoke and doesn't exhale any of it.

The smell of antiseptic is making me feel sick. This room is painted a dull grey. There are flyspots on the light. I bring my eyes down to him and smile, rigidly.

'Ahh, yes?'

'Immediately after amputation, we can attach an undamaged portion of sinew and nerve to this nyloprene socket.'

He holds out a gadget, spins it round between his lean fingers, and snatches it away again, out of sight.

'It is a permanent implant, with a special prosthesis that fits into it, but the child will retain a good deal of control over his, umm, hand movements.'

He sucks in more smoke and eyes me beadily, eagerly. Then he suddenly lets the whole, stale lungful go, right in my face.

'So you agree to that then?'

'Ahh, yes.'

Later, at night, she says, 'Are you still awake too?'

'Yes.'

'What are you thinking of.'

'Nothing really. I was just listening to you breathe.'

Her hand creeps to my side, feeling along until it finds a warm handful.

'I am thinking of the door,' she says thoughtfully.

You know the way a car door crunches shut, with a sort of definite, echoing thunk?

Well, there was that. Her hurried footsteps. A split second of complete silence. And then the screaming started, piercing, agonised, desperate. We spun round. He was nailed, pinioned against the side of the car by his trapped hand.

She stood, going, 'O my god! O my god!' and biting down on her hand. She didn't make another move, frozen where she stood, getting whiter and whiter and whiter.

I had to open the door.

'I know it's silly,' she continues, still holding me warmly, 'but if we hadn't bought that packet of peanuts, we wouldn't have spilled them. I wouldn't have got angry. I wouldn't have stormed out of the car. I wouldn't have slammed the door without looking. Without looking.'

'You bought the nuts, remember?' she adds irrelevantly.

I don't answer.

There are other things in her ocean now. Massive black shadows that loom up near me without revealing what they are. Something glints. The shadows waver and retreat.

They stuck a needle attached to a clear, plastic tube into his arm. The tube filled with blood. Then, the blood cleared away and the dope ran into his vein. His eyelids dragged down. He slept, unwillingly, the tears of horror and anguish still wet on his face.

The ruined hand lay on a white, shiny bench, already apart from him. It was like a lump of raw, swollen meat with small, shattered, bluish bones through it.

'We'll have to amputate that, I'm afraid. It's absolutely unsalvageable.'

'Okay,' I say. 'Whatever you think best.'

They say that hearing is the last of the senses to die, when you are unconscious.

They are wrong, at least for me. Images, or what is worse, not-quite images, flare and burst and fade before I sink into the dreamless sea of sleep.

I went out to the shed.

'Tea is nearly ready,' I call through the open door.

'Good,' she replies. 'Come in and look.'

She has made a hundred, more than a hundred, large, shallow wine cups. 'Kraters,' she says, smiling to me briefly.

I grin back, delighted.

'Well, they should sell well.'

She bends her head, scraping at a patch of dried clay on the bench.

'What were the cones?'

She looks up at me, the smile gone entirely.

'Nothing important,' she says. 'Nothing important.'

When she's washing the dishes, however, the magic happens again. For the first time since the door slammed shut, I look at her, and she looks willingly back and her eyes become deep and endless dark waters, beckoning to my soul. Drown in me . . . find yourself. I reach out flailing, groping for her hard, real body. Ahh, my hands encounter tense muscles, fasten on to them. I stroke and knead, rousing the long-dormant woman in her. Feel in the taut, secret places, rub the tender moist groove, caress her all over with sweet, probing fingers.

'Bait,' says a cold, sneering voice.

She gasps and goes rigid again.

'Get away to bed with you,' she says without turning round.

'I'm going to watch.'

An overwhelming anger floods through me. I whip around and my erstwhile gentle hands harden and clench.

'I'll . . . '

'No,' she says, 'no,' touching me, warning me.

She goes across and kneels before him.
(I see he's trembling.)
She kisses his face.
She kisses his hand.
She kisses the hook.
'Now go to bed e tama.'
He stands, undecided, swaying in the doorway.
Then, too quickly for it to be stopped, he lashes out with the hook. It strikes her on her left breast.
I storm forward, full of rage, and reach for him.
'No,' she says again, kneeling there, motionless. 'No,' yet again.
'Go to bed, tama,' she says to him.
Her voice is warm and friendly. Her face is serene.
He turns obediently, and walks away into the dark.

At the weekend, I suggested we go for a picnic.
'Another one?' she asks, her black eyebrows raised.
'Well, we could gather pauas, maybe some cress, have a meal on the beach. It'd be good to get out of the house for a while. This hasn't been too good a week for me, you know.'
They both shrugged.
'Okay,' he says.

'I will get the paua,' she says, and begins stripping off her jeans.
'You get the cress,' she says to him.
'I'll go with you and help,' I add.
He just looks at me. Those steely eyes in that brown face. Then he pouted, picked up the kete, and headed for the stream.
He selects a stalk and pinches it suddenly. The plant tissue thins to nothing. It's like he's executing the cress. He adds it to the pile in the kete. He doesn't look at me, or talk. He is absorbed in killing cress.
There's not much I can do.
So I put on my mask and flippers and wade into the water, slide down under the sea. I spend a long peaceful time there, detaching whelks and watching them wobble down to the bottom. I cruise along the undersea rock shelf, plucking bits of weed and letting them drift away. Eventually, I reach the end of the reef, and I can hear the boom and mutter of the real ocean. It's getting too close; I surface.
One hundred yards away, fighting a current that is moving him remorselessly out, is my son.

When I gained the beach, I was exhausted.

I stand, panting, him in my arms.

His face is grey and waxy and the water runs off us both, dropping constantly on the sand.

'You were too far out . . .'

He cries.

'Where is she?'

Where is she? Gathering paua somewhere . . . but suddenly I don't know if that is so. I put my mask back on, leave him on the beach, and dive back under the waves, looking.

When I find her, as I find her, she is floating on her back amidst bullkelp. The brown weed curves sinuously over her body, like dark limp hands.

I splash and slobber over, sobbing to her. 'God, your son nearly died trying to find you. Why didn't you tell us?'

She opens her brown eyes lazily.

No, not lazily: with defeat, with weariness.

'What on earth gave you the idea I was going to drown?' She rubs the towel roughly over her skin.

I say, haltingly, 'Uh well, he was sure that . . . '

(He is curled up near the fire I've lit, peacefully asleep.)

'Sure of what?'

'I don't know. He went looking for you, got scared. We couldn't see you anywhere.'

A sort of shudder, a ripple runs through her.

'The idea was right,' she says, very quietly. She lets the towel fall. She cups her hand under her left breast and points.

'Feel there.'

There is a hard, oval, clump amidst the soft tissue.

'God, did he do . . . '

'No. It's been growing there for the past month. Probably for longer than that, but I have only felt it recently.' She rubs her armpit, thoughtfully. 'It's there too and under here,' gesturing to her jaw. 'It'll have to come out.' I can't stop it. I groan.

Do you understand that if I hadn't been there, both of them would have drowned?

There was one last thing.

We were all together in the living room.

I am in the lefthand chair, she is opposite me.

He is crooning to himself, sprawled in front of the fire.

'Loo-lie, loo-lay, loo-lie, loo-lay, the falcon hath borne my make

190

away,' he sings. He pronounces it, 'the fawcon have borne my make away.'

'What is that?' I ask.

'A song.'

He looks across to his ma and they smile slyly, at one another, smiles like invisible hands reaching out, caressing secretly, weaving and touching.

I washed my hands.

I wept.

I went out to the shed and banged the door finally shut.

I wept a little longer.

And then, because there was nothing else to do, I went down to the pub.

I had been drinking double whiskies for more than an hour when Mata came across and laid his arm over my shoulder.

He is shaking.

'E man,' he whispers. His voice grows a little stronger. 'E man, don't drink by yourself. That's no good eh?' His arm presses down. 'Come across to us?'

The hubbub of voices hushes.

I snivel.

'Mat, when I first knew, her fingers were covered in clay, soft grey clay. And she smiled and said it's Charleston, we'll call him Charleston. It's too soft really, but I'll make a nice cup from it. Cups. Tall fluted goblets she said.'

His hand pats my shoulder with commiseration, with solicitude.

His eyes are dark with horror.

'I'll glaze them sea blue and we'll drink red wine together, all three of us.'

We never did.

BARBADOS—A LOVE STORY

Russell Haley

I have chosen to call this room Barbados. Ah – I can feel you shrink back already. Oh God am I going to be nagged by another of these madmen who is so confused about reality that he imagines his fireplace is a white sandy beach and that the brown bottle of beer on his table is a character named Nick Tromso?

It is not so. But all day I have been locked in here with myself, searching for a key to that place, Barbados, and all I keep turning up are nails or stones.

I began to think about Barbados when I made a visit to the South Island and stayed with a friend in Port Chalmers. He invited friends of his round to dinner and one of them, a man named Peter, came from Bridgetown before he emigrated to New Zealand. Our conversation developed when I mentioned that I was taking a trip to Europe by sea and that as far as I could tell we were going to call at Trinidad and Barbados before moving on across the Atlantic to Lisbon.

All this was five years ago and I cannot remember the details of our talk. He did suggest though that I caught only local buses and that I avoided all the usual tourist traps. He wanted me to see his island, as far as possible, as he had known it. Going to school. Trying to catch lizards as a small boy. Those bright green ones with a dark ring around the eye. It seems that I do remember something.

But before I go on I want to tell you one of my favourite stories.

It concerns a visit to a mental institution by a committee of aldermen. It was, if you like, a visit of inspection.

One of the elderly gentlemen from the committee drifted away from the main party. He was rather tired of looking at carefully clipped rhododendrons and immaculate kitchens.

The alderman sat down on a bench next to another elderly and rather well-dressed man.

'A pleasant day,' the alderman said.

'Perhaps for you,' the other man replied. 'But for me it is a misery.'

When the alderman expressed concern the man on the bench explained that he was a patient in this place and that he realised every patient told the same story, of wrongful incarceration (he used that word), but that in his case the story was genuine. He had been placed there, against his will, by his family so that they could have control of his business.

The alderman was shocked. He had often had a nagging doubt that such things might be possible. He questioned the man further and all of the man's replies were rational and coherent. He determined to do something about the case.

He rose from the bench.

'Let me assure you my friend that I will take this matter up immediately with my committee.' He shook hands and turned to walk away.

'You have made me a happy man,' said the elderly gentleman.

The alderman paused.

'I would do the same for anyone so wrongfully treated,' he said. And he walked on.

He had taken four paces down the path to rejoin his committee when he felt a violent blow on the back of his head. He fell to his hands and knees and stared at a large stone which had struck him. The alderman turned his head, dazed and bewildered. The elderly man with whom he had just been talking was dusting his hands.

'Now you won't forget will you?'

When I told Nick this story, standing at the rail of our ship, looking out over Bridgetown, he laughed and shook my arm.

'And you see yourself as the . . . patient hey?'

I remember looking past him to where the *QE2* was docked, over to our left.

'Well . . . no . . . I'd rather seen myself as the alderman.'

But let me tell you the real joke. I was lying to Nick. If I saw myself as anything in that story it was the clipped rhododendron – or perhaps even the stone.

Back to Barbados.

I suppose everyone who has ever travelled has experienced that curious thing I have come to call 'impersonations' in my notebooks. You are thousands of miles away from home and in a completely alien country. You understand neither the language nor the customs. Walking up a narrow lane in, say, Acapulco you look warily at small men in uniforms carrying automatic rifles. The walls on either side of you are of brick and they are almost the same colour as the mudstone cliffs around the East Coast Bays of Auckland. So, there is one touch of familiarity. But you cannot name a single tree or plant. A child offers you tortillas and, foolishly, you buy half-a-dozen. You eat them dry – without any meat. You have that much sense.

But then – suddenly – ahead of you there is a girl you used to

193

know in Auckland. You know it is her by the angle of her head, the colour of her hair, the carriage of her body.

You run, dropping your uneaten tortillas over a low wall, and finally, breathless with the humidity (your thighs chafed raw inside your too tight trousers) you catch up with Judy, or Jill or Helen – whoever you might have thought you recognised – and it is a total stranger who looks at you as though you were a stone and answers you with a monosyllabic 'No' in an American accent.

What happens when you travel are all these minute transmigrations of personality fragments – but never of people you know very well, close friends. Their psychic image is much more complex and cannot be impersonated.

I had suffered in this way since Rangitoto faded out of sight. So many unknown people had been greeted by my 'Hu . . . p'.

I walked into Woolworths in Bridgetown with Nick and suffered my first impersonation in Barbados. I saw a young man turning away from a counter and I said: 'There's Peter!' Peter, my Bajan acquaintance from Port Chalmers.

I ran up and grabbed his arm.

'Peter!'

'Er – sorry man – I'm Stewart.'

Of course. Peter was still in the South Island. And Stewart did turn out to be a valuable contact. He was a trainee teacher and had very little to do that day. He offered to show us a good beach out near where he lived in Speightstown.

I don't know how we would have managed without Stewart. I was still trying to cope with an internal complaint arising directly from eating those tortillas in Acapulco. Since leaving that port I had swallowed nearly a full bottle of Kaolin substance which was guaranteed to seize up the bowels. But the written assurance proved to be no magic talisman.

We were riding on the bus, out on Route 1, and I had made a note in my journal that I had seen a swan at Gibbs Beach, when I realised that I was not going to reach the terminus.

I sat rigid in my seat and sweat began to pour down my face.

Stewart was explaining that the casuarina trees were known locally as 'mile trees'. To our left were rows and rows of miniature houses. A kind of bach ghetto.

'Stewart,' I said. 'I'm sick.'

'You're sick man? You want me to stop the bus?'

'Actually Stewart yes that would be kind. I'm . . . really quite on the point of shitting myself.'

There was an immensely deep gutter at the side of the road and we crossed over a narrow log bridge. For a moment I thought I was going to have to crouch down in that storm drain but Stewart led me down a narrow path at the side of one of the little houses. I followed him marching like a marine – trying to press my three-dimensions inwards, sideways, so that I would be nothing but a two-sided figure, utterly contained.

Stewart called out in a loud, bubbling, laughing voice to a young woman who was washing clothing in a wooden tub.

She responded curiously. Or rather, in the state I was in I tended to see everything in a kind of hallucinatory clarity, an intense slow-motion. She withdrew her hands from the tub. Lather puffed out her arms so that she looked as though she was partially dressed in Elizabethan costume. She made a circle with her thumb and index finger and slid the lather from each arm back into the tub. Then she tipped her head sideways and smiled.

Stewart showed me to the privy and left me. There was no seat. Just a deep drop into the ground. I had to remove my trousers entirely to manage the situation.

Sordid though the subject may be I must say that I never experienced a purer pleasure than I did then, with the release.

But with my relief came another physiological problem. My prostate was obviously irritated. Without a single stray erotic thought passing through my mind I suddenly had an erection. Further, there was no paper in the privy.

'Er.' I called out. Stewart would come. Or Nick would appear bearing from thousands of miles away rangiora leaves.

The young woman handed me in a Coke bottle filled with water. . . .

Should I now make her smile? Cover her mouth with one hand? Exclaim? Avert her eyes? And what should I do with myself? Cover my private parts with my hand like an absurd hat? Avert my eyes?

It was the least I could do to pay the fares for Nick and Stewart and soon we were in Speightstown. What an odd little suburb that was. It reminded me of a very run-down Balmain in Sydney or, closer to home, Newton, before the motorway complex dashed it out of existence.

Men stood in doorways picking their noses. Women sold fruit at the side of the road. There were shops filled with bottles of rum and Falernum – a liquid used for flavouring.

And behind the shops were streets filled with neat bungalows where large black bees ate rather than collected honey from the many flowering shrubs.

Nick and I watched the green lizards which Peter had talked

about and an old lady came out of her house to talk to us about her life in the United States. Stewart drifted some distance away during this conversation and when we rejoined him he suggested that we go to the beach and drink rum.

'Oh but I'd like to swim too,' I said. 'Is it safe?'

'I dunno man. I never swim.'

We drank iced Rum Collins and then Nick and I slid into the perfect clear water. It was the temperature of blood.

Our second round of drinks cost us more than the first. I glanced at Stewart for confirmation and he shrugged. When Nick bought the third shout the price had tripled. For a moment only I considered questioning the barman but when I looked at his expression I gave that idea up. We were not at Paradise Beach but we were still tourists. We were with a local resident but what did that matter?

Nick and I sat in the sun but Stewart had found a patch of shade. Black birds flitted in and out of the trees.

'What are those?' I asked Stewart.

'Those are . . . birds.'

I laughed. My voice sounded strained. Almost petulant.

'No . . . Stewart . . . I meant what *kind* of birds.'

'Goling,' he said.

'Goling?' I reached for my notebook. 'How do you spell that?'

'You spell it Goling man – anyway you like.' He paused while I wrote. 'Hey listen man – you go on like this every place you been?'

'I don't understand you Stewart.'

'I mean asking about birds and talking to old ladies like some dumb-ass anthropologist. You think the barman rip you off and you think maybe he's my brother-in-law?'

'Stewart that is an offensive suggestion.'

Stewart rolled face-down in the sand and shrieked with laughter. I could hear the word 'offensive' spluttering out of his mouth.

Nick glanced at me as though to say it was time to leave. To head back to the ship.

Stewart suddenly jumped up and ran down towards the edge of the sea. He kicked at the water as though it was something solid. But all the time he howled with laughter. Finally he calmed down and walked slowly back towards us.

'Okay. Okay. You know I've been picked up before in town when the tourist boat in. And you people say "Show us around", but what you really mean is "Where can we find a piece of black chick ass-hole?" '

Then Nick amazed and frightened me. He stretched very slowly and looked up at Stewart.

'Well shit,' he drawled. 'I been waiting for you to . . . like ask. Where can we get some black chick arse-hole?'

The next second they were wrestling in the sand like two boys who had known each other for years. And Nick picked up Stewart and carried him down to the sea. He dumped Stewart into the water. But Stewart clung to his arm and he also fell in. They splashed each other in a frenzy and then ran back to me and shook themselves over me like two large dogs.

Stewart bought the next rums. He carried them over to us.

'My brother-in-law let me have these – same price as the first.'

Back in Speightstown we bought large polka-dot handkerchiefs, rolled them, and tied them round our heads.

'We'll go to a bar back in town,' Stewart said. 'Listen to some steelband.'

'I thought that was Trinidad.'

'It's all over. Here. There. London.'

In the bar I tried to talk to Stewart about literature. I was very drunk. I made the word sound as though it should have a capital 'L'. He had never heard of Michael Anthony nor of V. S. Naipaul. Stewart did know about Edgar Mittelholzer though and he told me a confused story about how that author had burned himself to death.

The whites of Stewart's eyes had turned red in the light of the bar.

'Death by fire,' he said. 'Bled and blood, squeak the weak bum, gleam the tree fang. Red the mud, bleat, bleat, bleat, for heat is a bitter flame.' It sounded like a quotation.

'Mittelholzer?'

'Leitmotiv!' Stewart hammered on the table.

Nick looked bored. He read no one except Malcolm Lowry and I don't think he liked the music.

My attention was drifting. I had drunk more rum than I had ever had in my whole life. I was trying to *organise* the evening. When drunk I have a kind of reverse paranoia. I don't feel that I'm being manipulated or the subject of some fully coherent plot. I feel that *I* arrange everything.

The woman whose dress slips down to expose one breast is the subject of my will. I loosened the strap. I made her inadvertently lean forward at just the right moment.

I could feel a plan forming to try to board the *QE2* which was still at anchor. I wanted all three of us to rush the elegant gangplank like crazed pirates. Possibly that was why I had persuaded the other two to buy the handkerchiefs in Speightstown.

'What about the girls?' Nick said. His mouth had slipped.

'I know some,' Stewart said. 'Have another drink.'

'Well why aren't they here?'

'Oh they'll keep. They won't move.'

'Unless we make them.' I know my face had an expression of low cunning.

'Listen – I didn't tell you guys before. I've got a brother in Canberra on a Commonwealth Scholarship. You think he's fucking white chicks over there?'

'If he isn't he's a bloody fool,' Nick said.

'Snake . . . red . . . grinning . . . uncoil . . . dark.' Stewart slapped the table as he articulated each word.

'How long are we here?' I asked Nick. 'Can you remember?'

'Till tomorrow . . . I think.'

'But that's probably now.'

'Another eight hours – at least.'

'You came in on the tide – you go out on it.' Stewart said. I was unconvinced by his logic. And the sea I could not organise. People only can be shifted around in my system. Didn't tides change by about an hour a day? Or was that only in New Zealand?

I had started to smoke again. Somewhere I had managed to obtain a packet of Drum and some Zig-Zag papers. I rolled them expertly. It is like riding a bicycle. Smokers are like alcoholics – they are never cured.

'Rice.' I said to the sailor on the yellow packet of cigarette papers.

'Every leaf perfect,' he replied. His black mustaches bristled upwards.

Drum is a mild, yet full-flavoured Cigarette Tobacco, manufactured from the choicest tobaccos, skilfully blended to give a perfect smoke. Its high standard is guaranteed by . . . Douwe Egbert.

I am happier with that guarantee than with the one for the Kaolin substance which was a terrible pink colour. I needed to go again. I made appropriate gestures and noises to Nick and Stewart and headed towards the rear of the bar.

I have never experienced such darkness. There was not a single crack of light in that place. I could hear the steelband from where I groaned. Other than that, the noise, and I fear that I might have suffered sensory deprivation.

What in fact I was deprived of when I returned was the company of my friends. In my absence they had flown. All signs of their presence had also departed. The table was empty. The ash-tray removed. The glasses gone.

Even the band seemed to be packing up. Or at the least taking a break. I went back to the bar.

'Have you seen my friends?'

'We are all your friends. Have a drink.'

There are places where you do not refuse a drink. This was one of them.

This town was now so familiar with alcohol. My casual encounters in the darkened street were all very friendly. If I may say so the feeling in the air was much less filled with menace than that of the pavement outside the Kiwi Hotel on a bad night. I could not see a single policeman.

I stepped into a dark passageway to urinate. Between my feet lay a dead rat. I pissed on it.

Faintly, at the far end of the passage I thought I heard Tromso's sing-song voice.

'*Uno mescalito por favor.*' One of his favourite Lowry lines.

Nick had bought a pottery bottle of mescal in Acapulco and one night, fearing that the European customs officials would seize it, we had drunk the whole flagon. I tried to do ineffectual headsprings on the dance-floor at 3 a.m. and had to be escorted to my cabin by the Master-at-Arms.

Was that his coded cry for help? Could I, a soggy thirty-five year-old do anything for him? The nearest I had ever come to violence or intrigue was to retain my seat in an Auckland bar while a fight progressed around me. In those days to get a seat was a rare pleasure which I did not wish to forgo.

But I headed up the alley. Trying to erase all memory of countless American films where places like this abounded with trash-cans and flick-knives. Bodies under cardboard cartons. I was in Bridgetown not Harlem: Barbados not the Bowery.

'*Uno . . . mescalito. . . .*' An audible will-o-the-wisp. It was my duty to follow.

All middle-aged males eventually come to a strip-joint. It is an axiom.

I found myself propelled through the doorway above which I had noted a neon sign which flickered in a curious, and I thought, an ambiguous manner. It said: ZEPHIRIN'S FOR BREAD. I could not work out if the apostrophe were correct. Was correct.

Many Caribbean dollars appeared to vanish from my hand. I bought a double whisky which tasted like rum. All the lights were red. I fell into a chair near the tiny stage.

Some of the whisky splashed on to my hand. It burned like fire. Like the red lights.

A negro in a white suit emerged from the wings carrying a cane-seated chair. He placed it carefully and sat down facing the audience. I began to applaud but soon silenced myself in drink.

A beautiful woman in a long gown came out next and sat on the knee of the man in the white suit.

Her mouth opened and shut. He spoke in a deep, resonant voice. An obscure ventriloquist act. But then she removed a glove and flung it into the audience.

'Hu . . . p,' I said. I thought I recognised her arm.

Another glove followed after an interminable time of deep talking and mouth opening.

Everthing else followed in rapid succession. The zip front opened. A breast was fondled. The dress was eased down to the floor.

Ah – I have converted this room into a night-club. I do not know Barbados well. I was there for . . . twenty-three hours. And because I do not know it well – as a friend – I have 'impersonated'. I feel as though I have been struck on the back of the head with a stone.

The dress was eased down to the floor. Have you ever had a lover for one night? Then never seen him or her again. All the way across the Pacific the juke-box played a tune called 'Knights in White Satin' by the Moody Blues. I hope I have that right.

Well – I felt like a Knight. I fell in love with that woman as a Knight might have been in love with his Lady. All they asked was a favour. A flower. A glove.

I see the crook of her elbow, the round of her knee, in every city street. In each dark bar.

She did not remove her G-string and so walked out of my life semi-naked.

I hit the wall opposite to ZEPHIRIN'S FOR BREAD with considerable force. It is quite possible that I cracked a rib. My journal records that I visited the ship's doctor the following day – the same day?– but I have not mentioned his diagnosis.

Under my note about the doctor I have drawn a very rough sketch-map. Across the width of the island, diagonally, there is a place called Cuckold Point. Also somewhere on the coast there is a lazaretto. Do you not feel as I do that those two facts combine into a sinister whole far greater than their individual parts?

That the man in the white suit was somehow a parody of me – the Anglo-Saxon intruder. That I was made a cuckold on the night I found my Lady. And leprosy is a disease which especially afflicts island races – a disease which turns healthy dark skin into an unhealthy white.

I begin to interpret myself and that is not my business.

We had been brought in across Carlisle Bay by ship's lifeboats, presumably because the tides were not right for docking.

I found myself in the wharf area where I imagined I would find the lifeboat to take me back, safely back to my cramped cabin on the orlop deck. I looked out over the dark waters to where my ship had been that morning – fully expecting to see the bright strings of lights. There was nothing but a dark space.

Someone had moved my ship. There were no lifeboats. I was an unwilling castaway.

It looked as though I would have to go ahead with my plan to board the *QE2*. I trudged for half a mile through unsavoury dock areas and I finally reached the bottom of the gangway.

Do you remember that story of Mussolini's room? When subordinates came to him with requests and pleas they had to enter a door and then walk for hundreds of feet before they reached his desk. By the time they reached him they knew they were inferior. I knew my situation was hopeless by the time I reached the top of the gangway. An officer stood there in a white uniform. He had a beard. Somehow he managed to stop me *below* him.

'Have you got a pass sir?'

I patted my pockets. 'No – I seem to have misplaced it.'

'I'm afraid we cannot allow anyone on to our vessel without a boarding pass sir. You are not a passenger.'

'No . . . actually. I seem to have misplaced my own ship.'

'Which is your vessel sir?'

'The *Northern Star*.'

'I see. That particular ship docked earlier today. I think you will find a taxi down there which will know the way. Some of our crew have been visiting yours.'

'That is most kind of you.'

'It is a pleasure . . . sir. Goodnight.'

'Er . . . good morning.' A humbled pirate I turned. The slope carried me down with a sense of speed and lightness. No insults, no dead dogs were cast down after me. My endings are pathetic rather than cathartic.

My own cabin was a sanctuary of sorts. I lay on my bunk with my eyes open and the light on. The room swum and spun. I closed my eyes and it twirled even faster.

The rhythms *were* changing. Something in the note of the engines and the movements of the crew in the passageway outside the cabin. There were strange knockings and rattles transmitted through the pipes and conduits in the steel ceiling of the cabin.

Elaborate and confused traveller's dreams which deal in arrivals and departures. Dark figures in wide straw hats who asked persistently: 'Is he in Auckland?'

But no. The ship was underway. I tried to catch the lift to an upper deck so that I could have my last glimpse of the half-moon of Carlisle Bay. Nothing seemed to be working. I climbed the stairs.

Once again I was afflicted with tourist's vision. All patchy surface and no real perception. The golden sun was lifting out of an airline poster. Across the bay the *QE2* was posed. Very elegant but somehow top-heavy. A reverse iceberg – most of the bulk above the waterline. And a single immaculate smokestack.

Behind the drifting town (a view partially blocked by a large warehouse) lay suburbs and then beyond, away after two lumpy hills was open country.

The many trees were an astonishment. I had not remembered them in this profusion. There were palms. And other trees shaped like poplars. There was a faint smell of smoke in the air – perhaps the aftermath of an evening cane-burning.

There was still some cloud about. Dark grey masses. As we moved out of the bay an almost vertical section of a rainbow hovered in the air.

There was that special hangover intensity about all visual things. Yachts. Launches. The disappearing line of beach. The island of Barbados finally a smudge of smoke on the rim of the sea.

We were now running away from the sun – latitude 19 degrees North and the air temperature was down to 76 Fahrenheit. The closest land was Guadalupe – 490 miles away on our port quarter.

I made notes like that. About Barbados I could not write a line. I made no attempt to make contact with Tromso – not even to find out if he had missed the ship.

After two days he emerged from hiding. He looked grey and shrunken. He refused to say anything about what he and Stewart had done – where they had gone. Tromso never apologised for leaving me in the bar. Our relationship deteriorated away to mere politeness.

I have met him since back in Auckland. We are cold and distant.

Barbados too is now . . . cold and distant. Odd flashes still occur to me. The flying-fish I saw being sold for fifty cents each. A starving donkey hauling an overloaded cart. But these bits and pieces cannot be integrated – they remain as scraps of local colour.

But this account does have a conclusion. Four years after my visit to Barbados I was sitting in a bar at the Hotel Intercontinental here in Auckland. It is not my favourite bar. I was there merely to see a radio producer who had expressed some interest in my journals.

The meeting had been unsatisfactory. There was so much cutting, so much editing, he wanted me to do. He talked about Durrell's book on Cyprus and I wanted him to talk about me. About Tahiti, Balboa, Acapulco, Curacao, Barbados.

We parted with the usual idiocies. I said I would think about it. He told me he would be in touch.

I was finishing my drink and about to go when across the bar I saw my Lady.

My hand trembled. I bought another drink and a packet of cigarettes even though I had given up smoking again.

I was terrified in case this was another 'impersonation' happening here in my own city. There had been no doubt in my mind that that oddity was a travelling syndrome. It should not happen to those who return. But I was afraid.

Most curious of all – she was wearing gloves. Here in sultry December in Auckland. It seemed so . . . out of fashion and yet so right for her.

Final confirmation came when she removed one glove to reach into her leather handbag.

There are times here in Auckland (and this is the main reason why I love this city) when an evening in a public bar turns, as though by magic, into a private gathering, a party. When you know . . . everyone . . . and all are in good spirits. We all moved into a smaller bar. This room.

Barbados.

'You are . . . ?' I asked.

'Yes.'

'Hey – and I was the washerwoman, remember?' My Lady's companion covered her mouth and averted her eyes.

Nick leaned over and punched me on the arm.

'If Stewart and I hadn't left you in the lurch. . . . '

Stewart grinned and introduced another young man.

'This is my brother. He's come over from Canberra.' I shook hands.

'We'd never have met.' My Lady said. And she slipped her glove into my pocket.

Stewart's 'brother-in-law' brought in another round of beers.

'They charged me the same price!' The room was filled with cigarette smoke and laughter. Over in one corner, dressed in his white suit, sat the ventriloquist. He opened and shut his mouth – happy that we were doing all the talking.

203

I put my arm around the waist of my Lady.
'I never did learn how to spell Goling,' I said.
'You spell it like it is man. Bar. Bad. Os.'

This is a love story.
I am not going to be the one to cast the first stone.

PALMS AND MINARETS

Vincent O'Sullivan

'You're the one who will have to decide. You're the one who knows whether you're run down or not.'

My wife sat under the lampshade made from a sheet of old monk's music we had brought back from Spain.

'I'll decide,' I told her. 'I'll decide before next weekend.'

Her needles clicked while she knitted. The shiny pages of a pattern book lay open on the sofa beside her, and even as she spoke her eyes moved from the needles to the instructions in the book, then back to her work. I looked past her to the red lines drawn on the curved stiffness of the parchment, at the heavy black squares to tell a monk's voice where exactly to go, where in the huge cool greyness of a church his voice was to rise or fall, the light from a high window over the shaved heads of the monks. Because I saw that once in Spain. My wife was looking for a shop that sold filagree work, the kind she had seen in Toledo and decided not to buy, and had then thought about and spoken about for the next three days. We were in a town whose name I forget, where we had not meant to be. She lay down in the afternoon and I walked through streets which were high white walls and stiff shadows. Then late in the afternoon she had decided to go after her filagree and I walked into a church, into the rise and fall of the voices behind the heavy leather curtain at the door, the black squares on the red lines behind my wife's head.

'If you don't decide to take a rest now who knows where we'll finish up?'

There had been a smell in the greyness like concrete, like water sprinkled on concrete. There was a young monk with a beard who looked like a movie star.

'I told you I'd go next week.'

'You know very well with a specialist you need to make an appointment well ahead.'

'I'm sure I'll last that long,' I said. My wife's needles clashed, they were steel and clashed softly but she may also have been cross that I kept putting things off. Her hair which once I had thought so lovely was drawn close against her head. It was red in the light from the monk's singing, from the music which had no tune to

205

follow, no notes I could read although I had learned the piano for several years. My mother had said *He'll never be a concert pianist mind you but he sticks to a thing*. She had said it to my aunt while she stood at the kitchen sink. She wore pink rubber gloves which almost made me feel ill if they touched my skin. *You can play that piece you did for the examinations* she told me, *the piece you played last night for your father*. But it was for *him*, I thought, I am not playing it for anyone else.

I'll play it when she comes round next week I told her. I watched her pink gloves shine each time she raised them from the water and their pale dry insides when she peeled them off. *Next week, auntie. I'll be better at it by then*.

Only a few times, once or twice in the Army and another time in a church group, have I been with men who talked about their fathers. I do not mean the way one reminisces with friends, because it is likely they would have known him or heard about him anyway. I mean the times when men try to tell others what their fathers were like. That doesn't happen very often, and I think that when it does, most men will tell lies.

My own father was short, his features as sharply fine as if clipped from paper. In these past months I have thought of him a great deal. I believe I remember the first time he walked down the street with me. He held my hand as I stepped across the dappled footpath through circles and patches of brightness and moving shadow, when I was still too young to know that the pavement wasn't shifting but the flickering was from the trees that grew right along the street. We would come to a puddle of light and when I paused he would take both my hands in his and say 'Over we go, digger'.

I am the only person I know whose father was a dandy, a man who failed at almost everything except keeping his shoes polished to perfection, and at a kind of kidding all the time that he was more melancholy than anyone understood. He loved standing on the back porch with his jacket off but his white sleeves rolled down, the cuffs held with slender jade cufflinks, his waistcoat buttoned and his watch–chain shining across his lean stomach. He would stand with a book open and resting on one palm and in the sunlight (it is never winter when I remember him), from the distance, he was lithe and solitary, a kind of figure from a western who held a book instead of a gun. But he would take books up and lay them down as though there were something in them which roughness would spill.

My father's single hobby was pool. Several nights a week he went out after we had eaten our dinner. My mother would say it was all very well having an interest but it would be nice if it was something that put food on the table. One of the delights of my childhood was to be taken to the saloon which was across the road from the library. Children were not meant to enter the bluish darkness with the great pyramids of light from the lamps above the tables, but my father nodded his head to the man at the doorway and said he's keeping an eye on me. He looked down at me and said *Don't you break the place up, do you hear me?* The tables were so brilliant and green that my hope for weeks was simply to touch one. It was my fourth or fifth visit before I asked if I might, and my father surprised me, he gave a quiet laugh and pressed my shoulder and said 'You just go ahead and touch it if that's all you want.' He spoke as though it was nothing at all that I had keyed myself up to ask, and I ran my hand along the side of the table on the smooth varnished wood, then on the table itself, backwards and forwards on the pliant crushed firmness of the felt.

My partner is the one who really makes the money. He brings ideas to me for new lines and especially for new promotion methods and at the board meetings he always begins 'We've decided' or 'We came to the conclusion' and the board believes that when he says 'we' he naturally means the two of us. He is loyal because ten years ago I brought him in against opposition. He had no official qualifications and he is as ugly a man, I suppose, as you are going to get. At the staff barbecues (it is there, I mean, one most notices it) he wears a short sleeved shirt and his guts sag over his belt. His arms are fat and pale and hairless, his hair has receded from a forehead which shines always in a slight glaze of sweat. One looks at him because one must. There is no way of working with a man, of sharing with him the responsibilities of a company, and avoiding his physical insistence. Nor would one ever call his wife attractive, but at least she is not gross, she does not make you want to reach out your hand to remove plate or glass, to spirit away both food and drink because one knows how it will sag and weigh against the strained belt, puff those disagreeable arms. She is a smallish woman and when she stands beside her he seems less than half his size. The lines of her clothes hang parallel from her shoulders to below her knees. It is of no consequence of course what she looks like, whether she were all rotundities or a breathing pencil, but I notice because she is so incongruous beside her husband. They are each a kind of distorting mirror to the other. She lays her thin fingers on the cushion of his forearm, he sometimes rests his arm across her shoulders, his hand hanging loosely in front of her slight breast as though to protect it. Perhaps because her skin is so sallow, so much the colour of a kind of tawny soap, I am reminded of an Eastern woman, perhaps an Indian I may have seen in *National Geographic*, with a plump snake relaxed about her neck. Yet I admit one has so little right to be fastidious with the lives or the choices of others.

Sometimes I see his eyes slightly puckered as against a drift of smoke, and he is taking in my wife and myself. I wonder why he is so meticulous to present me favourably to the board, to share with me what he has a right to keep for himself. Or why when he speaks to the staff in his joking way does he pretend it is my way as well? There is nothing more he can get from the company, he is my full partner although I took him in when the board said quite openly did I know what I was doing? Even then he was fat and smiled. When he covered his eyes with one pale hand at the very first meeting, had opened his fingers and looked at them like a child to see if he was going to be attacked before he explained his figures, they had laughed and they had loved him. Several times over the years they have said they have me to thank for him. And over and over when he begins in those meetings 'We decided' or 'We think it best', he is saying over and over too that he has *me* to thank for them.

I sat on the bench in the hospital corridor, leaning my head on the wall behind me. I wore one of those shapeless blue-towelling hospital gowns and sat cross-legged, while nurses pushed at the noisy swinging doors of the X-ray rooms. An old man sat a few yards from me in a wheelchair. His eyes were receded and his hands constantly smoothed the blanket across his knees. I feel uncomfortable among the sickly, but I continued to watch him. I was wasting the better part of an afternoon to satisfy a doctor I had visited because of occasional digestive pains in my chest. ('We don't know however that it's nothing until we see these,' he told me a few weeks later. He slipped a large negative from its brown envelope and held it against the window so we both could inspect the overlapping of shadow and outline, an aerial photograph it might as well be of a city I did not know, taken through cloud and gathering darkness.) I looked down at the incongruous shoes and socks which the attendant had told me I could keep on, and across to a young man opposite me who sat with bare feet, in a gown identical to my own. Again I glanced at my watch, I suppose with some impatience. A woman beside me said 'Would you like this to look at? It might pass the time.' She held towards me an *Australian Post* which had become dog-eared with handling by the bored and the ill. 'No, thank you,' I told her. I saw her own hands joined together on her lap, the band of a wedding ring on one of her fingers. Beneath the sleeves of her gown the bones of her wrists

208

stood up like little domes. I went back to looking at the old man, at the gleaming lino along the long corridor, hearing the squeak of rubber soles as the nurses came and went. The woman beside me was Eva, and for as long as I was to know her that was her way of sitting, knees together and the fingers of her hands interlacing as they rested across her skirt or her paisley house coat at home, or her naked legs during the summer.

We would joke that we met in a hospital corridor, in our ill-fitting gowns among the clattering of metal trays and the constant swinging of the doors. Later when she went for other X-rays or for tests, I would wait in the larger room at the end of the corridor. It became so much easier to take time away from my office than ever I had thought. I would leave at ten or at twelve or at three, whenever I wished, and I felt the freedom of a boy deciding simply to walk away from school. We would drive to Cornwall Park to the grey constantly stirring olives which Eva loved or to the kiosk in the Domain and once, on a flawless day in early September, we crossed the harbour bridge and walked on sloping paths between the dark green of native trees, above the glitter of the sea. Or more often, and what I preferred, was to sit at Eva's home, a small state unit on the other side of the city to where I lived. In our one winter we would sit on a settee in front of an open fire, burning thick lengths of pine which her brother had sent down to her from his farm. The ends of the logs hissed at the oozing sap and gave out a clean delicate scent. In the part of our one summer we sat in deckchairs at the back of the house, on the small square of grass, protected from neighbours and from wind by a screen of corrugated plastic sheets I had erected for her.

When I think of us it is seldom of one particular time, hardly at all of what we spoke about. I think of that simplest of things, the closeness neither of us needed to work at. It is as though when we were together we moved always under a canopy of content, like some ikon in a procession (which again I saw in Spain). And always Eva's physical stillness is in my mind, her voice which was almost harsh, which knew and carried more of life than any other I have heard. Yet she had not even been to the South Island, where her husband had settled with another family.

For the past eight years, since she came to the city from a small town in the north, she had worked at a warehouse I drove past every day. From the window behind her desk she could see our factory, with my name along the side.

I have said to my wife that I do not want to go out in the next few weeks, not to dinners nor parties nor to the Old Boys' Ball she has mentioned several times. 'You go by all means,' I tell her. 'We have gone with the same group for ten years, you will know everyone there.'

'I wouldn't dream of it,' she says. She smiles to let me know that her disappointment will never show. My partner has said to me several times 'She's a brick, that woman,' so I do not fuss when she is heroic. I say simply 'You may change your mind. You may want to go when the time comes.' She smiles again and shakes her head and there is the faintest of metallic sounds from the movement of her ear-rings.

My wife is the kind of woman everyone says has charm. The last time we were out together, the week before last at another company's social, the woman I was dancing with said 'Your wife's got him eating out of her hand.' She meant one of the directors who wore a hairpiece and who slid his spread hand over my wife's buttock when they turned into the shadow at the further end of the hall. She took the hand and raised it back to her waist. I danced with this younger female because I was obliged to. She was the wife of one of our up and coming men, a boyish petulant man who sat drinking in one of the booths at the side of the floor, his leg out stiffly in front of him in the swathed bandages of an ankle sprained while skiing. When his wife spoke she smiled at me and shook back her hair and I presume I was meant to be a little taken with her charm too. 'Oh,' I said to her, 'has she?' And the young woman I held and turned with and was bored to death by said 'There, every man with a lovely wife likes to play it down.' She gave her gay young executive wife's laugh, and it was like a stick being run across a child's xylophone. I thought as I glanced at the young throat and the breasts raised up by her dress and the folded lace handkerchief affair tucked like some small animal between them that Eva, without looks or charm, was all that mattered in my life after even fourteen months.

As on that night, dancing with the young wives of my staff, or at any other time I think of, alone with my family or going through the hoops with my equally well-trained guests, it is all much the same. I look at the faces in front of me as though at cardboard and plastic; I think of a woman who is nothing and nowhere, and she is more real to me than my own hand. Always as I think of her I am tapping my thick square nails (which Eva liked to play with, to snick her own nails against or press the bands of quick towards their base) on whatever happens to be near me. The vile marble thing on my desk at work or on an ashtray at home, until my wife says 'I don't like to nag but would you mind stopping that? It gets on my nerves.'

'So would breathing if you could hear it,' I answer her. Or once when she asked me if I did it simply to pass the time I said No, it was more than that, it was hearing time pass as well, and she and her daughter looked across at each other 'significantly', as I suppose they would think it. Their look is to say observe how husband and father is over-strained, is in advanced depression, when in fact I am bored, bored. Recently I dreamed of myself fishing a lake. I was sort of trawling with several lines from the back of the boat as we moved along. There was no water in the lake and the hooks dragged at the bottom like the teeth of a plough. As far back as I could see were the neat parallel lines of the dragging hooks. But while I tap my nails against ashtray or table or the wooden arm of a chair, my wife turns her head and raises her hands when she speaks, and her rings and ear-rings sparkle and her voice 'tinkles', as she likes to be told. She sheers like late-afternoon water, I see her standing in life and splashing as a child in the shallows of a river. That is where she speaks from, and I answer from the dry floor of my lake.

My father stopped with me one afternoon at a house much finer than our own. I had been with him at the library for the whole morning. At two o'clock he slipped his jacket over his long white sleeves with the jade links, and the dark waistcoat he did not take off when he worked. I liked to be with him in the room where he did his tasks, and breathe in the odours of glue and ageing paper and the shiny leather chair. His job was to sort out all the papers which came to the library, and put them in the wooden frames that held them together in bunches. There were brass hooks in the frames and the frames hung in rows, and between the rows was like being in a tunnel of papers.

He took his hat from a high shelf and turned it as he always did against his sleeve, while he held the edge of his sleeve in his hand. Sometimes on Saturdays we would go to the snooker saloon where I watched him play, or sometimes to the afternoon pictures. What I remember are stories about the desert and sheiks in long flowing robes and headpieces which flapped behind them as they galloped their horses in a smear of flying sand. There were often clumps of palms where they spoke to women inside silken tents, or cities with wonderfully white walls and high thin towers. After the pictures I would hold his hand when we came onto the street, and everything was so grey and ordinary and dull after what we had seen. But this day he said 'Nice afternoon to stretch the old legs, wouldn't you say?' Often I did not quite know what he meant. Yes, I would say to everything. He took up a parcel of books from the table where a stack of folded newspapers were still in their brown paper wrappings. We walked up the long street to the bridge and then across the tops of the trees. I looked down on the gully through the flicker of the gaps in the concrete fence. Towards the end of the bridge he lifted me right up and I held the small squares of wire and pressed my face close against them. I could look down to the rounded crowns of the trees, and in the bright summer light some of the leaves were shining like glass.

We walked until we came to a house with a verandah around three sides. A lady opened the door and when we stepped inside it was like going into a deep cool cave. My father placed the books on a small table in the hallway where there was a leaning white tower she said was carved out of one tusk of ivory. My father and the lady sat in a large room with heavy curtains folded like in a picture theatre. They sat in there and drank tea from cups which had little flecks in them that you could see through when they were held against the light. The lady took out to the verandah a little tray with a glass of lemonade, and cake I did not like with seeds in every mouthful. I walked round and round the verandah and put my hands through the spaces between the railings, and pulled over a stool from where wire baskets of trailing ferns and creepers were hanging from the roof. I knelt on the stool and leaned against the railing as though I were on a ship. I could look over the gully we had walked across, see the whole span under the bridge like part of a huge hoop. And far down was the harbour, so brightly blue I am sure I remember it as more brilliant than it was.

After our visit to the lady we walked back across the bridge and it was back to what was ordinary. We would just say we had been for a walk when we got home, my father said, this would be our secret. We waited on the safety zone for the tram to take us home. Usually my father let me sit on the thick curved end of the platform while I held on to his arm, but I remember that day we only stood. When we were walking down the small hill towards our own house my father said, as we came near the gate which always snagged for a second because part of the catch had come away, 'Mecca, eh, old man?'

'Yes,' I said to him. I knew that was a kind of secret too, long before I knew whatever else it was.

There is a marble inkstand on my desk, a present my wife brought me back from Mexico two or three years ago. I find that I tap my nails against it most of the time I am sitting at my desk. The lump of marble is off-white and yellowish on different sides, the veins merely darker unattractive streaks. It is like snow when it begins to thaw, that seeping and trickling and discoloration you see in diminishing banks stacked against the side of a road, when it is eaten at the edges and irregular and stained. This is what Zelma's present has reminded me of since the moment she placed it on my lap at home and said 'This is yours, senor,' while the children pranced about in their broad brimmed and sequined hats. She had loved Acapulco even more than she had thought she would, miles more than Spain on our trip before we had the children, when we had pretended to ourselves that we would return there to live.

'More than Honolulu?' my son asked.

'You don't have to compare things, silly.' She tipped the boy's hat forward so that the brim rested against his shirt front. The shirt was a present too, blue linen with eagles embroidered on the shoulders.

'I almost bought you a shirt, you know,' she said to me.

'Almost?'

'Would you have worn it?'

I looked at the bright embroidered wings and lied, I said 'You just never know.'

'Of course he wouldn't,' my daughter said. 'He'd die if he wore anything with colour in it.'

'You can see him with this hat on too, can't you?' The children held their arms stiffly and strutted as we used to for marching as wooden soldiers, but they were being their father. The boy put his head a little to one side as I suppose I do and gave the curtest of nods several times, his father acknowledging the neighbours. He and the girl and their mother became quite hysterical, 'The idea of him in that gear!' My wife had to sit back and flap herself with both hands until she said 'Now that will do, you've all had your joke.' I put my folded hands beneath my chin and watched them, the eagles moving when the boy's arms moved and the hats flashing as they turned.

'Did you see a bullfight?' I asked her.

'Do you think I'm sick or something?' she said. 'He says did your mother go and watch those barbarians torture a bull to death?' she exclaimed to the children. She closed her eyes at the thought of it and the girl said 'I'd certainly hate to see one, I know that.'

'What about you?' I said to the boy. 'Reckon you could face a bullfight?'

The boy was turning the hat in his hands now, his thumbs edging the brim round and round. He shrugged his shoulders when I asked him what he thought about it. 'Not interested enough to even know?' I said, and my wife and my daughter looked at each other and each raised her eyebrows at the same time. 'We'll leave it there shall we?' my wife said. 'Before we're fighting again.'

I have noticed time and again that they are so close they do not have to speak. I have seen them at parties, they circle and move about like two animals you think are unaware of each other, and yet once they get home each knows exactly what the other has done, to whom the other spoke and when. As they sit together and talk of something again they are feline, precise. They sit above whatever they speak of and nose it, as it were, prod it about with swift careful taps.

One night very recently they were discussing bridal patterns when I came into the lounge before dinner. They were speaking rapidly together, unaware that their husband and father had come into the room until they heard me at the bottles, and I asked them why there was no ice. 'There's ice all right,' my wife said. She moved to stub her half-smoked cigarette.

'Don't you go,' my daughter said to her. 'I'll get it for him.' While she banged at the refrigerator, inserting her arm behind the frozen vegetables and the television dinners to where the one small tray of ice was stuck fast against the back wall, my wife placed her hands palm downwards on the arms of the leather chair, and closed her eyes. She was like an Egyptian statue, something at the door of a monument.

'You'll have to get it for yourself,' my daughter called out. 'It's stuck too hard for me to move.'

'It must have been back there a long enough time,' I said.

'Hard to see how that could happen, the way you go through ice.'

'Well?' I asked her. 'Is that leading up to something?'

'The carving knife's there if you need it,' she said. I chipped between the wall and the metal tray while the girl went back to her mother. As I tugged at the tray to edge it free my hand slipped and my fingers caught against one of the sharp fittings inside the ice-box. Suddenly on the white encrusted ice I saw the small blooms of my own blood, splashes that opened like minute flowers. I looked at the drops for a moment, at the close sequence of stains across the ice, and felt my stomach lift with a kind of disgust. I must have stood for quite some time, fascinated at those vivid splashes that were myself. The others picked up the silence after my chipping with the knife and my daughter called out 'Managed, have you?'

'I've cut my hand,' I said.

'On the knife?'

'On the fridge.' I waited because I thought one of them might move. I pressed my finger in my handkerchief but there was no depth to the cut. Yet I still expected one of them to come across to say is it all right, even to take the tray out for me and put the cubes into my glass. When I turned towards them I saw that both of them were looking at me.

'There's plaster in that drawer,' my wife told me. 'That one right beside you.' I opened the drawer and moved my other hand through the jumble of papers and stamps and rubber bands and tins.

'Manage?' she called again.

'It'll be all right,' I told her. I had found the spool but when I took it from the drawer it was not plaster but masking tape. I left my finger wrapped in my handkerchief and attended again to my drink. I ran the hot tap on the frozen tray, the ice cracking under the stream of steaming water. Neither of the women – for she is that, too, I suppose, my daughter – asked me how it was when I went back into the lounge, my hand concealed in my pocket. I sipped at my gin, the ice-cubes nudging and clicking against one of the thin Danish glasses which my partner had given us last year for a Christmas present. 'Not that I believe in Christmas,' he had said, as he gave the box with its gay seasonal wrapping to my wife, 'but I believe in presents.' That was the first night – last Christmas Eve – when I knew how clearly I was watching something on a screen. I have thought of that comparison many times, each time I feel more strongly that what I watch does not really have much to do with me. I now watched the two women and turned my glass slowly to hear the ice. They spoke of whether my daughter's hair would need to be cut if that style were to suit. I watch them as if there is an audience between us, like a man who wonders when he sits in a cinema what those actors must be like once the cameras stop filming, is there any small movement, any inflexion in their voices, which tells him what they are really like? There is no one I know who is not behind make-up, not across a deep pit. I try to think of people who are not on a screen, and I think only of two, of my father and of Eva.

I have said that my partner's strength is that he can get on with people, whether he knows them or not. He tells me that is what selling is about. It is a way of putting your arm around someone's shoulder, talking to him so that he knows you're his friend. I have heard him explain this several times, to the staff or to the board. His hands open and close while he speaks. His face eases into its broad smile or he looks at whoever he is talking to quite solemnly, sincerely. When he opens his hands and shows his palms he has let out the dove of confidence and intimacy. It hovers over the heads of his audience and they feel its presence too, they look back quite as

215

solemnly. Then when his palms meet and close and his thick fingers interlock or rub over each other in a kind of love-making with themselves, the bird has returned, it has disappeared into the magical hands, and those who have listened smile back, or laugh at his own laughing. It is like a man performing in front of a mirror, and his mirror is people.

Once my partner said to me 'I know you think my methods are brash but they are also twenty-six percent better than those anyone else in this outfit would think of using. That's not a bad return on brashness.' He sat opposite me while I tapped my nails against the marble inkstand. His hands were folded across the rise of his guts, as they usually were when we spoke together. He is far from being a fool and I believe he knew very early on that I did not believe in the dove. He had just delivered his latest advertising thoughts on to the broad unstained blotter of my desk. What he had placed there was a coloured photograph of a foetus, the tiniest veins in the creature's disproprotionate head quite visible through its surrounding transparent sac. There were words typed beneath it. *Nobody packages more carefully than we do.*

'I can't claim it's my own idea altogether,' he admitted. 'I've seen it in an American magazine, but no one here's to know that.'

I looked again at the glossy photograph and the words on a narrow strip of paper gummed beneath it. The hands in the picture were like small fins.

'It's a logical extension, though,' he went on. 'Remember that one we used last year of a girl sealed in cellophane for the new Airtex Lunchwrap? Remember that?'

Yes, I told him. There was still a lifesize enlargement of it on the wall of the staff cafeteria.

'We're all a lot more ecologically aware now than we were even twelve months ago,' he said. 'That free advertising we did for the Beech Forest buffs on our food cartons for example. People associate our name with caring about such things.'

'The public?' I asked him.

'People,' he repeated. 'That's why we can't go wrong with this one.' He leaned forward on his thick thighs and a length of pale pink cuff was exposed as his hand spread above the foetus. 'You don't use a photograph like this lightly,' he told me. 'It's something pretty important, after all, pretty delicate. People would know we were serious because we're serious about what we market. Serious the way nature is when it wraps this up, if you like.' The features on the oval face were obscured by the square jut of his index finger. 'We want them to know we take packaging as seriously as that.'

I continued to look down at the photograph when he removed

his hand and settled back in his chair. His legs were crossed and one foot jerked slightly as he waited for me to speak. I was amazed at the clarity of what I looked at, the fine detail of the utterly vulnerable and trusting curve of the incompleted body. I had read once how an embryo goes through the whole of evolution, through various stages of fish and other life before it reaches the fully human. I remembered how appalled I had been twenty years ago when the doctor had called me into my wife's room and shown me my newly delivered daughter. The nurse was washing her with a wad of dampened cotton wool, and there were streaks of blood and foam over the tiny chest and legs. The doctor had said *Well aren't you pleased with her?* and I watched the wad move under the mottled arm, the look of discomfort or even pain on the tight screaming face.

'We'll go ahead then?' my partner asked.

'You'll go ahead anyway,' I told him. 'Everyone else will think it's splendid whether you kidnapped it from an American magazine or conceived it yourself.'

He laughed broadly and said, 'But you think it's shit?'

'You know what I think of it,' I said.

'Like a bet sales are up fifteen percent at a minimum on this line within three months?'

'I'd rather bet we'll be into glass coffins before the year's out,' I told him. 'Your concern for the living and the unborn can be carried further than this.'

He stood with one hand on the handle of my door and his other rubbed the back of his neck while he clucked and shook his head. 'Don't know what we're going to do with you, pardner,' he said in a drawling voice.

Before he shut the door I called to him 'Don't you need the photo?'

'I've had half a dozen run off for Friday's meeting,' he said. 'You're welcome to it.'

I slanted the photograph towards the light to examine it more closely. There were even little fingernails on the hands, branched veins in the sac which enveloped the body. I wondered at the minute and intricate being which in time would become one of my partner's people, one of our tenfold profit increase for total additional production costs of maybe five percent. And then a curious feeling stirred in my stomach as I realised that of course the thing was dead. There could not be a photograph like that unless the child had been removed from its mother. The idea disturbed me, and yet I was amused at my partner's self-congratulation that our care for the people was a huddle of human meat perhaps an hour or two from the first workings of decomposition.

As I said, I watch them. And now they are watching back, even addressing me, which people on a screen or stage should never do. And I remember once I had said to Eva when we were in Wellington together, standing at the window of a hotel from which we could look across the clutter of streets beneath us, would she like to go to a play? I had seen one advertised in the *Dominion* we read together in the taxi from the airport. The paper was spread out over our knees like a sheet, and her hand had rested on mine while she leaned close to the page to read it, because she would not wear glasses. I had kept the play for a surprise. Through the afternoon, between two meetings, I found my way to the theatre and bought the tickets. We could never go out together like that in Auckland and so now I said, as though I might have asked it any night, did she fancy the theatre? *Love* she said *let's not waste our time together*. I said nothing about the tickets and instead we simply walked about the city. She held my arm and we strolled along the finely curved road beneath the hotel. Every few minutes she would press my arm, bring us to a halt as she pointed or remarked on something which held her eye. When it was dark the lights twinkled up and down the hills. Right above where we stood, as though supporting itself, was the large cross illuminated on the wall of a monastery. I began to say something about religion. Eva said nothing and we were walking on, her hair lifting and blowing across her face and touching my own cheek. She raised her hand to draw back and smooth her hair, and her skin seemed so pale against the darkness. A little further on she said *Do you mind if we rest a while?* She sat on the wall which ran along the seafront, and now we were drenched in the orange glare from the lights along the Parade.

'Tired?' I asked her. And she said to me *Never, I just want to soak it up*. The harbour was streaked with the broad flowing band of a moon which had risen above the hill across the city. It seemed almost exaggerated, like an enormous backdrop. I sat beside Eva on the wall and I said we would never be more contented than this, which of course was true, but at the time Eva said, teasing me, it was because like so many rich people I am sentimental.

'Not that rich,' I said to her. The sea slapped against the wall a few feet beneath us and Eva sat with her head rested against my shoulder. A little later I said that it was turning cool, and although she said she did not notice it, when we stood she asked *could we take a taxi back, love? was that all right?* At the hotel she lay on the bed and told me to switch on the television, it was the night of a programme she knew I usually watched. She lay there with her hair spread across the pillows. *You'll wake me if I nod off?* she demanded. *I don't want to miss a minute of this.*

Eva's brother was a tall man about my own age, his face lined and weathered, with the same grey eyes as his sister. He waited on the top step leading up to the foyer and reception desk, and he moved down the steps as I came towards him. It was eight o'clock in the morning, March the twenty-third. There was a cool wind coming in from the mudflats which lifted the soft corners of the man's checked collar. The girl at the reception desk was standing and looked down on us. She must have pointed me out to him as I left my car in the car-park on the other side of the road.

'I'm Eva's brother,' he said. 'I don't want to spend any more time with you than I need.' He looked at me with the hard stare that some men who work the land seem to take on, a hardness that dismisses all divergence as weakness, other ways of life as directly hostile to its own. I have seen his face a hundred times at football matches and on the streets of country towns. Eva had told me, when she first spoke of going to stay with him for a few weeks, that he belonged to some small religious sect. His wife was his only help on the farm, they worked difficult land with the singleness of prophets. She had felt the rest and the country air would help her pick up some of the weight she had lost in the last few months. I said I would drive her north but she had demurred at that, she said her brother wouldn't approve of us, it was better if he didn't know. 'I've come to see you because I could not avoid it, because Eva is dead.' I saw the blue-checked collar rising with the wind and lean back against his jaw. I saw the girl still looking down at us from behind the shine of the plate glass, and Eva's brother cleared his throat. 'The service and the rest of it is over,' he said. 'She wanted to make sure I saw you.'

'She knew?' I said. The words were like dry flakes in my mouth, they were colourless sounds.

'She knew she was pretty sick,' her brother said. 'I'd have thought you'd have known that much. I thought there was more between you than sin.'

'She didn't say that?' I asked. His tongue moved quickly along his lips, he turned from me to look over towards the sea. 'She said nothing very much,' he told me.

There was nothing now I wanted to say to her brother, nothing more for him to say to me. I walked up the steps and through the doors with their gentle hushed closing and into my office. I sat among the routine noises of the morning, looking out between the various factories and across the open patches of land to the slight

Vincent O'Sullivan

caps of foam on the shallow inlet, the mud-brown shoreline. I watched the odd movements of wind from inside the stillness of a closed room, watched the rocking of an empty drum in the yard behind the factory. There was the stretched emptiness of the sky above the buildings and the low slope of the hills. 'Eva,' I said. *He would scoop the coloured balls into their wooden triangle and then lean at the end of the table for only the slightest moment, because he seemed always to know what to do, while the other men waited and took practice shots and stooped until their chins were tucked back and quite disappeared, and their eyes were level with the table. His cue was back resting upright in his hand before I had seen it move, the packed balls were scattered and brilliant and flowing across the cloth. Then he would pick them off one by one,* tock *and* tock, *then the soft catching noise as the first fell into the pockets, and the different kind of click as one after another bulged out the nets in the corners or in the centre of the table.* As I said Eva's name I had stood for a second in the intensity of what never comes back, in the curling bluish drifts of smoke and under the bright pyramid of light which I had not thought of for years. And yet now I seem to think always of two things at once, or of one person who immediately brings to mind the other. They are not ghosts, they are what everything else is seen by, is paled against, until what I look at in front of me is not even a film. It is a negative hung at a window, I see by the light from the other side.

They have come to look at me and so to sympathise, to take my elbow on one side with the wifely hands of concern and duty, my elbow on the other with the feeling and the intimacy of having spoken with me daily for a dozen years. I am part of their rights. I am what they have worked at and are entitled to. I am their guarantee that *they* are sane. I let them take me across the yellow earth to where my daughter's fiancé holds open the door of the car.

My daughter with tears in her eyes and my wife who does not wear make-up because her paleness is the marking of her grief, now sit one on either side of me in the back seat. My fat partner accelerates and the white line in the middle of the road disappears beneath the long shining bonnet of his car, an endless ribbon he devours. I sit quite calmly and consider how I am branded because I have stood for longer than usual in one place among the machines and graders of the extended motorway, looked down into a hole where a beautiful house once stood. There was a verandah on the house, and leaning on its rail, my knees supported by a stool, was like leaning over the rail of a ship. I stand on the wet clay and remember my father, and a woman I loved, who are also gone into smaller but identical holes. To think of that seems to me the very

220

best of reasons to stand so still, to wonder what there can be to make moving a matter of any consequence. I have looked things in the face because they are not there.

Yet my wife and my daughter, my partner and my daughter's boyfriend, for all their love of things, their touching and their endless talk and their hating to be alone, do not believe in what they see. All *that* – the bodies, the cars, the Mexican ashtrays – is for them no more than a sketch of what is real, of what might be. They believe that reality is something they shall make from all these things, not these things themselves. They now look at me from either side, in discreet glances in the rear-vision mirror. I am smiling slightly which confirms all that they suspect. I am smiling because I am with four people who think that our travelling at forty miles an hour along Great North Road, in the silence of tact and apprehension, will make some difference to anything at all. They are like those mad saints of centuries ago, men who would not believe that the world is what it is, but a distortion from its true shape that love and charity and worship could somehow wrench it back to.

We are now travelling past the used-car marts with their bright strings of flapping plastic flags, with words spelled out in little metal discs which shimmer endlessly against the light and wind. We are coming towards the turn where a church sits high on one's left, a tall grey finger of stone against the sky. I consider for a moment with some amusement that we are a procession from that old time I was thinking of. My partner who is like St. Francis opens his thick hands and the doves of fifteen percent hover at his shoulder, move with their strutting walk along his extended arms. My own wife with her eyes cast down, my daughter like a novice, my devoted son-in-law of two months' time, beside and behind that franciscan flesh as he leads me to where I shall be questioned, dressed in a special robe, touched and tampered with by men who will work towards that miracle, to turn my world to theirs. They shall give me the cool pastures of a private room, the quiet waters of their choice. And on the green slats of their garden seats I shall be silent as a boy who walks from a picture theatre holding his father's hand, who looks at the bald streets with eyes fresh from palms and minarets.

AFTER THE REVOLUTION

Michael Gifkins

She was undoubtedly the most astonishing woman he had ever met. To discover her by running out of petrol outside her tennis club was of course fortuitous, but beyond this the sequence of her unfolding seemed designed to guarantee his unflagging curiosity and pursuit.

It would not be true to say, as some did, that he worshipped the fairer sex. Indeed, the bosomy matrons who bounded and flexed under his apparently approving eyes aroused not wonder but a kind of fear that such unbridled aggression could be condoned on a modest suburban afternoon. It must be something in the air, he thought, sticky after rain and with a biting sun edging its heat through the haze. To walk for petrol on such a day might be to invite prostration. What was the source of the tumultuous energy displayed before him? Then another doubt assailed him. Would he be mistaken as a peeping tom? He wriggled lower in the seat, affecting nonchalance. The action must have contributed to the feared image, for the matrons threw themselves into a frenzy of service and return.

Her arrival was like a salvation to him. The car throbbed into the kerb in front of his own derelict vehicle, totally out of place, so flagrantly slumming that he caught his breath at the driver's audacity. Ten to the gallon, he mused, and watched perhaps a quarter of that amount disappear into the complex and cockeyed manoeuvre by which she endeavoured to park.

His second surprise – and here his romantic interest did quicken – was her choice of clothes. Not to be exposed to the obscenity of short skirts and coloured cardies she had donned mannish gear – baggy shorts and a good cricketing jersey, several sizes too large. She paused to hitch a collapsing sock, and Antony's loving gaze was rewarded by a pair of delicate olive legs, and the poignant marbling of a varicose vein behind one slender knee. Yet for all this she played like a demon, gave no quarter and was sullen in her manners about the court. The other women seemed to fear and respect her, and her irritation when her partner betrayed them to defeat was positively tigerish.

Antony transferred himself rapidly to the large car. He sank back in leather and feigned sleep as she approached. Seeming oblivious to him, she threw herself into the driver's seat.

'Damned women!' She jumbled her gear into the back. Antony opened one eye and looked across at her.

'I thought you played very well!'

She fumbled in her trouser pocket for the key.

'I suppose you think you're coming with me? What about that?'

Antony found himself suddenly quite faithless to his own car.

'I'll just forget about it. It's not going to go away.'

She looked searchingly across at him. He tried to rest an easy and unassuming gaze on the road ahead. She seemed reassured.

'Would you like a cigarette?'

They drove for a while in silence before she spoke again.

'I do find it necessary to beat those women.'

Antony felt it more prudent to say nothing.

'It's learning what makes them tick that I'm here for, but I find I need to beat them too. Does that surprise you?' She glanced across to gauge his reaction.

But Antony knew how to listen, and could reward her with his attention. It was with greater assurance that she continued.

'When the revolution comes there could be violence and even a period of famine. Of course we won't be affected. But most of those women, along with their families, are going to suffer.' She paused, drawing deeply on her cigarette. 'It's imperative that I understand how they're likely to react.'

Antony felt a twinge of sympathy for the buxom ladies back at the court.

'What does your husband think?' His curiosity was now real. 'Does he know about this?'

'He hasn't got the time.' The answer was quite flat. 'This is my department. This and the kids.'

Antony had visions of a militia of flaxen-haired children.

'They're not old enough yet.' It was as though she could read his thoughts. 'And I'm trying to have more, but. . .' As she trailed off to silence Antony felt a new excitement. Perhaps this was where he came in.

'These children of yours.' He tried to sound genuinely involved. 'Will I get to meet them?'

'Of course you will. When they're home from school.' But she had sensed the insincerity. 'Now tell me – ' She paused, and the question hung heavily between them. 'Why did you get into my car?'

'I think I fell in love.' It was the first thing that came into his head, and was not strictly untrue. She snorted. Sensing the demands of propriety, he introduced himself. The car slid into a green street. From somewhere in the bushes came the lush chortle of a blackbird.

'Well, it's going to be hard work.' Swinging the car up the drive she glanced sharply across at him. 'Not what you think! I mean tonight.'

'Tonight. Of course.' Antony nodded, trying his hardest to appear wise. An astonishingly colourful woman materialised suddenly in front of the car.

'There's Mother.' He noted the anxiety in her voice. 'I hope that she's all right.'

The strange creature advanced springingly on Antony. Her daughter forestalled her.

'Mother, I'd like you to meet Antony.' Her tone was very formal. 'He's going to help us with everything tonight.'

Antony smiled in his most suitable way, drawing from reservoirs of charm. But there was little time for nicety.

'Antony! Come with me. I'll have to change. Mother! I'd like you to see to the children when they get home.'

They hurried through the considerable mansion. Antony had an impression of a kind of taste, slightly ragged at the edges and even a bit grubby. Her room was the same. A chenille spread lay crumpled at the foot of the single bed. She threw it hastily over unmade sheets. Ignoring him now, she pulled her jumper up over her head, unbuttoned her shirt and shrugged it to the floor. Her breasts were luscious and she smelt very sweaty. She undid her trousers and stepped out of them, took off her knickers and walked through into the shower. He had decided that he should not be aroused. For one thing, children were arriving home from school in the rooms below. But as he waited on the bed the picture of her body niggled in his mind. He had to admit himself checked. The shower hissed on endlessly. Kicking off his shoes and socks he climbed in amongst the crumpled and slightly gamey sheets.

He woke with a start to find her standing at the foot of the bed.

'How long have I been asleep?' The discontinuity disturbed him. She thrust him a mug of coffee.

'Here. Drink this. It'll wake you up.'

Her evening clothes were of severe and formal cut. Massive blue stones clasped her ears. But before he could take a sip, her husband was advancing on the bed. Tall and athletic, he was holding out his hand.

'Alan Sater. Glad you could come.' He seemed very boyish. 'I know my father will want to meet you.'

Antony shifted awkwardly to his other elbow to reciprocate. The children were shepherded forward by their grandmother. The little girl's short skirt revealed a pert behind.

'I don't think much of him! I bet he stinks.'

Antony felt at an increasing disadvantage. He glowered at them over his coffee.

'*If* you don't mind, I think I'll get up.' He reached forward to place the mug on the bedside table.

'I wonder what his muscles are like.' The boy glanced warily at his father while sidling over to the bed. 'Show me your muscles – please.' He snuggled into Antony's side.

'Let him get up. Go down and make sure everything's ready.' She shooed them all to the door. 'Are you all right?' She looked down at him from beside the bed. 'You really had better get up and tidy yourself. The workers will be here soon.' It was said with a frown of distaste.

Antony seized her by the hand and pulled her down towards him. He had not allowed himself contact and felt he had to remedy the situation. She shoved him hard in the chest, forcing him back on the pillows. Breathless, he was unable to complain. A haze of Chanel enveloped him. She kissed him quickly but lasciviously on the lips. Then she was at the door, looking back at him with some severity. He tried to speak but she had gone.

It was not to be his day. He cleaned his teeth with her toothbrush and tidied his hair with her brush and comb. He was starting to feel an acute isolation. Attempting to relax, he read all the contents of her toilet cabinet. People were beginning to arrive in the rooms below. Overtaken by an obscure sense of purpose Antony took the mascara and lightly blacked his lashes, and then brushed in shadows above his eyes and rubbed a hint of foundation into his cheeks. It was not an improvement. Alienated by his own face, he turned out the light and went downstairs.

The party started on the patio, which was lit with guttering flares. Guests spilled over into the garden and across to a barbecue area on Antony's right, where tall trees and thick vegetation played havoc with the light, shrouding knots of people in heavy shadow. Fat dripped and spurted on hot coals. The effect was bizarre, a whirlpool of dark movement frozen in rushes of light. Fireworks exploded in diamond sprays. The husband was quickly at his side, thrusting a large tumbler of whisky and water into his surprised hand. Antony mumbled his thanks. The whisky was good and he drank of it deeply. Alan waited attentively, bending over him with concern etched deep in his face.

'Is it all right?'

The warmth of the whisky was a familiar cue. Antony nodded.

Visibly relieved, Alan took him by the elbow and ushered him across the lawn. A cracker exploded close by, causing Antony to wince. Alan seemed not to notice, steering him towards the central mass of people.

'Why can't I have some with my lemonade?' It was a birdlike elderly lady, crumpled in a wheelchair and dressed in a froth of purple tulle. No one paid her the slightest attention. The trim and obviously distinguished gentleman who stood by the chair with his hand resting fondly on the bar smiled generously. Well-wishers pressed forward to shake his free hand and offer halting congratulations on his success.

'This is my father.' Alan looked anxiously down into Antony's face for approval. 'You can see for yourself – it's his night.' Parting the crowd like a traffic officer he moved Antony closer to the shrine. A hush fell around them. Antony confronted the old man, who looked to his son for an explanation of this unwarranted interruption in the evening's tempo.

'Congratulations, sir!' It was Antony who took the initiative, speaking with as much sincerity as he could muster. 'Alan's been telling me how well you have done.'

The older man relaxed, finding the formula impossible to resist. He took Antony's outstretched hand and held it for a moment in both his own.

'Thank you, my boy, thank you.' His gaze from beneath the bushy white eyebrows was firm and clear, his manner direct. The grip tightened on Antony, drawing him closer. 'I'm sure we all have it within us to do as I have done.' He paused and looked searchingly into Antony's eyes. A conspiratorial grin made his face suddenly sly. 'God willing,' he added insinuatingly. 'God willing.'

Antony felt a hand pluck at the edge of his jacket. He reached down to hold the old lady's brittle fingers. She stared back up at him with a malevolence of self-pity and blind greed. Alan looked anxiously to his father, who clapped Antony firmly on the shoulder.

'There, my boy. There.'

They prised Antony away from the wheelchair. Others pressed forward to take his place. The old lady began to wail, staring straight ahead.

'I want it! I want it now! I want it!'

Antony found himself gaping like an idiot. Alan's father nodded understandingly to him, and then winked. It was the signal of his release.

'Are you hungry?' She was there beside him, carrying a plate of food. 'Alan! Don't just stand around! They need some help with the drinks!' She pressed forward upon Antony, holding the plate high out of reach of the jostling crowd. He could feel her body mould against his own and stay there in the crush.

'Hungry?' She kissed him.

'I don't know.' There was so little time to think. She lowered the plate to just below his chin. It overflowed with an enormous steak and was topped with salad and barbecued chicken legs. The smell caused a shock of recognition in his belly.. 'I want you,' he thought. He disengaged himself from her body and took the plate. She watched him closely as he ate. With each mouthful his curiosity returned. 'I'm not so sure any more,' his naivety overwhelmed him, 'I'm not sure that I know exactly what is going on.'

Immediately she was serious, and shushed him with a finger to his lips. She seemed determined not to arouse suspicion, though everyone round them looked too drunk to care. Blood ran down his wrists and chin. She whispered in his ear.

'The old man. He's retiring. Alan's taking over. Alan's hopeless. I know that but *they* haven't guessed it yet. There's bound to be unrest. They hated the old man but he could understand them.' She paused, then concluded rather lamely, 'I love Alan. That's why you're here.' Her hand moved sharply up his thigh and cupped against his groin. No emotion was betrayed upon her face. The words she had just mouthed whirled nonsensically in his head. He felt fire spreading through his lower belly. 'Come on!' It was an urgent whisper. 'There's someone you've got to meet!'

They moved through the crowd as if it were a dream. People fell silent as they passed by then buzzed in speculation behind their backs. Another whisky appeared in Antony's hand. He placed his arm possessively about her waist. The heady smell of determination rose from her armpits. He drank it in, with the whisky fumes and the charcoal, and the softer scents of the night. Her mother was on the terrace, lurid in a columbine dress. She waved happily. Children appeared from the darkness to throng their passage.

The confrontation could scarcely have gone against him. It was true that under different circumstances the man would have been an adversary to fear. Yet with much of the anger and confusion in his gaze deflected on to the boss's wife it was a contest to which Antony felt more than equal. He heard himself speak coldly as he shook the other's hand.

'Mr Sater has mentioned you before.'

It was a strong face with full beard and good eyes and the handshake did not lack power. Yet uncertainty was there.

'There are things we need to discuss.'

The man nodded reluctantly. Antony let his eyes wander over his partner. She was an attractive woman, dressed clingingly in silk. Leaning to her man, her look was for Antony alone.

'Most importantly there is the matter of loyalty.' The words were selecting themselves on Antony's tongue.

'I thought I would discuss that with Mr Sater junior.' The bearded man was preparing to be defiant.

'Mr Alan Sater will not have time for *your* doubts.' Antony played out the words with heavy emphasis. 'Tonight he is concerned that we should honour his father. Personal problems have no place on an occasion like this.'

His words served to exasperate the man. He addressed his next remarks not at Antony but to Celia Sater. Her face cold, she stared blankly back at him. Antony recognised the opening and played to it.

'And then there is the question of productivity. Perhaps we should hear your opinions on that.' Without pause, but allowing his manner to soften, he shifted his stance towards the man's wife. 'And later possibly we should discuss your eventual prospects within the larger organisation?' The question was ambiguous, but he allowed promise in his tone. Almost as much promise, he thought wryly, as he allowed himself, when Celia squeezed his groin.

It was a foregone victory, and Antony left the perplexed employee at the pressure of Celia's hand upon his own. Old Mr Sater was mounting the makeshift dais in the centre of the lawn. Spotlights played on him from the children's upstairs rooms. Antony did not listen to his speech, conscious only of the warmth within him. But she was urging him forward to join the half-circle of men at the foot of the platform. There were cheers and clapping as the old man descended. Alan followed his father from man to man, valiantly dragging two large cardboard boxes along the grass behind him. Antony found himself shaking Mr Sater's hand for the second time that evening, and recognised on Alan's face the familiar plea. So he accepted everything that was pressed upon him, and taking the first opportunity to withdraw moved his booty to the edge of the light. An envelope contained the firm's cheque for fifty dollars and a formal note of thanks. The cheque he folded carefully in an inner pocket. The parcels held a gift-wrapped selection of supermarket cheeses and six half-bottles of a local champagne. These he would dispose of in the bushes.

Almost instantly he found himself surrounded by sibilant children, led by Celia's daughter. They laughed as they took him by the hands and led him further into the trees, away from the light. Fingers plucked at his trousers. He could hear a whispering behind him.

'I'll bet he's not as good as the other one!'

They formed a fairy ring, dancing with him, and when he was exhausted and cried halt threw themselves at his legs and tried to bring him down. There were a dozen children at least. Party hats tilted drunkenly across their eyes and their faces were smeared with food. They twirled like dervishes in the faintest glimmerings of light.

Then he was down on one knee. Hands were jerking at his shoelaces. The little girl threw herself against his chest.

'Let's get him! Let's get him!'

The squealing was shrill about his ears. Now they were clutching at his genitals and fingers tugged at his hair.

'He's frightened. Don't let him get away.'

Taking himself by surprise Antony cracked her across the face with his open palm. There was a split-second silence and then a piercing scream. The other children melted back in terror.

He had to find Celia. Bursting out of the bushes, he struggled up the garden, leaving a chorus of howls behind.

'Antony!' They were in the living-room, farewelling chosen guests. She was so delighted to see him. 'We'd been wondering what you were up to!'

A small voice that was about all that was left inside him urged him to withdraw. He was getting to feel chilly. Like a thief or a beggar (it was his own image that he used) he pulled his torn jacket tight about his chest.

'Well then. I'd best be off.' He was careful to smile equally at them both.

'Are you sure?' Alan was still anxious. 'If there's anywhere I can drop you. . .'

'Don't be ridiculous, Alan.' She silenced him with a wave of the hand. 'Of course Antony must take the car. And I'll want to see him tomorrow and thank him.' There was a moment of panic in her eyes. 'You will drop by, won't you?'

With the greatest clarity that the day had allowed him, Antony saw both himself and this beautiful woman as victims of the same delusion. The keys were in his palm.

'Oh Antony!' Her voice stopped him a pace short of the french doors. 'Would you mind very much dropping Mother on your way?'

He handed the aged columbine, wrapped now in furs, into the sumptuous interior of the car. The engine grumbled powerfully to life. He would at least make it to his bed. The strong lights swept the trees as they slid out of the driveway. The streets were empty. Surrendering to a growing sense of *déjà vu*, he flicked the lights on full and punched his foot down to the floor. The car surged forward with a bellow of excitement from the exhausts. The old lady cackled merrily and snuggled in close beneath his arm. 'Harridan!' he murmured. His lap was alive with the sparseness of her hair and street lights rushed to greet them like strings of shining pearls.

ASTRID OF THE LIMBERLOST

Yvonne du Fresne

Our school was divided into many groups, like the nations of the world. Some fought great battles against each other and then made loud treacherous Peace Treaties. These groups were the Gangsters. They spent playtimes and lunchtimes crawling through thickets of hydrangeas and shrubs seizing victims. Cherry Taylor was seized once. Anna Friis crawled into the hydrangeas and grabbed Cherry by her other arm.

'Release your victim, you nincompoop,' said Anna Friis in her cold, still voice. And the Gangsters, confused by Anna's long words, let her go. The Gangsters were always confused by long words. Inside school they drooped and died when it came to the *Journal* readings. We read in turn, one sentence each. A bumpy road it was; first one Gangster – then another – stumbled on in their poor hoarse voices. The first Gangster announced 'Angela's Cold'.

'At first you could hardly tell it was a sneeze, it was such a tiny one.' He dropped into his seat as if he had been shot. Then another Gangster clambered to his feet.

'Angela tried hard to think it was not one; but when it came again, it did indeed seem like a sneeze.'

He too dropped as if he had been shot. Then the biggest Gangster stood up with hunched shoulders like Pretty Boy Floyd. He growled –

'Just then Mother came in and pulled up the blind. "Good morning, Angela," she said, "slip on your dressing gown and run along to the bathroom." '

The Headmaster watched from his table by the fire. The strap lay by his hand. I leaned back and admired the scene. It was straight from *Les Misérables* by Victor Hugo – the flickering light from the fire, the high windows, the grey winter afternoon and a distant sound from the road outside of somebody breaking stones . . .

After the Gangsters had stumbled into silence, a representative of the next group stood up. This was the Grown-Up Girls' Group. She balanced on her high heels, bit her lip and tossed back her Ginger Rogers' hair-do. She wore a great many bits of her

Moder's jewellery and pink fingernails made by colouring them in with a red pencil. She read in a wonderful, highly offended lisp,

'An-ge-la began to say some-thing, but a . . .'

'Middle-sized,' grated the Headmaster.

'Middle-sized,' lisped the Grown-Up Girl, 'sneeze stopped her.'

She tinkled some bangles on her arm.

I regarded her through half-closed eyes. Anna Karenina. A head crammed with pretty trifles, and that railway track at the end. At breaks I hung around the Grown-up Girls, observing them. The Grown-Up Girls longed for their last day at school. And until that day came, they practised. They wore stockings and shoes with highish heels, so they could not run. They spent the breaks slowly writing, in fancy letters, 'By hook or by crook I am first in this book' in each other's autograph albums, and they did each other's hair, absorbed in combing and fluffing, with hairpins clenched savagely in their teeth.

The rest of us, who were not Gangsters or Grown-Up Girls, ranged around looking for something to read. We tried the school library, a small grim storeroom, where the barred windows had ivy growing over them. There were two rows of thick black books. When we picked them up they fell open with a sigh of years and dampness, letting fall small, dead, transparent spiders. My book had on its opening page –

'*What's your name?*'

'*Diggory Trevanock.*'

The whole class exploded. This incident, one of the little pleasantries occasionally permitted by a class master, and which, like a judge's jokes in court, are always welcomed as a momentary relief from the depressing monotony of the serious business in hand, happened in the Second Class of a small preparatory school, situated on the outskirts of the market town of Chatford, intended for the sons of gentlemen.

I shut the book.

But at home, Tante Helga had a little surprise: a whole box of books someone had given her.

'*Girls*' books,' said Tante Helga, 'of the Colonies, the Antipodes and so on.' Already she was deep in a book. She waved vaguely at the heap, while I peeped at the cover of her book. *The Family at Misrule* said letters cleverly constructed from branches of a tree. There was a picture of a gentleman in boots striding out of a house on fire. He had a beaming baby in his arms. Did that baby not know that its house was on fire? Underneath, more tree branches said: by Ethel Turner.

'Try that one,' said Tante Helga in a vague, drugged voice. She gestured at a khaki book with black irises on it. *The Girl of the Limberlost*, said flowing, scarlet letters.

'What is Limberlost?' I asked.

Tante's eyes raced along the lines of her book, her lips moved. She surfaced only enough to give a taste of the family at Misrule.

'Nell is letting down her muslin,' said Tante mysteriously. 'Too young. She is but fifteen. Meg is distressed. Nell walks up and down. Frou-frou go the muslin frills above her shoes. The Cook likes Nell's new long dress.'

'Who is Cook?'

'They are English aristocrats,' said Tante, 'a lady cooks their food. She says things like "La Miss Nell." Now please read your *Limberlost* . . .' Her voice trailed away. She would read without breathing, without food, without sleep, until the book was finished. Then she would be the heroine for two days. Then she would be Tante Helga again.

I started my *Limberlost* saga. I read of a white-faced girl, forced to go to school by her cruel Moder, wearing thick boots, a shabby black hat, and a skimpy calico waist, whatever that was, and carrying a tin bucket with her lunch in it, to a new high school in some place called the city. My eyes raced along like Tante Helga's. The girl Elnora, white-faced, but crowned with shining dark red hair, walked blinded by tears, climbed a snake fence and went along a trail worn by feet of men who guarded the precious timber of the swamp – *with guns*.

'Tante,' I quavered.

'Mmm,' murmured Tante.

'Tante . . .'

Helga raised blind eyes. She murmured, 'Meg has been left to look after the whole family. She teaches the little ones and wrestles with the Cook.'

'Fighting!' My heart stopped.

'Nej, nej,' said Helga impatiently. 'Disputes. About the food that is to be cooked.'

'What did they eat Helga? What did they eat?' Helga looked brighter.

'Lots of meat – boiled meat and roasted meat. The heat in Sydney it is not to be borne. The blow-flies get at the meat. The Cook is angry. Meg is distracted. Then they had . . .' With animation, Helga flipped through the pages. 'Ah!' she said, 'beef-steak pie, sweet potatoes and a Cabinet Pudding. No greens!' said Tante Helga, scandalised.

'In my book,' I said excitedly, riffling pages, 'there is a dainty lunch baked by her kind aunt to make her respectable before her new classmates who wear dainty dresses and hair-ribbons and scorn the Girl of the Limberlost. In her new leather lunchbox. Listen!' I

233

read, getting hungrier and hungrier – '*Half the bread compartment was filled with dainty sandwiches of bread and butter sprinkled with the yolk of egg, and the rest with three large slices of the most fragrant spice cake imaginable. The meat dish contained shaved cold ham of which she knew the quality. The salad was tomatoes and celery and the cup held preserved pear, clear as amber. There were two tissue-wrapped cucumber pickles.* And then she says – Tante Helga? Tante Helga? Listen! This bit says, *She glanced around her and then to her old refuge, the sky. "She does love me!" cried the happy girl. "Sure as you're born my little Mother loves me!"* '

I went to get a drink of water to offset the thought of the cucumber pickle, which would undoubtedly burn the mouth. I read on, leaning against the sink, swigging great gulps of artesian water. Elnora did chores after supper. It was ten o'clock when the chickens, pigs, and cattle were fed, the turnips were hoed and a heap of bean vines was stacked by the back door . . . At four o'clock next morning Elnora was shelling beans. At six she fed the chickens and pigs, swept the cabin, built a fire, and put on the kettle for breakfast . . .

I felt so tired that I went into my room and lay down on my bed to give me strength for the next bit. Worse was to come. To get dress-goods, shoes, hat and books for school Elnora had to comb the swamp, and find moths, butterflies and arrow-heads. These she sold to somebody called the Bird Woman who lived in the city, but the Indian arrow-heads she sold to the manager of the Bank of America. The money gained thereby, Elnora stashed into a hollow log, and brooded a little upon the swamp which was lying in God's glory about her. That night, saying her prayers, she noticed lights flashing by her hollow log, far off in the muck and ooze of the swamp.

I looked at those words, 'muck and ooze', and went to find my Fader.

'Fader,' I quavered, 'where is the Great Swamp?' Fader straightened and swept an arm from horizon to horizon.

'Aw,' he said, 'all around us really. What a time they had!'

'Time?'

'Draining it, and so on,' said Fader cheerfully. 'But those Danes, my word, how they *worked* . . .'

'Fader.'

'Ja?'

'Will we have enough money for me to go High School in the city?'

'Mmm,' said Fader, 'well – you'll have to work your fingers to the bone, be a model child and laugh at all my jokes . . .'

It was enough. I trailed to my bedroom and read a little more. Elnora was weeping to her uncle about her cruel Moder. Her uncle explained – '*You see,' said Uncle Wesley, 'I was the first man there,*

234

honey. She just made an idol of him, your father, I mean. There was that oozy green hole, with thick scum broke and two or three bubbles slowly rising that were the breath of his body. There she was in spasms of agony, and beside her the great heavy log she'd tried to throw him. That's why she just loses control of her soul in the night, and visits that pool, and sobs and calls and begs the swamp to give him back to her . . .'

I shut that book so quickly, and lay and looked at the ceiling. Tante Helga drifted in with *The Family at Misrule* slackly between finger and thumb. Tante Helga was sated with goings-on and happy endings.

'What happened?' I asked glumly.

Tante Helga said in a tired-out voice, 'Ja, well, Nell went to dinner unlawfully at the home of a new-rich neighbour when Meg said Do not go. They are vulgar. Their cook had diphtheria. The only ornament poor Nell wore was a knot of wild-flowers tucked in her bosom. She carried the diphtheria home. Little Esther caught it. Meg caught it. Poor Nell wept in the moonlight and prayed to God that the crisis would come.'

'The crisis was still to *come*?'

'The crisis,' explained Tante Helga with dignity, 'is when the body throws off the poisons of the fever and the skin gleams with sweat. Then they hug each other and praise God. Bunty the boy did not break the school window or steal the five sovereigns and was found months later, washing dishes at a low eating-house in Sydney. The family is happy at last and thanks God yet again.'

'Ah,' I said, and rolled on to my stomach. Tante Helga arose. 'Dinner now!' she said, and went. I noticed she had a small bunch of wild flowers tucked into her bosom.

I gazed bleakly at the distant bush. Tomorrow I would have to start trying to find the Great Swamp of the Manawatu. Then I would start the arduous task of collecting moths, butterflies and Indian arrow-heads, dodging the pool covered with green slime, around which my Moder paced at night calling my Fader's name. I would spy on the flickering lights of the Carson Gang signalling to each other where the best Redwoods were for smuggling out, and finally trudge along the twenty miles to the High School in Palmerston North, carrying my bucket of lunch and a load of Indian arrow-heads carefully bunched in my skirt to sell to the Manager of the Bank of New Zealand, to pay for books, dry goods, and my tuition. It would be a terrible life, but with grit and spunk I would pull through. As I knocked on the door of the Bank of New Zealand I could see a faint curve of sadness on my young lips, half concealing a smile – one for sweet buried childhood, and one for the broadening days.

THE DAY HEMINGWAY DIED

Owen Marshall

YYou'll be wary of too much coincidence I know, but I had been reading a good deal of Hemingway about that time. We weren't doing it in lectures either. The Faerie Queene was what we were doing in lectures. The Faerie Queene is suitable for university study because people wouldn't read it otherwise. The lecture in the afternoon was on arachnid imagery in book two. The lecturer had the habit of lifting his head from his notes and glancing despairingly around the tiered seating, as if he feared we were drawing closer to suffocate him.

It was raining that day, and the streets were softened with it, and the cars hissed by. I rode very slowly because my bike had no front guard, and the faster I went the more water the wheel flicked up at me. So I was in the rain longer, but the water coming down was cleaner than that coming up. When the rain began to run down my face I imagined I was neanderthal, and persevered with sullen endurance. The cars came from behind, and hissed like cave bears as they passed.

Mrs Ransumeen complained if I dripped inside. So I stood in the wash-house and dried off with a pillow case from the laundry basket. I wriggled my toes and they squelched inside my desert boots. I put my feet down very flat when I went inside, so they wouldn't squelch. 'Don't you leave wet socks in your room,' said Mrs Ransumeen.

'I don't really think neanderthal was a dead end,' I said. 'More and more research seems to show that they added to the gene pool that carried on.'

'I'm not doing any washing tomorrow. I'm not.'

'It's subjective I know, but I feel the stirrings of neanderthal at times. Some atavism of the mind I guess.'

'Oh shut your blah,' said Mrs Ransumeen. Her face was like an old party balloon that had been left strung up too long: become small and tired with stretch marks and scar tissue in it. Yet still more air pressure inside than out. Mrs Ransumeen's face was like that; looking blown up and deflated both at the same time.

'For three pounds ten a week I don't have to listen to your rubbish,' she said. 'And I don't have to pick up wet socks from your room either. Stop dripping on the floor will you.'

Mrs Ransumeen had beautiful hair. She had hair that girls would steal for. It was black and heavy. When well brushed it had a secret gleam, like water glimpsed in a deep well. Every woman has something of beauty I suppose.

I went up the stairs, squelching. The party balloon stood at the bottom.

'It's a cold meal,' she said. The rain drifted into the window on the stairway landing. I should've gone back down and had it out with her about one hot meal a day. I owed it to myself, to keep my self-respect. For a moment I thought I could do it.

'Oh well,' I said. 'Yes, okay.' Even neanderthal genes can be recessive.

Neddy's door was open. He was lying on his bed with his hands behind his head. He was grinning at me. As I changed my socks he mocked me through the wall. 'Okay Mrs Ransumeen. Yes Mrs Ransumeen. Cold tea, how delightful Mrs Ransumeen. Let me lick your bum Mrs Ransumeen.' Neddy was an engineering student. He lacked any culture, but had prodigious courage. He even took on the Ransumeens once or twice. Got beaten, but at least he took them on. He had to get worked up to it mind you, with drink, or the desperation of academic failure. He had no culture, but a certain vision of self did Neddy. He had that hopeless courage that arouses both admiration and pity. In all other ways he was even less than ordinary.

The radio in the kitchen was always on. It was on when we came down for the cold meal. The party balloon liked to listen to the talk back shows. She loved to hear people making fools of themselves. 'Listen to that silly bitch,' she said.

'Arp, barp,' went her husband.

'For god's sake stop that face farting all the time,' said Mrs Ransumeen.

'It's natural isn't it? A natural function for christ's sake.' Ransumeen's face was the evasive, plural face of a man who had no self-respect. A face pushed forward by impetuosity without talent, and worn back again by constant disadvantage. It was the face of a man who gets by how he can. It was the face in which you fear to look in case you see yourself.

The radio said that Hemingway had put a shotgun in his mouth and killed himself. 'It's a poor show that's all, if a man can't express his natural functions in his own home,' said Ransumeen. When it said about Hemingway, each object in my line of sight assumed a derisive clarity. There was first the Belgian sausage sandwich on my plate. Its pink edge peeped like a cat's tongue from the uncut side, and the top piece of bread had a smooth indentation in one corner from a bubble in the dough.

'I saw the old tart next door putting rubbish in our can again,' said the party balloon. The salt and peppers were faceted glass with red, plastic tops. The salt had five holes, and two were blocked because of the humidity. What I felt had less to do with Hemingway as a writer, than with the idea that no-one cared if he lived or died anyway. There were better writers than Hemingway, but he was the one who died that day. In homes all over the country there would be the news about Hemingway; and no-one cared. On the bench was a pie dish with water in it to soak the burnt apricot on the bottom; and a biscuit tube of golden macaroons. The price was marked with felt pen on the cellophane.

'Lincoln is always a hard team to beat in the forwards,' said Neddy.

'I'll take all the rubbish I can lay my hands on, and the next time she does it I'll follow that old bitch back and turf it all over her floor.'

'It said Hemingway's dead,' I said.

'Bread,' said Ransumeen. He had his hand out for it.

'Because she lives by herself, she thinks she can do what she likes.'

'And with this rain there'll be a heavy ground all right, and the forwards will tell.'

'I said Hemingway killed himself.'

'Barp, arp. Ah, that's better out than in as the actress said to the bishop.'

I quite like macaroons actually, but the party balloon never put more than two each on the table. When I'm working I can eat a whole packet easily. The first Hemingway story I ever read was 'Indian Camp'. Hemingway wasn't always beating his chest. Mrs Ransumeen had a broad, yellow ribbon in her hair. When she turned aside to criticise her husband her hair had a sheen so dark there were hints of purple, as had the skin of a Melanesian bishop I heard preach once in Timaru. Sometimes I thought her hair must be false, and that underneath was the real hair that suited an ugly woman. Neddy asked if he could have a stronger bulb in his room. He said he couldn't see to do his work, and he had two assignments due that week. 'Oh, you shut up,' said Mrs Ransumeen.

'Yea,' said Ransumeen. 'You shut your cake hole. You're just a boarder here.' Vulgarity was a natural property of the Ransumeens, and to deplore it was like criticising wetness in water or the smell of methane.

The salt sloped high left to low right, and the pepper the other way. It must have happened as Mrs Ransumeen carried them to the table gripped by the tops in the fingers in one hand. The cellars tend to angle out when they're carried that way. The butter had marmite on its top edge like an ink line, and one pendant of water dithered from the cold tap. The radio had finished with Hemingway, and begun on political instability in Italy. It was a lot more important perhaps. I don't know. 'You're not going out tonight,' said the party balloon. Ransumeen gnawed his sandwich and said nothing. It was a silence of hope rather than subterfuge. 'Are you deaf or bloody something?' she said. 'I may have to go out for a bit,' he said. She started on him, but with an underlying boredom from countless victories. Neddy and I went upstairs.

Nothing in my room had changed for Hemingway, and the houses outside looked the same as ever. Mould stains always showed up on the roughcast when it rained and the knuckled camellia bushes moved a little in the drizzle and the wind. Nothing flamed in the sky for Hemingway. Not even an aurora of picadors, or quail in the sun.

Mrs Ransumeen's voice reached a competent fighting pitch. She could sustain it as long as she wished. Her virulence was that of self-pity rather than active hatred. 'And why the hell you can't get some better job anyway I don't know,' she said.

'Ah, for christ's sake,' said Ransumeen.

'S'obvious you won't get anywhere again. We never even get invited anywhere.'

'Who's going to invite us, for christ's sake.' Ransumeen went out, and left her talking.

'That's right. That's right,' she said, 'You bloody go on out. Whether you get back in is another story.' She began banging the dishes in the sink, and talking to the radio again. 'Will you shut your face I say. Prouting on,' she told the announcer. She traded him for a tidal flow of film themes. She seemed to be banging the utensils in time with them.

It was colder in my room as the darkness deepened outside. The bulb of small power seemed to grow even dimmer in the cold. Neddy came in. He wore two jerseys which gave him a stomach. 'The troll has turned off our heaters at the switchboard,' he said. 'It's unbearable.' His hands were yellow with cold, and his fingernails lilac. Mrs Ransumeen had become quiet below. She had laid the snare and was content to wait. 'We can't put up with it. Why should we? We can't work like this,' said Neddy.

'Today I won't stand for it,' I said. Neddy was encouraged by my support.

'Let's have it out with her.' Neddy had a square, practical face and a feeling for natural justice. 'We'll do something about it. The troll has turned the heat off again and it's the middle of winter.' He swayed and marched on the spot, partly to keep warm and partly in rising militancy.

As we went down together, I felt that the day had to be marked in some way. As the lightning wouldn't strike, some risk was necessary on the day that Hemingway died. Mrs Ransumeen sat with her arms laid before her on the table. The twin bars of the kitchen heater glowed. 'Our heaters are off,' said Neddy.

'Yes,' I said. It was a token of our alliance. Mrs Ransumeen's fat arms were dimpled, and spread on the table as if filled with water.

'So,' she said.

'It's cold,' I whined. Hemingway knew all about the cold.

'It's too cold to work in our rooms,' said Neddy.

'Horseshit,' said the party balloon. She began to breathe more noisily through her nose, and she stirred in the chair. She was getting ready to really let go I thought. Neddy and I stood shoulder to shoulder. Then her mood began to change; as visible in its way as a change of weather. Her eyes dulled like the surface of a pond beneath a breeze, and her shoulders settled. Her expression was for a moment surprised as she felt the change spreading from within; the new imperative. Her hands spread out like a star-fish, and despite herself she began to cry. 'Oh I don't know. I just don't know,' she said. As she cried she lifted her hands and began rubbing her face; smearing the tears from forehead to chin. 'Sometimes I just wish to god I was dead,' she said. 'One lousy thing after another. One lousy day after another. A rented house, and a husband who becomes less and less a man.' She stood up, and her breathing was broken with hiccups from her sobbing. She went over to the fridge and opened it. From the rack behind the door she took eggs one by one and flicked her forearm and wrist to send them against the window, the bench, and the cupboards. Her throwing action was restricted, and her defiance half-hearted. The eggs broke with the sound of black beetles being stood on. Mrs Ransumeen seemed to find no relief in doing it, and it shamed us to watch.

It should have been very comic: my landlady throwing eggs in the kitchen on the day that Hemingway died. Yet the thing is that it wasn't in the least funny. On the radio a man explained the importance of mulching shrubs for summer. The party balloon rather dully cast the eggs, and they crushed like beetles. 'Now I've bloody done it,' she said. 'I've started now and I've really done it. He'll notice something when he comes home tonight.'

'Will he ever,' said Neddy softly. He was afraid to disturb her apathy. She began to cry again, and her mouth opened into the speechless square that accompanies the onslaught of tears. She closed the fridge door, and stood with one forgotten egg in her hand.

'Horseshit to it all anyway,' she managed to say. The situation was in advance of her response. She was struggling with a crisis the significance of which didn't provide her with any greater means to confront it. Smashing eggs and crying were the outlets she could think of. Neddy and I left her there. We had nothing to offer as a consolation. Contempt and fear were stronger than our pity. We went quietly up the stairs. Neddy was uncertain.

'I've never seen her like this before. She's packed up properly.'

That's how it was for me on the day that Hemingway died. I had meant to give it all a humorous gloss, and get in a bit of sex; bed springs and muffled cries. That's what people like in a story. But it remains much as it was. Cold and wet, horseshit and broken eggs, no heat in my room and a landlady I disliked crying aloud in the kitchen.

VISITORS

John Cranna

My grandfather was a large man with a strong laugh who grew pomegranates for pleasure, but for reasons that only gradually became clear to me, and certainly were not clear to him, it was felt necessary from time to time to strap him to a bed and apply electric shocks to his head.

When I saw him after his treatment he had difficulty in recognising me, so I stood at his side for a while, repeating my name until the dullness had gone from his china-blue eyes. Although I was only fifteen, I was careful to arrange my face into a mask of apologetic innocence, in fear that he would begin to link my appearance with the treatment he was receiving. When the Pale Suits had gone away he would get up slowly and go out into the garden, where he would walk for a time, occasionally stopping at one of his fruit trees to touch the skin of a pomegranate that had hung there all summer, as though extracting its smooth permanence from the wreckage that had been made of his immediate past.

My grandfather had travelled in the time when this was still possible, and had collected musical instruments from around the Pacific. They stood in the dim corners of the house, or hung on the walls, a great Javanese gamelan in the hallway, and a Chilean lute on a shelf above. In the long afternoons when our visitors worked on my grandfather in the front room, I could hear the instruments in their other lives singing to me. The gamelan I knew well; it sat on the edge of a clearing in the jungles of Java, played by smooth-faced boys, its heavy sound mingling with the trees and the soil. The sound was very clear to me; it lodged in my chest as a kind of ecstasy, and it would only fade when the surge of voices from the front of the house told me that the men had finished with my grandfather. They went then to the kitchen and spoke to my mother, although I could never hear what they said to her. I watched from a window as they walked down the drive, two men in pale suits, one of them carrying an aluminium case, which was laid carefully in the back of the waiting vehicle.

The house and the garden were too large for the three of us who lived there, we had unused rooms, some still locked and containing the possessions of members of the family whose whereabouts were no longer discussed. On one side of the long hall that ran through the house my grandfather and I had our rooms, and on the other, at the furthest end of the hall, was my mother's room, a sanctum that no one was allowed to enter. My mother was a graceful person who moved about the house without ever seeming to touch it, and who each afternoon following lunch would brush my cheek with the lightest of kisses, before retiring to her room for the remainder of the day. After she had gone the long hall held a trace of her perfume, lingering there amongst the instruments, as though the house was reluctant to concede her departure.

At the edge of the orchard my grandfather sat and watched his pomegranates ripen, indifferent to passing showers. In a murmur that carried across the lawn to the house, he spoke endlessly of his years travelling the Pacific in search of instruments for his collection, struggling to prevent the treatment he was receiving from unravelling the thread of his memory forever. I sat beside him on the grass and tried to follow the path of his reminiscences. From Java and the jungles of Indochina it would lead suddenly east to Mexico, then south to the deserts of Chile, before veering west again to the island chains of Micronesia. A story that began in Djakarta might end in Santiago without his being aware that the location had changed, and fragments and characters from one tale would find their way into others, so that his monologues were jigsaws of confusion that held me entranced for hours, but which I could never fully understand.

Some things, however, were clear to me. He had always stayed among the ordinary people, whether it was in the shanty towns of the great cities or in the small, poor towns of the interior. He was obviously welcome in these places, and because of his enthusiasm for the music of the people, instruments would be produced and impromptu concerts arranged. He was often invited to join in the music-making and in this way he became a competent performer on dozens of the instruments he had collected. I could only dimly recall the times from my childhood when he performed for the family in the front room, but I have a clear memory of his large figure stooped forward slightly, playing a lute made from the shell of an armadillo, and holding it so carefully in his arms that he might have been cradling the shell of a massive rare egg. The lute, which was from Chile, now rested in the hallway, where it had remained untouched for many years.

One of my grandfather's remaining clear memories was of his

time in Chile and he told me of the year he had spent there in the northern deserts, studying the ancient music of the Atacameno Indians. The language of their songs, he said, was so old that the performers did not understand it themselves, and he described the strange sound of the great side-blown trumpets that accompanied the performance. He had lived in the home of one of these musicians and he spoke of the stark beauty of the deserts and of the resilience of the people who had lived there since the dawn of time. One day, as we sat in the orchard, he told me with surprise in his voice that he had never been happier than when he was with the Atacameno, but when I asked him why he had left, his eyes dulled and his story slid off once more into confusion.

The men in pale suits were visiting twice a week now, and as I sat there beneath the fruit trees, I heard the quiet sound of their vehicle pulling up at the bottom of the drive. My grandfather fell silent at their footsteps on the gravel, and was suddenly very still in his chair. We could hear the Pale Suits talking with my mother, and then her breathless voice calling to us across the lawn. My grandfather got up and walked slowly towards the house, where our visitors would now be waiting for him in the front room. I waited for a while, then went into the hall and sat there in the gloom amongst the dead instruments. I concentrated very hard, until the loudest sound I could hear was the steady beat of the blood in my ears, then softly, across a great distance, I heard the strains of the lute singing in an Atacameno village, and the music grew stronger and more clear, until I was there among the scatter of low huts, listening to the lute as it cut the thin air of the desert. I saw my grandfather, dressed in the clothes of the Indians, working with them in their carefully irrigated fields on the desert's edge, and returning each night to study their ancient music in the household of a master musician. I saw him crouched by an oil lamp, taking down the music of an evening performance in his notebook, and writing out the unknown language that was used in the ritual songs of fertility and death. And then the lute began to sing of strange Indian tribes my grandfather had never mentioned, the Aymara and the Pehuenche; it sang of their languages, of their music, of the rich collection of myth that held together their pasts, and it sang of their struggle against the lethal promises of a new order that had come recently to their land. I was so absorbed by the tales of the lute that I almost missed the babble of voices from the front of the house that signalled the end of my grandfather's session, but the moment the Pale Suits opened the door into the hall, the lute fell silent again.

When the men were in the kitchen, speaking in their sing-song voices with my mother, I went in to see my grandfather. He lay on the bed, the straps loosened at his sides, staring up at the ceiling with unblinking eyes. An acrid smell hung in the room, and a circular stain lay around him on the sheet. I stood there for a while, listening as the kitchen door closed and our visitors' footsteps receded on the drive. I watched the stain spread out across the bed, and thought, They've embalmed him and the fluid is already beginning to leak out. His body seemed a long way off, as though it was withdrawing into the angles of the room, and I felt a sensation of falling. I put a hand out to the wall, and as I did so my grandfather turned his head to look at me, his face blank and his eyes empty of all life. He made a weak gesture with one hand. 'They're very kind to take so much trouble with me. I feel I should be more grateful...' I had never spoken to him about his treatment before, and now, hesitantly, I asked what they had decided was wrong. He frowned, as though trying to remember a complicated diagnosis that had once been fully explained, but eventually he shook his head and lay back, his eyes fixed once more on the ceiling. Behind me the door opened and my mother came into the room in a cloud of perfume. She opened the curtains with one hand while holding a handkerchief against her face with the other. 'What have you done, father?' she said. 'You know you really can't behave like this in front of our visitors.'

That evening, as though in protest at my grandfather's lack of discretion, she failed to appear for dinner, so the two of us ate alone. Although he had bathed and changed his clothes, a faint odour still hung about him, and when I sat down to eat I found my appetite had gone and I could not bring myself to finish my meal.

It had been six years since my sisters and my father had gone away to the mountains. I was too young to understand at the time, but soon after that the schools closed down and before long the Pale Suits called at our house for the first time. My mother would not allow me to go into the city, so the only Pale Suits I saw on foot were the pair who came to visit my grandfather. At other times I saw them passing the house in their long vehicles, and always they were on the wrong side of the road, driving very fast. When I asked my grandfather about the Pale Suits in their vehicles, he was unable to tell me anything. He was fully occupied, it seemed, with his dissolving past, and the only energy he had left for the present was expended on his orchard. There his pomegranates hung thickly on the trees, the best crop there had been in years, he told me, and the fruit were at the point of cracking from within with their own ripeness.

My grandfather spent many hours in the orchard, inspecting the bark of the trees for disease and the leaves for the first signs of summer blight. Often he would stop and stare at a ripening fruit for a time, touching it with his open palm, before moving on to the next laden tree. The longer his treatment continued, the more important the orchard became to him and sometimes he would call me over to a tree and explain his methods of soil preparation and pruning. It was important, he said, that there was someone to take over the orchard when he could no longer manage it. From the bottom of the orchard I could see the outline of the distant mountains, and I began to watch them more closely, thinking of my sisters and my father, trying to imagine them eating and sleeping somewhere among that jumble of pale shadows.

On the next occasion that the Pale Suits visited, the gamelan sang to me, and it sang from a shanty town on the edge of the great city of Djakarta, the music of its gongs shimmering and dancing in the Javanese dusk. Behind the knot of musicians the shanty town stretched away until it disappeared in the haze of cooking fires. The music of the ensemble was very solemn; it spoke of the land the people had struggled for and lost, of their flight to the city, and of the new poverty they had found there. The steady chime of the gongs reached into the corners of the furthest houses, so that it seemed in the end that the entire shanty town echoed with sadness for a time when better things had been promised, and the promises had come to nothing. As night fell, the music faded into silence, and I saw a small boy, asleep on the dirt floor of a hut, clutching in his arms a perfectly made model of the great gongs my grandfather had spoken of. Although he was fast asleep, he held the gong so tightly to his chest that it was possible to believe it was his only possession in the world. But now that the gamelan had ceased, the shanty town was slipping into shadow, and before long I was back in the gloom of the hall, waiting again for our visitors to emerge, the instruments lifeless shapes around me.

I no longer had the courage to visit my grandfather in his room, so I went out and waited for him by the orchard. Eventually he came across the lawn, moving like a blind man, groping his way to his chair beneath the trees. I watched as he tried to speak, his tongue lolling between thickened lips, and I knew then that if his treatment continued in this way it would eventually silence him altogether. I never thought of discussing any of this with my mother. For some years now she had been so detached that her presence in the house seemed almost accidental. We did not discuss the Pale Suits and my grandfather's treatment because we did not discuss anything of importance. It seemed that some part of her had become too fragile to exist in the world of the Pale Suits, so that she had retreated to the sanctuary of her bedroom, a room whose only concrete reality for me was as the source of the mysterious scents and beautiful clothes she wore.

Then something happened which changed the course of the summer. One evening I looked from my window and saw a glow on the horizon, a glow which flared gradually brighter until it lit up a great section of the central city. At one point I thought I heard the distant sound of explosions. It was nearly dawn before the glow subsided to a dull red. The next day there was increased activity on the road outside, with the long cars of the Pale Suits travelling faster and in greater numbers than I had ever seen. In mid-afternoon there was almost an accident, when a driver approached our bend too fast and had to struggle to keep his vehicle under control. I saw a momentary look of fear on the face of the Pale Suit at the wheel, a look that stayed with me for long afterwards. It had never occurred to me that Pale Suits might be able to experience fear. The activity on the road outside continued into the next day, which was a treatment day for my grandfather, and the two of us sat in the orchard and listened to the steady sound of the passing vehicles. My grandfather was slumped in his chair, watching the drive in silence. Even the most halting reminiscence now seemed beyond him. Flies from the orchard settled on his face and arms and he did not seem to have the strength to wave them away. The hot afternoon stretched out for an age, and to pass the time I counted the vehicles as they took the corner. By dusk I had counted 142 and yet the Pale Suits had still not arrived, so at last we went inside to eat. There was a feeling of unreality about the meal that night, I could not recall the Pale Suits having ever missed a treatment day before.

This feeling continued into the rest of the week as the Pale Suits still failed to call. Outside the vehicles came and went on the road, sometimes alone, sometimes in great convoys, but none of them pulled up in the drive, and by the end of the following week the Pale Suits had missed five treatment days in all. By now I had begun to notice small changes in my grandfather. He moved among the trees in the orchard more freely, his shoulders were straighter and he no longer trailed the faint smell of urine that once had followed him about the house. Before long his reminiscences began again, and now they were a little easier to follow. Tales that had once baffled me with their shifting locations and broken plots started to hang together, as though a fragile thread had begun to run among the scattered pieces of his memory. Some of his stories stirred in me a strange feeling of recognition, as though I had heard them before but when too young to remember or to properly understand. He spoke of his voyages among the endless atoll chains of Micronesia; he told me of the time he had contracted a rare strain of malaria in the Mariana Islands and of being paralysed by village liquor in Guam. The liquor had been drunk at a celebration to mark his mastery of the rare stomach bow after months of apprenticeship to the leading musician on the island. He had lain in a coma for ten days, and, on coming to, had been presented with one of the oldest bows on the island, cut from hibiscus wood and strung with finest pineapple fibre. Through some special reasoning that was never explained to him, his coma had been taken as a sign of exceptional suitability for the instrument.

My grandfather told his stories with a new vigour now. There was no stopping him once he had begun on a tale, as though the long months of his treatment had diverted his memories into a dammed lake of the imagination, and the obstruction that had been holding them back had now been cleared away. Instruments which had lain in dusty corners of the house for years and whose origins had been a mystery to me became suddenly recognisable – I identified the stomach bow from Guam at once. The instrument hung in one of the unused rooms, a length of curved wood with a split gourd halfway down its length. My grandfather explained that the gourd was placed against the musician's stomach to amplify the vibrations of the fibre string. From his tales I also identified a shawm from Guatemala, a nose flute from Truk and a log drum from the Philippines.

We would sit in the orchard until after dusk, the trees turning to dim shapes around us, the line of distant mountains catching the last of the light, as my grandfather exercised his returning memory and the fruit flies gathered in clouds above our heads. It was very peaceful there in the orchard, the vehicles on the road outside were another world away, and I began to believe that the Pale Suits had bypassed us, that we no longer had any place in their scheme of things. We had come to a silent agreement not to discuss this, however, for fear that we might alter some delicate balance of invisible forces that was keeping them away.

My mother was unaffected by the absence of the Pale Suits. She came and went in the house in the way that she had always done, appearing in the morning and for meals and retiring to her room for the rest of the day. The house, however, had changed. The windows now let in more light, the dust on the floor did not seem so thick, and the doorways of the unused rooms no longer gaped like mouths onto the hallway. The house was breathing again. I could sense the sweeter air moving among the rooms and, although the instruments were no longer singing to me, they rested more easily in their corners and on their shelves. I felt sometimes that the instruments were beginning to replace my sisters and my father, and I thought of them as more real in some ways than those distant members of my family who had gone away to the mountains so many years before.

In the orchard my grandfather's pomegranates had reached their full maturity, and the branches of the trees bent almost to the ground with the weight of the fruit. The days had come to taste the first of the fruit and we decided to hold a small celebration to mark the occasion. We set up a table under the trees and spread it with a white cloth. My grandfather laid out two plates and a cutting-board, and I hunted through the drawers until I found the sharpest knife in the kitchen. We knew which of the pomegranates we would choose; we had been watching it for weeks. It hung on a tree near the bottom of the orchard, perfectly formed and with an unmarked skin of deep crimson. My grandfather took the fruit from the tree, placed it in the middle of the cutting-board, and we sat down facing each other across the table. We had agreed that I would carve the pomegranate and he would be the first to taste its flesh. When I cut into the fruit I thought that I had never seen a brighter splash of red, and the juice ran in rivulets across the board and stained the white of the tablecloth. My grandfather lifted the pomegranate to his mouth and bit into the flesh, his hands trembling a little as they always did when he ate. I was watching the pleasure spread across his face, when a movement in the direction of the house caught my eye. At the edge of the orchard, standing very still and watching us intently, was a Pale Suit. My grandfather was so engrossed in the fruit that he did not see the expression on my face, he went on eating the pomegranate until he had finished it, while I sat there across the table from him, unable to take my eyes from the stain of the juice on the white tablecloth.

When they had gone inside with my grandfather, I dragged the table around the house and placed it under the windows of the front room. By standing on the table I could reach the level of the window, and although the curtains were drawn, I found that by positioning the table carefully I was able to see a part of the room. At first I could not pick out any details, but as my eyes began to adjust I made out my grandfather's feet on the end of the bed, shoeless and still. Beyond his feet something winked in the gloom of the room, and after a while I realised that it was the light catching the turning reels of a tape machine. I stood there, mesmerised by the reels, my face against the window, and I might still have been there when the curtains were thrown back, if a pale shape had not moved between the machine and the window and broken into my trance.

I carried the table back to the orchard, and set out the cloth and plates as we had left them. Then I went inside to where the stomach bow hung on the wall. I concentrated on the instrument, listening for the hum of its fibre string. Nothing disturbed the quiet of the room. I tried again, straining into the silence, searching for the echo of the distant atolls, and knowing now that it was more important than ever to communicate with the instruments. But the bow would not sing to me; it remained mute and still on its hook on the wall, and I realised then that in my weeks away from the instruments I had lost my old intimacy with them, and I did not know how I was going to close the gap that now separated us. I thought of the pale shapes moving in the gloom, of the turning reels of the tape machine, of the other, unseen contents of the aluminium case that our visitors always brought with them. And I thought about the change that had come over them while they had been away. The Pale Suits had been impassive before; they had come and gone without showing any sign of emotion in their work. But there was something different about them now, a new tension, as though a deep anger lay behind their bland faces. Our visitors were in the front room for longer than I could ever recall, and eventually, exhausted by the knowledge of their return and by my attempts to rouse the instruments, I fell asleep on the floor of the unused room. Much later I seemed to hear the sound of my mother calling, and because she was calling something that was strange to me I could not decide whether I was dreaming. I lay still, and after a long pause I heard her voice again and realised that I was awake and that she was calling to my grandfather in the orchard. I got up and went outside to where the evening light had begun to illuminate the back garden. When I saw the orchard I stopped. Not a single pomegranate remained on the trees. In the middle of the orchard, swaying slightly on his feet, was my grandfather, and around him in all directions lay the remains of the crop of pomegranates. In his hands he held a heavy stick, and his shoes were crusted and stained from trampling the fruit as they lay on the ground. He was squinting into the trees, inspecting each in turn to make sure that he had not missed any of the fruit, and then he threw down the stick and walked past me towards the drive. He stumbled a little, regained his balance and went off down the drive like a blind man, leaving behind him in the gravel a trail of seeds and red pulp. I saw my mother, pale and motionless, watching us from the porch. She seemed to be looking past the wreckage of the orchard to the mountains beyond, and I knew then that she was thinking of the others, but I could not tell from her face whether she believed we would ever see them again. Then she turned and went back into the house. My grandfather was nearly at the road now and I ran after him down the drive. Although the traffic had fallen off a little in recent days, the road was busy, and the great vehicles of the Pale Suits still came and went at speed. I had almost reached the bottom of the drive when my grandfather crossed the pavement and went out onto the road. A vehicle that had just rounded the corner made a wide arc to avoid him, its horn blaring and its tyres crabbing on the asphalt. My grandfather followed it with vacant eyes as it pulled to a halt further down the road. The driver looked back at us through his rear window. By now I had my grandfather by the elbow and was leading him to the pavement. I raised an arm to the driver in the hope that he would drive on. As I led my grandfather back up the drive, I heard the vehicle pulling away into the stream of traffic. Back at the house my grandfather sat in the kitchen looking into space. He did not move or speak for several hours, and eventually I had to lead him like a sleep-walker to his bed.

As though making up for lost time the Pale Suits returned the next day and on this occasion they brought their vehicle to the top of the drive. When they got out I saw why. On the back seat, in place of the usual case, there was a much larger case made of the same bright aluminium and heavy enough to need both of the men to lift it. They were too concerned with getting the case into the house to notice the condition of the orchard. They carried the case down the passage and past the gamelan to the front room, and as they did so I imagined I heard the low chime of a gong, as though the instrument had been brushed in passing. My grandfather sat in the kitchen, watching the Pale Suits come and go, his blue eyes sharp and feverish. When the front room was ready the Pale Suits came into the kitchen and waited for my grandfather to get up. He remained in his chair, his arms limp before him on the table. The three of them seemed to be there an age, the men standing silent by the door and my grandfather motionless in his chair.

At last he got to his feet and went out into the hall, and I knew then that his resistance was over, that his last defence lay in the wreckage of the orchard and that the Pale Suits would now be able to do with him what they wished. When the door to the front room had closed behind them the house became very quiet and I tasted the stale air moving once more through the unused rooms, ebbing and flowing among the inert instruments. Then from the hallway I heard the chime of the gamelan, and as I listened it came once more, a low echo on the dead air. The instruments were waking again, and they had not waited for me to try to reach them first. The chime of the gamelan was solemn and regular now, welling up through the house like a heartbeat, until I could feel it through the soles of my feet and sense its heavy pulse in the pit of my belly. I saw again the shanty towns of Djakarta, the smoke haze low over the huts, and my grandfather sitting cross-legged in the circle of gamelan players; and then through the sound of the gamelan like a sharpened blade came the pure tone of the lute, singing from the deserts of Chile, telling of the ancient music that anchored the past of the people against the shifting sands of the desert. And now other instruments were waking and crowding in on the lute; I heard the sigh of the Guatemalan shawm and the rapid beat of the Filipino log drum. Instruments that had never sung before were breaking their years of silence, emerging from their dusty corners of the house for the first time in order to jostle for place in a chaotic rising choir. The air around me was alive with rhythms that broke in on other rhythms, with melodies that surfaced briefly before being drowned by the surge of some new voice joining the chorus, as instruments struggled to find their true voices after years of disuse. Slowly the milling sounds began to take on some order, the instruments were beginning to complement each other, as though fumbling their way towards a common voice. And then they began to sing in concert, sometimes one taking the lead, sometimes another. They sang of the howl of the typhoon in the tin roofs of the great shanty towns of the East, of the blinding rains and steaming heat; they sang of the harsh lives of the shanty town dwellers and of the peasant farmers on their meagre plots of land. I heard then of the hopes of the people for another life, of their struggle to make a new, better order from the old...and suddenly the music of the instruments grew dark and discordant, and the gamelan sang of blood on the grass of the teak forests of Java, the lute spoke of burning huts in the Chilean deserts, and the drum beat out the rap of midnight fists on the doors of Filipino slums.

And like shadows appearing in the cities and in the countryside, I saw men in pale clothing who emerged from the dusk, who stood on street corners and listened in market-places, who went quietly among the people with their soft, sing-song voices, watching and waiting, and who moved when they were ready with deadly swiftness to still the struggles of the poor. I knew then as the dark chords of the music swirled around me that my grandfather had been touched by these things, that his life of travel among the peoples of the Pacific, the secrets he had learnt from them, the music he loved and its sacred place at the heart of their cultures – all this had eventually led him to the dim front room of his own house, where the pale figures of our visitors attended him on a urine-soaked bed, while a lifetime's knowledge slipped through his mind like water through sand.

At that moment the chorus of instruments stopped abruptly and I heard the door of the front room burst open and the sound of feet in the hall. The Pale Suits stood in the doorway, looking about them at the silent instruments. One of the men wore gloves of pale rubber that came halfway up to his elbows. The Pale Suit with the gloves went over to the stomach bow and gently plucked its fibre string. The instrument gave out a low, dull sound, as though it had hung there untuned and unplayed for twenty years. He listened as the note faded into the corners of the room, watching me closely as he did so. 'A young musician,' he said. 'Following in the footsteps of his grandfather.' The Pale Suit walked among the instruments, sometimes running a gloved finger across a dusty body or plucking a slack string. When he had finished his inspection he stood once more in the doorway with the other man, gazing thoughtfully around the room. Then he turned and the two of them went back down the hall to the front room.

Later I sat in the chair at the edge of the ruined orchard and watched the Pale Suits load the instruments into their vehicle. First they packed the gamelan, after dismantling it into its various pieces, and then added the stomach bow, the lute, and the Filipino log drum. When they had stripped the house of the last of its instruments they climbed into the vehicle, backed slowly down the drive and moved off in the direction of the city.

I set off for the mountains that night; travelling only by darkness and avoiding the roads, I estimated that it would take me ten days to reach them. I did not know how I would find my sisters and my father when I got there, or even whether they were still alive, but I knew that I could not stay to watch the final decline of the house. I saw it then as the Pale Suits would eventually leave it, gutted and open to the weather. I saw the wind lifting the iron of the roof, the rain beating through open windows onto the floor... I saw my grandfather wandering through its empty rooms and I saw him going out to sit by a blackened orchard overgrown with weeds, freed at last of the intolerable burden of his memories.

DISCONTINUOUS LIVES

Barbara Anderson

I am pouring the tea at my cousin's house after her funeral and there are many special requests. – No milk please, just a dash, is there a stronger one, where's the sugar. But that is how it is wherever I am pouring so why not at a funeral. We have brought extra cups. There are green ones with primroses, wine-coloured ones with gold rims and Andrea's blue and white. Most people have one by now, the women that is, the men have whisky. Amber curls in each glass for comfort for that is how it is at funerals, though maybe a sherry later for some of the girls. Another cousin, Maureen, says into my ear as I turn my head checking for cupless female hands – That's Morris Baker.

– Morris who? I say, then remember. – Morris Baker! Where?

– Over there, Maureen points.

– But it's a woman!

– Didn't you know? A pseudonym.

– No! Goodness me, how extraordinary, and I have to re-group, my cousin's silver-plated teapot left hanging because I am so surprised, like when I found Auden's 'Lay your sleeping head my love' was written to a man, to say nothing of Shakespeare's sonnets. Why not, and many men have most beautiful hair but it is a different head I see laid human on that faithless arm, and now Morris Baker.

Morris Baker is a large woman, deep bosomed. It finishes not far above her belt having swelled out at the usual place. She wears an expensive easy-care which has small purple and black checks. Her dark-grey hair is swept back from her strong features and her expression is serene and what on earth is this world-famous novelist (albeit of yesteryear) doing at Diane's funeral on Bluff Hill, I gasp.

– Didn't you know? says Maureen again. – She was born in the Bay, at Clive.

– No indeed. Fancy that. Fancy *A Man In Grey, A Nettle Grasped, Whither Stranger* and all the rest of them coming from *Clive*, for heaven's sake!

– No no no, says Maureen, rescuing the teapot which has begun to dribble onto Diane's brown carpet of which she was so proud. – They left years ago, went back to England, her parents were English, they got fed up. It must have been after you left. I can remember when she went. What a party, she was a beautiful girl.

– And still is. How amazing, I must meet her. Why is she out?

– There's a brother or something. She lives in Burford now, you know in England.

But this cannot be. I lived in Burford for years and if anyone came from New Zealand, let alone a famous novelist (I was there in yesteryear), I would have met her because everyone would have said – There is another New Zealander living in Burford you must meet her.

Whether you want to or not.

– Perhaps it had an E or something, says Maureen.

– Yes perhaps, though I am puzzled.

By now people are coming back for second cups and I am pouring again and reboiling the kettle and Morris Baker has to keep.

We stack the cups on the steel bench, looking out over the grapefruit tree which did well for us all because Diane was generous. – We'll do them later, we say, nodding wisely at the cups and saucers and each other. We know what to do. I wipe my hands on a tea towel I sent Diane from Burford which has a picture of Anne Hathaway's cottage on it and move back to the front room which is crowded with my cousin's friends and relations. A neighbour shows me the spot where he found my cousin. – It was *there*, he says, pointing. – There. I stare at the carpet beneath his craggy finger and nod. – Yes, I say. Yes.

There is quite a lot of noise by now. – Diane would be pleased, we say, but do we know. We know she liked people and parties. – Where would I be without my friends, she would ask as we arrived with another jar of soup to stuff in her refrigerator and always on New Year's Eve she let her hair down but we still don't know. Like when middle-aged children say at a parent's demise, Mother would hate to have been a nuisance. Have they seen it in writing.

Morris Baker is by the window, the neighbour is pointing at the carpet, Morris Baker is nodding. I move over quickly, my hand outstretched. – Hello, I'm Elaine Wilkinson, I just want to say I've always loved your books. Morris Baker is pleased. She puts down her empty cup which we must have missed and holds out her hand. I remember from Burford about women shaking hands, it does not happen in Napier so much though occasionally, prize-givings for example. Her hand is warm and soft, the bones beneath are strong. If Morris Baker shakes hands like this in Burford the ladies must be surprised and I bet she does. She smiles at me, a beautiful warm wide embracing smile. Her eyes are large and brown and I am delighted to meet her and this shows as we beam at each other holding hands.

– Which book did you like best? asks Morris Baker. – *Whither Stranger*, I say. – Yes that is my favourite, she replies.

– Tell me what you meant at the end did Rupert...

Morris Baker flings back her smooth coiled head to laugh deeply. – Ah no, she says, you mustn't ask me that, how do I know.

There is too much noise.

– Come into the spare room, I say, so we move to the door into the hall, touching people gently to show respect for my cousin Diane who is dead.

The hall is narrow and empty, there are coats on the hooks and a beater which someone brought for the cream but didn't need lies on the carpet. The telephone my cousin loved sits round-shouldered and silent, grieving on its table.

My cousin was not a believer. She was bonny and blithe and good and gay and saved me when I returned from Burford in despair, having tried matrimony and failed.

Morris Baker and I have reached the spare room. It is very simple. Every penny my cousin Diane had she earned in the library, unqualified and cheerful. There are two single beds covered in a glazed chintz 'all over' pattern of pink rosebuds and blue ribbons which loop and scroll to encircle each bud. She made these on her ancient Singer inherited from Auntie Dot when the more affluent were converting them into wrought-iron Outdoor Tables. She frilled the valances and attached them firmly so that the crass hot pink of the sprung base was hidden. She ran up the curtains. All this I know and ignore as Morris Baker and I sit one on each bed knee to knee though mine are higher and we continue our in-depth discussion of Morris Baker's books.

– I always thought that you left the ending of *Whither Stranger* so *unresolved*, I say.

– Well of course.

– Yes I know. I mean I know you meant to but...

Morris Baker laughs an in-depth gurgle of pleasure. She stabs a hand down the front of her dress and produces a small white handkerchief. I am not to be put off.

– I know you meant to, I say, leaning forward with my hands

257

on my knees, but I still think... I mean we don't even know if Rupert *stays*.

Morris Baker dabs at the end of her dry nose with her handkerchief.

– I have left you, that is the reader, she says, imaginative space.

– Yes I know and I like that, I say, – but don't you think that in this case you might have just... The unspoken word 'cheated' stains the silence. I have gone too far. I am now an anxious placating figure, a shadow of that switched-on bibliophile whose behind creased the roses opposite Morris Baker's.

But Morris Baker is an old pro, a trouper, she takes the rough with the smooth, she wins some she loses some, she rides with the punches, she takes it on the chin and comes back fighting.

– How can you, she says, smiling with large white teeth (I envy to gut bitterness those with the white sort) – How can you say in the same breath that you like imaginative space and yet you feel I've cheated by leaving you, the reader, just that.

– Goodness me! I gasp. I didn't say that.

– No you didn't say it, says Morris Baker, but I heard it.

This is better than ever. Morris Baker is an opponent worthy of the steel of one who has slogged through extramural English and a hard time we had of it I'm here to tell you.

– What I meant was, I say laughing with my yellow teeth for amiability, what I meant was that I think there is a difference between the author leaving the reader imaginative space and just not knowing... Again the words melt and fizzle. The cut and thrust of literary criticism is one thing, a tea-pourer being rude to a famous author at her friend's funeral is another. How can I say '... not knowing how to finish'.

– Not knowing how to finish, says Morris Baker.

I toss my head to show how merry my laugh is. The curls bounce in the three-sided mirror attached to the dressing table. I look away quickly and focus instead on three mats embroidered by my late cousin which lie upon its horizontal surface. The larger one lies in the middle, a smaller supporter graces each side. Embroidered upon each is a lady in a crinoline. Three faces are hidden by poke bonnets, three flesh-pink mini hands hold parasols, six tiny feet wade among buttonhole stitch forget-me-nots, lazy daisies, and blades of single stitch grass. The two smaller mats have proportionally smaller ladies but the blossoms of their flowering fields are the same size. Each mat is edged with crochet in a colour called ecru. As a diversion from Morris Baker's acuteness I heave myself up from the bed and hold up the large mat.

– Diane made these, I say.

– Good Lord, laughs Morris Baker.

This comment has the small shock of a cobweb in the face. It clings. It won't do. I brush it away.

– Tell me about your life, I babble. When did you leave the Bay? What was your real name?

– Beryl Hollings, she says.

The years slough off, a crumpled discard. – Beryl, Beryl, I scream, seizing her hands. – I'm Elaine Nimmo! We are hugging and laughing and laughing and, No, Go on, Of course, Of course, I knew I knew you, we lie, but not quite, I did have a feeling. We laugh some more, touching for warmth, touching for contact, touching for old times and remembering and for the wonder of our lives and reunion after so long when we had almost forgotten we existed, the other one that is.

They were different the Hollings, being English for a start.

And they weren't at Clive as Maureen said, just Greenmeadows like we were, but too far to bike so Beryl and I played together on parent-arranged visits, the worst sort.

– Aw hang Mum do I have to go, it smells. It is not the smell which worries me but I don't know how to express unease, and hope to touch a sympathetic chord. My mother dislikes smells. – It *whats*? – Smells. – Nonsense! My mother lifts her head momentarily from her bedmaking demonstration. Her hands continue their origami-like pleating and tucking of the blankets; she insists on hospital corners. – What a fuss pot, she laughs. I spot the contradiction, but though hospital corners may defeat me I know about answering back.

The Hollings' house did smell; a close, layered smell, airless and nicotined. The french doors never opened onto the wide verandah except for the huffing exit of Dinky the canker-eared spaniel.

They had brought their things with them from Home and crammed them into the small square rooms. The Drawing Room was the worst. A mahogany bureau faded beside a brass-bound sea chest (male) and a small davenport (female). Occasional tables teetered at a touch. There was no room to move. – No space, no space, moaned Mrs Hollings, drifting and dreaming of height and width, of gentler suns and softer airs. She cut up cucumbers and 'applied' them to her pale skin. She did what she could.

Captain Hollings was a small explosive man described by my Uncle Bob as a no-hoper and thus watched with interest as he stumped about clutching a stick for support. He had lost a leg in

259

the war. Where? How?

The Captain rose late. His pretend leg, its attachment end slack-jawed and empty, waited beside his disordered bed as he made a good breakfast and Beryl and Mrs Hollings scurried in and out with replacements in response to his roars. – Marmalade! – Toast! Dinky lay at his feet, a golden lump beneath the eiderdown, buried deep in his foetid smell.

After several false starts Beryl and I became friends. My father and I swept up the drive in the Buick, hammered the bored lion's head knocker against the door till Mrs Hollings, distracted and unnerved by any summons, yanked the door open, her fingers fluttering against her mouth for protection. She apologised for everything, anything, the stuck door, her apron, the lack of decent rain for the farmers, her very existence. She made me want to cry. My father waited hat in hand and departed as soon as possible. Beryl appeared behind her mother and stuck her tongue out at me in greeting. Her mother's hunted glance fell on us. – Well now chicks what would you like to play? There was no need to answer. We skidded to the heavy-lidded chest in the back hall full of the Captain and Mrs Hollings' discarded finery, presumably also shipped from Home. I wore black velvet and a solar topee. Beryl sailed along the concrete paths in front of me trailing green lace, clumping along in ankle-strap Minnie Mouse shoes, her head high as we progressed towards Making Up, our discontinuous unwritten lives beneath the lemon tree.

– Where had we got to? she asked on arrival, adjusting the set of the peplum above her knees.

– You're still in the cave, I said. – I haven't broken free yet.

– Well hurry up, said Beryl, sitting down in butter box confinement.

Our real life was carefully hidden at school. We were in the same class, with Miss Lynskey who taught me right from left and ran a ballot for the class monitor. We voted according to sex and sycophancy. I voted for Beryl who voted for Ann Henare who voted for Glenys Ashwood who voted for the next girl up.

My visits to the Hollings increased in frequency. Happy, wreathed in night smells, we lay in our narrow beds telling. – I'll tell if you tell. I flaunted my double-jointed thumbs. Beryl skited her tap steps. We swapped comics, *Dick Tracy* for *Phantom*. We investigated Romance, our stomachs flat on the sun-baked verandah. ('She has dirtied her face to hide her beauty,' cried the Sultan. 'This shows intelligence. A rare thing in a slave girl.') We attached one end of a long rope to a hook on the verandah wall. –

Your turn, bossed Beryl. I swung the other end yelling – Apple jelly jam tart/Tell me the name of your sweetheart/A,B,C,D . . .

Beryl jumped, then tripped sprawling on the hot wood at M. – Mervyn, I squealed, – Mervyn Colley's your boy. Mervyn with purple painted school sores who squinted in the front row and still couldn't see. Beryl's bush of black hair shook as she leapt at me. I turned to flee and cannoned into Mrs Hollings' wet apron.

– Elaine, she gasped, winded. – Beryl, look who's here.

We stared at my cousin Diane in her frock with apples on it, five years younger, smiling and golden. We untied the rope, hooked it round her shoulders and ran her deep through the garden behind the garage to the lemon tree. Her cheeks were pinker than ever from the enforced gallop. She glowed with pleasure, proud to play with the big kids. Beryl moved to me, stiff fingers shielding her secret.

– The Ward of the Sultan is in our power! she hissed.

– Yes!

– We'll tie her up.

– Yes! Yes!

– For ever. Beryl's usually pale face was scarlet. My legs were hot with excitement. My cousin smiled, safe as houses. Beryl seized one end of the rope and we twirled the captive around twisting and tugging, one at each end. – She is our slave. – Yes! – For ever! My heart was bonging, too big for its space.

– She can take your father's toast in! I screamed. Diane's smile faltered. She tried to reach out a hand to me. Beryl slapped it back and tugged harder on the cords. – Eelaine, panted my cousin.

– And help him on with his leg! shouted Beryl.

– No! squealed the terrified child. We dragged the struggling kicking bawling four-year-old to the post of the clothes line and slammed her against it, my knee in her stomach my hands busy while Beryl loosed and retied the rope. We cobbled the ends together, our fingers tense and eager. My pants were wet with mob violence, my throat harsh with blood lust. Diane's eyes never left my face.

– Eeelaine! Eeelaine! she sobbed. 'The bleating of the kid excites the tiger.'

– Shut up, I said, my face stiff with rejection.

– Mum! screamed my cousin with the hysterical despair of the betrayed.

– Belt up! said Beryl, her hands tugging at the knots.

– Or we'll sock you! I yelled, jumping up and down in damp chilling delight.

All this Morris Baker and I remember as we sit facing each other in the still room and our relationship shifts and slides and does not resettle. Author and reader, admired and admirer have vanished from my cousin's sparsely-furnished lovingly-furbished spare room. The room is empty. There is no sound.

Morris Baker's strong left hand, the nails pink and curved, touches her powdered cheek. The hairs on her arms are no longer dark like they used to be. Her ear lobes are rounded and puffy, modelled from play dough, the chunky gold earrings too heavy for old ears. Her handkerchief is a tight ball.

   – Do you remember . . . says Morris Baker.
   – Yes, I say. Yes, I do.

AN ANGEL ENTERTAINS THEATRICALS

Anne Kennedy

(*Acquiring angels*)

A woman, human, going about the world all in her arms and legs and her trunk and her best head, and everything functioning apart from the little stumps where wings once were, found two angels, one of flesh, the other stone; and she took these angels to her in a manner which might have suggested she would never let them go. But perhaps this was truer said of the stone angel. And because she was a writer she said, 'Everything I write for the rest of my life will contain angels.'

And it did, but it will not.

(*Word made flesh*)

She once thought there was one writer who had existed in the whole history of the world; that the desire to write was one idea, like any other idea, like the spreading of wings in the presence of a vision, like the touching of skin in the presence of a person; a moment, never to be repeated.

And how could it be that many people had come to this idea at the same time, come to it quite independently of each other? The woman preferred to think that one person wrote once, and that was writing. That is writing. And perhaps it was she and perhaps it was not. Is not.

And if it is, that is because there are words and flesh and they must be seen to be the same because they are the same; everything is linked, there is nothing that is not linked. And there is nothing quite like the contents of her head for making these things the same, for making them into angels, which are, anyway, almost nothing.

And like nothing they will not go away, and that is at once the greatest paradox and the most annoying thing in this world – that a thought is nothing but it cannot be destroyed.

And it is the same with angels.

(*The afternoon of an angel*)

He often asked her what she was thinking about, but it was

impossible to tell. (Once he complained that the blurb on the back of a book of women's fiction said, 'What women are writing *about*' (his italics). 'It should say "What women are writing",' he said). She said, 'I am not thinking about anything, I am just thinking.'

(A declaration of the independence of wings)

She was once a member of a choir aloft, this as a child dressed in the cast-off beliefs of her older siblings. Later she said she would write of angels for the rest of her life, because someone had to and it had fallen to her, from God, like a vocation; there was no question of choice in these matters, the physical matter of what angels are made of. Not that she would write of angels exclusively, but there would always be an angel hovering, like a motto in winged letters, its span of attention across the apex of a building.

But although she *said* this, there did come a time when she let herself be persuaded by certain people (people with an umbilical cord never severed from Heaven (or from Earth)), and also by the events in her life, the strangeness in her flat to do with electric lights and their own *a cord*, and also the painful beating of wings confined within her soul, attacking it from the inside as if it were her heart; a soul attacked by something approaching angles – persuaded that angels should not be in her possession, whether stone or flesh. And this started her thinking, and she thought, How everything is linked!

And it is; there is nothing that is not linked.

And like thoughts, they were not easy to put aside, these angels. Like the stacking of plastic containers – the obsessive collection of what will never go away, their everlasting lives in rubbish dumps – the angels were impossible to dispose of.

This despite the fact that everyone she knew wanted the stone angel for themselves – even the other angel, the one clothed in human flesh; he wanted it. But she found that if she were to part with the angel (stone), on account of the idiosyncrasies it left in its flight-path, the vapours, it could not be to anyone she knew, who would out of the blue give her reports of it, a description of the greenness of the moss growing on its one whole wing.

Also, they did not want it enough in that they do not now *have* it, these dilettantes, their half-souled attempts to possess it no more than a passing fancy for an angel. They did not want it as she had wanted it. Right from the beginning she had wanted the angel (stone) so much her determination to get it would have known no bounds. Nothing would have stood in her way.

And it did not.

(*The angel of the Lord viewed at a sharp tilt*)

There was one person who did not want the angel and that was the man who had first given it to her. Like certain saints he had entered the over-populated order of the recluse, and he existed in the Waitakeres where mists were his intimate friends. And even the inhibited presence of an angel – not speaking, eating, or asking anything of him – would have been an invasion on a scale of choirs visiting at Christmas together with the thronging crowds of their carols.

When she first laid eyes on the angel (stone), it was standing at the top of a flight of steps at the top of a steep incline; and it seemed to the woman, ascending towards it, that it was about to fall on her from a 45-degree angle.

(And a man she had just met had written, '*The angle of your hair will be an education*,' and another man, who gave her a quotation every time she saw him, said, '*Not Angles but Angels*.')

And even though it did not fall on her, the angel, there was something of the calamitous, the divine, and also of the familiar about its particular slant. It was as if she had known it all her life and she threw out her hands, involuntarily, in a mirror image of its wings.

And its owner, her friend – who had taken the angel first from a Devonport cemetery which had been mown into rubble (as if someone had mistaken it for a lawn cemetery) to Grey Lynn, and then to the Waitakeres to mark not a death but the possession of land – said to her straight away, immediately, with no pause for thought, that she could have it. This as if she were a member of the royal family and, according to custom, anything she expressed a liking for must be given her. She could have the angel, and take it away with her, that day, back to town.

And although there was no need to, because of the manner in which it was given, it was the first object she had ever coveted in her life; had wanted more than anything, more than the moment of wanting itself; even that she would have given for it. On a scale of wanting, played on a piano pitching between the snowy lowlands and the sharp angles of the black-capped alps, the angel was at the extremity, where the air is thin and things are desired because they are necessities: words, flesh, angels. She embodied the angel and all the words in its wake.

And accordingly she drove it back to town, and walked in on a lunch party thrown by her flatmate on a Sunday (it hitting her between the eyes); and the Party was engaged to move the angel from the boot of the car. And mid-air there was some discussion about where it should land, on the terrace or at the bottom of the garden, and the woman was in favour of the terrace where it could be seen from all angles, but her flatmate – also the owner of the house, the terrace, the garden and all the air above it reaching up into the sky, and also the earth beneath tunnelling through to Spain – was greatly of the opinion that it should reside at the bottom of the garden, among trees. Having proved herself not an ardent fan of the angel (a man), his nocturnal visits, this moving-in of an angel (stone) would perhaps be a constant reminder of his presence; or his actual presence, the object of it.

And so it was stationed at the bottom of the garden among all lunch-time admirers and was dappled by the sunlight of their various gazes. A garland of flowers encircled its inclined head; its gown fell to its bare feet, undisturbed by the wind; its right index finger, held aloft and pointing heavenwards as if to prevent the dead ending up in Spain, was but a flight-path, as the angel had at one time sustained the loss of its lower arm; also the tip of a wing.

Next morning it was found on its side, felled by the will of the other woman during the night. Its gown still hung straight down, demurely, unconcerned by gravity; the embodiment of softness in stone.

But this object, even though it is stone, substance, of the physical – it is, after all, an *angel*.

(The wings of a mosquito disturb an angel sleeping)

According to the Penny Catechism, which in 1968 was converted to decimal currency along with the sweeping changes the Caretaker Pope had instigated after Vatican II, his late-spring cleaning, angels do not sleep, nor do they think, nor do they procreate; they merely sing.

Once in a tent in the upper North Island, the woman and a man were plagued all night by swarms of mosquitoes – this after the locusts, the drought, and the floods of tears. While she slept fitfully, her face covered with a gin-soaked handkerchief they had earlier thought might deter the insects, he held the naked flame of a candle against one mosquito after another, and watched them explode into choirs of black notes. She thought, sleepily, this might be a little cruel to the mosquitoes, and also inflammatory to the covering of her face.

But towards dawn the mosquitoes went back to where they

came from and at last the man and the woman slept in the absence of these wings.

(*A chronicle of the dark side of angels*)

They were once both angels, only he was a white angel and she was a black one, the angel of death visiting like the seventh plague, the plague that came after the mosquitoes; and their various addresses (she knew three people in Auckland whose street number was 4/50, and whereas 666 denotes the devil, 4/50 was allied with catastrophe) – their various addresses were marked with a cross above the door.

She had seen many deaths in her life, including the deaths of those still living – to all intents and purposes they were alive, but to intent and to purpose, dead. And he had seen only birth, and he was white and she was black.

(A fortune-teller once gazing at the flattened city in the palm of her hand said her childhood had been like the Great Fire, and she had done cartwheels through this fire, which was how she had emerged only singed, blackened.)

The first catastrophe in the presence of the angel (stone), corresponding with the first time she wrote of angels ('... *thinking they were angels and dressing them accordingly in winged gowns*'), was that the moment it arrived at the little house she shared with another woman, the physical make-up of the house, its atomic structure, suddenly became impossible and it exploded, blowing the woman sky-high. And she landed in the flat (4/50) of the angel (a man), and he watched over her, a *Guardian* newspaper wrapped about her body on a parkbench, while she slept off some sleep she had swallowed, and in the middle of the next afternoon he said, 'I know of a flat' – that recently vacated by his (religious) sister – and the woman moved into the flat (4/50), leaving the angel (stone) lying on its side in the dark recesses of the garden of the devastated house.

And then the angel (a man) began living at the flat too, with the stain of blood on its door.

The second catastrophe to befall her was that of the car which had transported the angel (stone) over the paths of stars being smashed in in the boot, right where the angel had once lain. It was written off, and she has written often of angels, archangels and the Angel Gabriel, and pondered how many angels can dance on the head of a pin, and pins will never be the same again; she will never touch them again without strewing a constellation of their comets and dashes across the hem of a skirt, all in their

267

wings and their white robes, disturbed in their singing.

And the man who drove into the back of the car while it lay parked (the manager of a K. Rd strip club) had no insurance – instead, a Filipino bride. At least, that was the woman's interpretation of her accent over the phone, but perhaps the interpretation was given a little to excess, a gift to it. The Filipino woman said her husband was down at the shooting gallery (and every three minutes a shooting star passes every single point in the sky).

Eventually the written-off car was translated into a cheque and then, as if by magic, into a new car, red, which the angel (a man) thought was a good buy because it was such a bright colour. And one night while the woman was at work proofreading, earning the money to run to such frivolities as cars, the man drove another woman – recently arrived to visit her sister – around in it, and this was the third catastrophe.

(And if only she had known that *good buy* meant *good bye* in Filipino!)

(*The movement of land masses and an angel is a small mass of the holy days of lands*)

It takes three people to lift it, or one angel (a man) who once had a job moving china dogs the size of dogs from the factory to the home of childless couples.

On the eve of a trip he had planned to the South Island, she asked him if he would move the angel (stone) from the little house where she had once lived, where it had been lying on its side for the winter. Here it had seemed quite peaceful, and her life also had been quite peaceful, relatively so, and the angel (a man), his life, of course, was peaceful. But she said she needed the angel to keep her company in the flat while he was away. And this perhaps heralded the ringing of a change of heart ('*The angel of the Lord declared unto Mary . . .* ').

So he picked it up in one movement (a quick one) and moved it to the flat he had once found her, and found himself, and while she scrubbed it down on the doorstep, he played the piano, a slow movement learned at the age of ten, because it was covered in moss from the lawn, the angel.

And she, the prime mover of this escapade, cannot even lift an angel (stone).

And the next day the angel (a man) went to the South Island with a photographer on an expedition of photographs and interviews with writers – of capture; himself the movement of land masses, plate tectonics; and there he met a woman (the woman who was later to travel in the red car at night, also the owner of a green car, its opposite) and he wrote to the woman of this new woman that she was very interesting to talk to. And the woman written *to* knew straight away, immediately, with no pause for thought, that there was more to this woman written *of* than her conversation.

And it was as if, after moving the angel (stone) to the place where their existence was, he never returned to it; that there could not be two angels.

And there are not. There never were; there were not.

(The absence and difference of avoiding angels)

A man she worked with who gave her a quotation each night and once said, '*The banana is bent with care, it fritters its life away,*' also told her Gregory the Great said, as he arrived in England and for the first time saw blond heads, '*Not Angles but Angels.*' And this was very much to the point.

And an angel entertains theatricals, or was it they who entertained it with their pyrotechnics? (And after all, that was what the woman had come from, from fiery explosions all year round and at a Guy Fawkes' night party, a plot to blow up the Houses of Parliament, and all Party, backfiring on the young soul rebel.)

The angel has watched everything. There is no one knows more than the angel does, even one who has written of angels.

At first it stood just inside the bedroom in a direct line from the front door, so that anyone who came to the flat, the first thing they saw was the angel; they were greeted by an angel. And the woman and the angel (a man) skirted round it during the day and stubbed their toes on it in the middle of the night, but never did they think of moving it. It seemed to have more right to be there than they did, by its very nature, that it was heavy and also an angel; both these things.

And an angel of the Lord is a void and is also not a void.

And when he had gone she took the angel (stone) and moved it, symbolically, in the only way she could – walking it across the room, its heaviness, as if showing it how to put one foot in front of the other; giving the inanimate animation; also the spirit, limbs; and teaching your grandmother to suck eggs (which has been said). And it came to rest beside the other heavy object in the flat, the piano, which was against the south wall collecting dampness to add to its dampeners. And together they orchestrated a singing through the air of black and of white.

269

And the man she worked with who gave her a quotation a night, the next time she saw him, which was that night, the night of the worst day of her life (She cried, 'This is the worst day of my life!'), the night after the night of the red car – he said, '*The lights are going out all over Europe; we shall not see them lit again in our lifetime.*'

And the following night in her flat, she sat with a woman, a proofreader and also a viewer of ghosts in her past; and this woman screamed because the lights flicked off and then they flicked on and then they flicked off again, all unattended. And the woman (*the* woman) said it was nothing to worry about, that the wiring must be faulty. But when the other woman had gone she lay uneasily in her bed, and after that, every night, late, around twelve, the lights in the two rooms and the hall tapped out a message constructed of the presence and absence of light.

It was then that the woman decided to call in the services (Masses) of a Catholic priest.

(The Church of St Mary of the Angels and of the Madness of Wings)

Because of the writing off of cars and the sudden elopement of electric light switches and the general escapement of everything including the action of a piano, the woman concluded that she should no longer have this angel (stone) in her possession; she took heed of those who had warned her a long time ago of the mysterious properties of tombstones, no matter how angelic they might appear (also, no *matter*). And because it was Christian icon and she was once, if not Christian, Catholic, she sought the appropriate channel to unburden herself of it (also to unburden the angel of theatricals).

But the Catholic priest, when approached, said that this was the fruit of the nonsense of superstition.

(And she once wrote, '*How our lives bow to rhyme,*' believing her own life was lived according to the links in the language used to describe it; and everything is linked, there is nothing that is not linked. And what if this rhyme happened to be a nonsense rhyme? What of that?)

And she had thought it was her very upbringing in the Catholic Church taught her there is no difference between sense and nonsense, between fact and fiction, that everything is the same; the inside of the head is the same as the outside. And that was something to be thankful for, for the small mercy of never doubting, to have never had The Doubt when it came to these matters of what is matter and what is not; that word and flesh, body and soul, are all towards the same point (angels dancing upon it). And the priest was the last person she thought would leave her dangling with this angel, its heaviness and the levity of its gaze towards Heaven.

But she is left with the angel (stone). Like a thought she once thought, it cannot be destroyed.

(A film, light from a flat surface, fills their bodies)

She went to a film, *Wings of Desire*, and it was a miracle in the tradition of Lourdes, Fatima, Garabandal. In the foyer three people came up to her and said, 'I just saw him,' as if he were an apparition (I *saw* him!), warning her in case she too should see and be knocked flat to the floor with the power of such a vision. And she had known anyway that he was there because she knows these things, and also she had seen his sister of the religious order in the service of this particular Church. And all through the film, embodied by this film, she felt the presence of angels.

And in the film an angel, invisible to humans, comes down from Heaven in the body of a man in a great coat, and he walks about Berlin helping people in need and others about to pass from this world to the next; a guardian angel, but touching none of it and touched by none of it. And this angel, he falls in love with a woman, a trapeze artist, the wearer of wings, and because of this love he wants to become human. But perhaps the desire to become human was there before the woman, and it was the woman who walked into this desire.

And she once said to him, the reason they were there, together, was the propagation of the species, and the propagation of the species is why people fall in love.

(She once met a woman, a banker from Iraq, who every time she said 'lot of', it came out sounding like 'love'. For instance she would say, 'There are a love people out of work in this country.' She had come to New Zealand wanting to acquire another citizenship, to turn this country she had never before set foot in, into the country of her birth. She said an Iraqi passport was useless; that everywhere you go, they ask you questions. Already, after fourteen months, she spoke like a New Zealander of the turmoil the country was in, and she was fast acquiring a New Zealand accent to go with her promised passport – apart from the words 'lot of', which she had entirely misconstrued.)

But what of the propagation of angels, and of the faith, and of the screenings of films?

He sent her a card, a little later, on her birthday and they talked on the phone and got very upset, she first, covering him with a veil of tears. And the card said he had thought of her watching that film with him; he was once an angel, and had become human.

But for her it had been the other way round, almost; that before she was human, had made herself become human, the propagation of the species, etcetera; and with him, she became infused with the language angels use, which is singing, and the billowing of a wing.

And the point where they passed each other is where so many angels dance.

(*Guardian angels and newspapers blow about the streets*)

A high wind on the morning a photographer photographing writers came to the flat, blew outside their heads and inside their heads, causing a theatre of the flurry of tempers.

The photographer was looking for the person who took it into their head to write once, and he thought the camera would tell him, because the camera has no perspective on sense and nonsense. And perhaps it was the woman and perhaps it was not. And in the case of the latter, the way the photographs came out was under-standable because they did not look like her – either that, or her appearance set off in another direction immediately they had been taken (*taken*). He had taken her former appearance away.

And just before his arrival, the photographer's, she had had a fight with the angel (a man), because of the wind, for no other reason. And they made it up, inventing a reason for the argument after the event (and it was always worth the trouble (of the argument) for the way their heads, afterwards, formed the inter-secting subsets of breaths), while the photographer who was about to detect her unpacked his camera in the other room watched by the angel (stone); an eye observing an eye, and all ears for what was going on in the kitchen, especially the angel's ears, although angels do not hear (as she was taught), they only sing. But perhaps this angel (stone) sang in order to hear.

And because of what had happened, because of the wind, she couldn't keep her eyes off him (the laying on of eyes), and when the photographer photographed her, it was as if the camera received the image of a woman receiving the image of an angel (or was it the camera divining the writer through the woman, a forked rod?). And eventually the photographer said to the angel (a man), 'Go and sit on a rock and look out to sea.'

Which he did – sucked out the door first of all by the Mistral in the yard. And he looked all the way down to the South Island, not seeing, perhaps, but singing as is the wont of angels.

And the photographer and the woman were left alone in the flat with the stone angel. And the photographer took 97 photographs, thereabouts, of the woman, some of them with the angel, and in these ones – in the presence of the angel, or of a tip of its wing – she did not look herself. And people said to her later, 'That is never you!' (And it never will be now, no matter how long she waits.) And she was pleased that it was some other woman who was photographed in the presence of the angel (stone).

And months later when a photograph of this other woman happened to appear in a newspaper together with the angel, her friend the filmmaker (*a* filmmaker, not the maker of the film *Wings of Desire*, although perhaps it was; that there was one person once who had the idea of putting images on celluloid and filling a room with them, and they did it, and it is done) wrote to her (he was going to Italy, the *whenua pai* of angels), and he said, 'Your *angel* looks pretty real.' (Her italics)

(Cherubim and seraphim and the dull little lives of the heads of pins)
After the Catholic priest, still she must relieve herself of the angel (stone). But was there any higher authority?

A man she knew, of Devonport, who had just won $US6,500 for the drafting of a script (first draft, second draft, etcetera), obviously knew something of the drafting of patterns to be pinned, cut, and then cast, as in metal, by the blackness and light of thousands of angels.

Also, the woman who was in the flat the night the lights started to alight, she told her of a woman she knew, a woman of the spirit, who once propelled a poltergeist from her house (or was it sucked out by the sudden absence of ghosts, by comparison, outside?).

The woman of the spirit, on first hearing of this angel, the circumstances of the possession of it, or of its possession (and possession is nine-tenths of the law), said, Yes, it must go back where it came from. And she told the woman to cover it in the meantime, while it was still in the flat.

And draped in a cloth it is suddenly human.

And the scriptwriter (who also is awarded $40,000 a year to discover mistakes in the *Herald*, running after its loose pages as they blow about the street, crying, 'Here's one! Here's one! I found it!'), he helps her to walk the angel up the steps and into the boot of her car, and at this he proves very good, having a two-year-old daughter. And when he tries to get the angel to say 'Daddy', and it will not, he says, 'Why can't you fly, damn you?' The spirit is given limbs if it will not use its wings. (And after all, they have both of them written for a flat surface to come out and engulf people.)

And they prepare to take the angel (stone) to the Devonport Cemetery, which is where it came from according to the recluse in the Waitakeres (once she had taken the angel he wanted nothing more to do with her, with anyone, for a long time, but he wrote, 'Please, Anne, don't put her back in the mud!' And all along she had thought it was a boy.) And the woman of the ghosts, and the woman from the little house way back at the beginning, also the woman of the spirit and the man of the scripts – all said they would come on this pilgrimage of the delivery of angels.

But on the appointed day, first of all the woman of the ghosts rings and says she cannot face it. And then the woman of the angel itself, her back half-turned, finds she cannot face it either. Something has happened, another catastrophe, but this time, nothing to do with anything – at least, not with the physical, the flesh, or of the moment. Something past, or imagined; or perhaps it is the reallest thing, the presence and absence of angels.

And she rings the woman of the spirit, and the woman of the spirit is obviously relieved that there is to be no removal of angels today, because she has a migraine.

(A dancer she knew once and meets again quite by chance in the Lizard Lounge, opens a green literary magazine lying between them on the table (in front of its editor who also sits there, an entrepreneur of the greenness of lizards and of the moss growing on the wings of angels) and reads about Hildegard, the visionary, something the woman has written, or the writer wrote once, and he says he knows of a theory that visionaries were also migraine sufferers, the vision the meeting place of pain and enlightenment. And he says that he, also, is obsessed with angels, but it is not a problem, it is a delight.)

And because the angel is not to be moved that day, it spends the night in the boot of the red car parked outside the house of a friend where the woman also sleeps. And in the morning they look to see if the car is still there, if it is intact, if it is still red. And it is all these things, and it is a miracle.

The next day the scriptwriter from Devonport rings her to arrange, once more, for the disposal of the angel (stone), but her phone seems to be out of order; it is engaged for a long time. And it is perhaps a matter for faults that she is talking to the other angel, the one clothed in human flesh. And it is another last conversation they will ever have.

And the angel does not get put back in the cemetery that day, and that night, the scriptwriter decides he would like it in his garden; that he wants it. The woman advises him not to, that it is dangerous for humans to get mixed up with angels. But he wants it more than anything. He is quite determined to have it, and in the end the woman agrees to let him have it, because there is something in the urgency of his desire for the angel that reminds her of herself, and she could not deny herself an angel.

And because the woman is about to go away for a fortnight and there is no time to move the angel to Devonport, it is loaded, temporarily, into the car of the woman she is lending her car to; moved from the roadworthy car into the car that has no registration, that theoretically does not exist. And there is a moment of intimacy between these cars, back to back, and their exchange of an angel.

And the story of this angel is becoming so enormous that the woman wonders if it will ever come to an end. She has already written thus far – the writing of angels as she said she would do – before she knows the outcome. She is waiting for something that will be written to happen, although it has not always been this way – she has written of things not knowing they would happen and they happened. And she has written of things not knowing they were there and they were there all along; and that is perhaps where writers meet, and are one writer.

When she gets back to Auckland, they load the angel (stone) into the boot of the scriptwriter's car and he drives slowly over the bridge to Devonport, dragging the mass of the dancing upon pins. As she watches the angel go, she catches her breath.

And now she has no angels in her possession.

(*A lateral thinker, the span of his wings*)

(*The Angelus rung at six and twelve and at six and twelve*)
As a child she was sometimes disturbed in her sleep by the ringing of bells by the sisters of the Home of Compassion ('*The angel of the Lord declared unto Mary . . .*'); not often, but according to the way the wind blew, which everything was dependent on. And in the morning she would ask, 'Did you all hear the bells?' but no one else would have heard. Only the child of six heard them plainly. And at twelve they were dimmer, and at eighteen

they were dimmer still, and at twenty-four, when she had gone, the bells, also, had gone.

On the subject of the lights chiming in the middle of her sleep according to some authority other than the national grid: this is nothing – nothing, light, the absence of it – compared to the real comings and goings of an angel.

And whereas there was once a queue of people waiting to move into her flat, should it be vacated – camping just outside in order to be first in the doors at a fire sale – now that it is to become empty, the woman first in line (the same woman who once screamed at the fickleness of the lights) her nose pressed against the glass, clasping her rug and her thermos of tea and her purse, and her picture appearing on the front page of the *Herald*, has decided not to move in because of *what has gone on here*.

What has gone on in this flat! The woman is amused; she finds this amusing. Also a little disturbing, like the massed choirs of mosquitoes, of sleep; that she and her past have now acquired the quality of the unknown quantity of ghosts. And when the woman next in the queue, due to move in, decides not to at the last minute, the fingers of the woman vacating slip from their grasp on the dwelling-place of angels.

And the next time she sees him is at the very moment of the blessing of the Holy Ghost to begin Midnight Mass – the meeting quite by chance, apart from they have perhaps both come to church with the express purpose of beholding a vision. And for a moment she believes she is looking into her own eyes. And they do not attend Mass, they leave Mass immediately, without thought, pushing their way through the crowd in the foyer, and instead they talk, bringing all the Weight of their past to bear on these small hours.

And among it all, among this talk parked in a red car at night, he tells her that the woman he once drove in this car and who now drives him in her car (green) (knowing nothing of mechanics for so long, apart from how they get you from A to Z, he is now an expert on the A to B of the car (red) and the car (green)) – her *sister* has moved into the flat. (*Her* sister.) And she says, 'I wish you hadn't told me that,' and he says he visited once but cannot visit any more, the flat where an angel (stone) once resided.

(Angels, archangels and the Angel Gabriel)
Like the Angelus, she rings, every six hours, a publisher (he is difficult to get hold of apart from over lunch in the Lizard Lounge while the angel (stone) reclined in the boot of a carbody without

soul). When she finally gets through she asks him if he can retrieve the photograph of the angel (stone) and a strange woman on the particular day when the wind blew. This photograph has been replicated and sent to newspapers, and she is worried about bad luck.

And he did get it back, but he did not.

She was once infatuated with him, with the publisher, from a place where angels are, only he was not an angel, and she wanted an angel. And she had one – two; also the impossibility of the two angels co-existing, the angel (a man) and the angel (stone). The publisher tells her he is about to get married. He is marrying a human.

And the angel she loved – *loved* – he also now is human. And the woman is now human. All are human. It is far too late in their lives for the matinées of angels. They are done with angels, and this is the last word she will ever write on the subject of angels.

A STORY ABOUT SKINNY LOUIE

Fiona Farrell Poole

THE SETTING

Imagine a small town: along its edges, chaos.

To the east, clinking shelves of shingle and a tearing sea, surging in from South America across thousands of gull-studded white-capped heaving miles.

To the south, the worn hump of a volcano crewcut with pines dark and silent, but dimpled still on the crest where melted rock and fire have spilled to the sea, where they have hissed and set into solid bubbles, black threaded with red.

To the west, a border of hilly terraces, built up from layer upon layer of shells which rose once, dripping, from the sea and could as easily shudder like the fish it is in legend, and dive.

To the north, flat paddocks pockmarked with stone and the river which made them shifting restlessly from channel to channel in its broad braided bed.

Nothing is sure.

The town pretends, of course, settled rump-down on the coastal plain with its back to the sea, which creeps up yearly a nibble here a bite there, until a whole football field has gone at the boys' high school and the cliff walkway crumbles and the sea demands propitiation, truckloads of rubble and concrete blocks. And the town inches away in neat rectangular steps up the flanks of the volcano which the council names after an early mayor, a lardy mutton-chop of a man, hoping to tame it as the Greeks thought they'd fool the Furies by calling them the Kindly Ones; inches away across shingle bar and flax swamp to the shell terraces and over where order frays at last into unpaved roads, creeks flowing like black oil beneath willows tangled in convolvulus, and old villa houses, gap-toothed, teetering on saggy piles, with an infestation of hens in the yard and a yellow-toothed dog chained to the water tank.

At the centre, things seem under control. The Post Office is a white wedding cake, scalloped and frilled, and across the road are the banks putting on a responsible Greek front (though ramshackle corrugated iron behind). At each end of the main street the town mourns its glorious dead with a grieving soldier in puttees to the north and a defiant lion to the south, and in between a cohort of memorial elms was drawn up respectfully until 1952 when it was discovered that down in the dark the trees had broken ranks and were rootling around under the road tearing crevices in the tarmac, and the Council was forced to be stern: tore out the lot and replaced them with plots of more compliant African marigolds. There are shops and petrol stations and churches and flowering cherries for beautification and a little harbour with a tea kiosk in the lee of the volcano. It's as sweet as a nut, as neat as a pie, as a pin.

Imagine it.

Imagine it at night, a print composed of shapes and shadows. Early morning, January 24, 1954. The frilly hands on the Post Office clock show 3.30 so it's 3.25am, GMT, as everyone knows. (Time is no more thoroughly dependable than the earth beneath one's feet.) It's unseasonably cold. A breeze noses in over the breakwater in the harbour and in amongst the pottles and wrappers by the tea kiosk, tickling the horses on the merry-go-round in the playground so they tittup tittup and squeak, fingering the bristles on the Cape pines and sighing down their branches into a dark pit of silence. Flower boxes have been hung along the main street and as the wind passes they swing and spill petals, fuchsias and carnations. There are coloured lights and bunting which, if it were only daylight, could be seen to be red white and blue because tomorrow, the Queen is coming. At 3.05pm the Royal express, a Ja class locomotive (No 1276) drawing half a dozen refurbished carriages, will arrive at the railway crossing on the main street. Here, Her Majesty Queen Elizabeth II and His Royal Highness Prince Philip will step into a limousine which will carry them up the main street past the Post Office, the banks and the shops which have all had their fronts painted for the occasion (their backs remain as ever, patchy and rusted). By the grieving soldier the Royal couple will turn left towards the park where they will be formally welcomed at 3.20pm by the Mayor and Mayoress and shake hands with 45 prominent citizens. They will be presented with some token of the town's affection. At 3.25pm they will commence their walk to the train and at 3.40pm they will depart for the south. The moves are all set out in the Royal Tour Handbook, the stage is set, the lines rehearsed, and the citizens, prominent and otherwise, are tucked under blanket and eiderdown, secure in the knowledge that everything has been properly organised. If they stir a little it is because the wind tugs at curtains, or because through the fog of dreaming they hear some foreign noise outside the windows where their cats and dogs have sloughed off their daytime selves and stalk, predatory, the jungles of rhubarb and blackcurrant. The sea breathes. Whooshaaah. Whooshaaah.

BRIAN BATTERSBY WITNESSES A CURIOUS PHENOMENON

Midway up Hull Street on the flanks of the volcano there is one citizen who is not asleep. Brian Battersby is sitting on his garage roof. His legs are wrapped in a tartan rug, his thermos is full of vege soup, and with stiff fingers he is trying to adjust the focus on his new 4-inch Cook refractor. Thousands of miles above his head a civilisation more advanced than any on Earth is constructing a canal and by muffled red torchlight Brian is tracing the line of it: from the Nodus Gordii SE in the direction of the Mare Sirenum, at mind-boggling speed: a hundred miles a day? Two hundred perhaps? What machines they must have, what power! Above the Cape a meteor flares, green and white, and Brian pauses, waiting for the shower that will follow, but the meteor grows in brightness. Brighter than Mars. Bigger. A fireball as large as the full moon! For a moment the whole town is caught in brilliant silhouette and Brian sits motionless on the garage roof, vaguely aware of music, an odd percussive ticktocking. He cannot identify it, but the fact is that every hen in the town is singing. Necks stretched, tiny eyes like amber beads shining in the warm darkness of their fowlruns, they chorus: Wa-a-a-chet auf, ruft uns di-e Stim-mm-e, Awake! Awake! Out on the Awamoa Road a Hereford cow more sensitive than her sisters is levitating above a hedge and cats and dogs have forgotten the jungle, and kneel paws tucked to soft belly. The meteor explodes at last into a sequined fall of shining particles and the town recovers: hens tuck heads beneath wings, the cow descends with a soft thud and cats and dogs stretch and look uneasily about them into the night, ears flattened. Up on the garage roof Brian is shaking. He knows suddenly and with absolute clarity that those canals are not the work of superior beings who might offer solutions to fallible humanity but are mere ripples of dust blown this way and that by howling wind, and he knows that he, Brian, is a small rather pompous accounts clerk who will spend the next 30 years in the offices of the Power Board, and that his wife wishes now that she'd married Don Barton, former All Black and successful stock and station agent, when he'd asked as a promising junior back in

1948. She stays for the kids and takes out her disappointment in housewifely perfection. It's too much truth to handle all at once. Best not confronted. Brian reaches for his notebook. 'January 24, 1954. 0357 UT.,' he writes with trembling hand. 'Mag. – ?? fireball in clear sky. Green and white.' What amazing luck! What a coup! He peers up into the darkness, eyes still dazzled and sparkling and attempts accurate estimation. 'Travelled 30°–35° start 25° altitude 140° azimuth. Approx. 1 min. 58 sec. duration.' What a note it will make for *Meteor News!* 'Accompanying sonic phenomena,' he adds and reaches for his thermos and a shot of hot soup.

Two miles from his garage roof in the Begonia House at the Public Gardens, Louie Symonds, Skinny Louie, aged 15, is giving birth.

SKINNY LOUIE HAS A BABY

The Begonia House is warm, steamy, sticky with primeval trickling and the sweet-sour smell of rampant growth. Louie has managed to drag some coconut matting into a corner and squats there, full-bellied and bursting, hands clamped to a water pipe while her body tears in pieces. No one can hear her groan. The Gardens are empty. Only beds of pansies and petunias wheeling away from the glass house along the edges of gravel paths, circling the Peter Pan statue and the Gallipoli fountain and the specimen trees with their identity labels tacked to their trunks. Louie is on her own.

Far away to the south is the dark little warren where she lives with her mum Lill. Lill isn't in tonight either, as it happens. She's been off for three weeks or so on a Korean boat and she won't be back till it leaves for the north with its cargo of snapper and squid, and the girls are put ashore. Lill says she's got a thing for the chinks: she likes them small and smooth and she likes the way they pay her no trouble and she likes the presents: whisky, stockings, a nice jacket. It's better than hanging around the Robbie Burns anyway taking your chances with any poxy John who fancies a bit between jugs. Louie came with her once or twice down the boats, but she gave them all the pip, got on people's nerves being so quiet, hanging around like a fart at a funeral, so Louie stayed home after that while Lill with her Joan Crawford lips and her hair curled went into Port. At this moment she's bobbing about two miles off Kaikoura wondering if she's got enough to go eight no trumps and Louie is in pain. She has walked for days to this place, travelling by night, and by day when the sun slammed down like a pot lid, she has curled round her belly and slept under a bush or a bridge.

She has often done this: got the jumpies, set off walking till she's quiet again, then turned for home. This time she's had them bad. She has walked and slept for days, sucking a stone for spit, following the road up from the city to the hills, past the white rock where she lay once months before to warm herself in the sun. She'd been sprawled, dozing, light tangled in her lashes in tiny scarlet stars, when a shadow fell upon her like a stone. Louie looked up and there was a hawk hovering. She lay very still. The hawk flew closer, settled. She took the weight of him, gasping as his talons drove tiny holes in her breast. He dipped his tail feathers in her open mouth. She smelled the dry bird scent of him. Then he rose wings beating into the sun and she lost him in the glare.

She passed the rock two nights ago. Yesterday morning she stopped near a country store where she got a whole Vienna slipping it quick as winking under her coat while the man was lifting trays from a truck. She'd sat under a hedge in early morning half-light and picked out a hole, chewing slowly, and a plump grey mare had come to her from the mist and stood while she squeezed its titties and took the milk, licking it from her fingers, glutinous, sticky, Highlander Condensed. When the sun was up, she slept. It was wise to hide by day. She didn't trust cars. When she was little, cars came to their house, crawling like grey beetles round the road from Port and when they saw them they'd run away, her and Alamein and Yvonne, because the cars meant questions and picking at their hair for cooties and icecream sticks forcing their tongues back and where? And why? And how often? And Lill in a paddy, though she was as nice as pie to the lady clearing a space and saying would she care for a cup of tea? But as soon as the car had gone it was bloody cow and why the hell couldn't Louie learn to smile instead of standing there like some mental case because if she didn't they'd have her out to Seacliff, she looked that daft. Lill slammed around them savage, so they learned to scatter when cars came, hiding like the cats in the smooth places beneath the hedge or the washhouse. But once Ally and Yvonne weren't quick enough and the lady got them, took them away somewhere and they were never seen again. So Louie hid from cars. You couldn't trust them.

Tonight, Louie has crossed some paddocks sniffing for the sea and found herself on a hill above a railway line which curved down into a crisscross pattern of light. Her body was heavy and her back ached. She'd been picking at the bread rolling doughballs when she went to the lav suddenly, no warning, right there in her pants, so she peeled them off and stuffed them steaming into a bush. Cough said a sheep. Louie began to walk along the railway towards the town. The pain in her back was growing and another tiny nut of it pressed at the base of her skull.

Clump clump clump sleeper by sleeper careful not to fall between and have bad luck. Around her everything was coming alive: trees tapped her shoulder, fence posts skittered by on the blind side and the grass lined up and waved. The weight in her belly heaved and she had to stop at the bottom of the hill for everything to settle. The railway line crossed a street. Louie stepped from the sleepers onto tarmac and ahead was an arch of flowers, framing black shadow.

Then the pain came up from behind and grabbed her so that she had to cry out as she used to at school when Wayne Norris chinese-burned her arms or stuck her with a pen nib saying cowardy custard cry baby cry only this was worse and she tried to run away through the archway into the dark. The pain lost her there for a bit so Louie took her chance, stumbling across a lawn to the shelter of trees and a cage where a bird asked her who was a pretty cocky, along paths frilled with grey rows of flowers to a glass house gleaming when the moon came from behind cloud where Louie hid, sneaking into a corner. But this pain was too smart. It had slipped in beside her already and was squeezing sly, cowardy cowardy custard, driving her into a black hole where there was nothing but a voice groaning over and over and her body ripping and suddenly silence. A slither. And silence.

On the coconut matting between her legs lay a sticky black thing, wriggling in the sweet stench of blood. Louie crouched waiting for the pain to jump her again but it had gone, sidled off shutting the door silently. Louie wiped some jelly from the black thing and it mewed under her hand.

They lay quiet together. Slowly the glass about them turned to grey squares then white and Louie felt her legs twitch. The warm air here settled round her head like a thick blanket and she needed out. She took her cardie, and wrapped it round the thing then stood carefully, wobbling a little, and went outside where the grass was shiny and her feet left dark prints as she walked on water past the bird and the flowers to the archway and the street. She moved slowly past houses with their curtains drawn still and the cats coming home to sleep, down a long street to the shore. The sea was stretching and waking too and the clouds as she walked up the beach were golden bars with the sun slipping between. She stopped from time to time to wash blood from her legs. She ate the last of the bread. In a cleft in the low clay cliff were a wheelless Ford, some mattresses stained and spitting fluff, broken boxes, a pile of rotting plums. Louie was tired. She dragged a mattress into the car, and curled up to sleep. On the gearshift a nursery spider had spun its web. Baby spiders jittered under the membrane, hundreds of them. Louie prodded gently at their opaque shell and they scattered at her touch but she was careful not to tear a hole because then the cold could come in and kill them all.

That's the story of how Louie Symonds, daughter of Lilleas Symonds popularly known as Shanghai Lill, gave birth. The paternity of the child is in some doubt. It is possible that the father is Wayne Norris, an acned youth who, since primary school, has paid Louie in bags of lollies for a quick poke in the cemetery on the way home. She's particularly fond of gob-stoppers. She likes lying back in the long grass beside the stone IN L VING   MORY of Isabella Grant 18 blank blank OH D TH WH   IS THY   NG while Wayne wiggles his dicky about prodding hopefully, and when she's had enough of that she can say get off, roll over and see how the lolly has changed from red to yellow to blue.

Wayne is a definite possibility.

It is equally probable that the father is a hawk.

THE QUEEN COMES BY TRAIN

The Queen was coming. Maura stood with her mother and father and Shona down by the railway crossing at the very end of the route. She would have preferred to be in the park suffering torments of jealousy while some other little girl with perfect curls and a perfect dress handed the Queen a posy while performing a perfect curtsey, but they'd been late and this was the closest they could get.

Dad hadn't wanted to come at all. 'Load of poppycock,' he'd said. 'Mrs Windsor and that chinless cretin she married riding along waving at the peasants and mad Sid and the rest of them bringing up the rear kowtowing for all they're worth. Lot of nonsense.' 'I think she's pretty,' said Maura who had a gold Visit medal pinned to her best frock and a scrapbook of pictures cut from *Sunny Stories* in her bedroom: The Little Princesses at Play with the Royal Corgis on the Lawn at Balmoral, The Little Princesses in Their Playhouse which had a proper upstairs and wasn't just a made-over pig pen with ripped sheets for curtains. 'Mrs Barnett says the Queen has a peaches and cream complexion.' 'Peaches and bloody cream!' said their father, thumping the table so his tea spilt. 'There weren't too many peaches around back in 1848 when her lot were gorging themselves in London while our lot ate grass, and don't forget it.' Dad hated the Queen, Oliver Cromwell and Winston Churchill because of the Troubles and the Famine and because they-came-across-and-tried-to-teach-us-their-ways. 'That's years ago,' said Mum. 'Now turn around Maura so I can brush out the other side.' Maura turned, glad to be relieved of the tight ringlet sausages which had dug into her scalp all night. 'And what about during the war?' said their mother, who was pink-cheeked today and ready for a fight. 'They stayed in London didn't they? They stayed with the people in the East End right through the Blitz and the Queen Mother even said she was glad the Palace got bombed because then she could feel they were sharing the suffering.' 'Suffering?' said Marty. 'What did she know about suffering, one of the richest families in the world and you know how they got there don't you? Murder and betrayal and half of them illegitimate into the bargain, born the wrong side of the . . .' 'Shh,' said their mother, her mouth tight-lipped round a blue satin ribbon. 'The children . . . Hold still, Maura, for pity's sake.' Marty drank his tea morosely. 'Eating grass,' he said. 'Eating dirt, so some English bugger could go in velvet.' A final tug at the ribbon and Maura was released. 'Well, are you coming or not?' said Mum driving a hat pin into her pink church hat, and Dad said he supposed he would, if she was that set on it, but he was damned if he was going to get dressed up. The Queen would have to take him in his gardening clothes or not at all, and Mum said nonsense, you're not leaving the house in that jersey, so go and get changed, there was still time, but of course there wasn't and they could hear the crowd roar like a wave breaking before they were halfway down the hill and they had to run and push even to find the place to stand by the Gardens gate.

The pipe band was wheezing and wailing a few yards away and Maura would have liked to go and stand up close to watch the men's cheeks puff and the rhythmic flap of their white duck feet and to feel her ears buzz with drum roll and drone. But they were inaccessible through a dense forest of legs and bottoms: fat, skinny, trousered, floralled and striped, milling about so that she felt as frightened and inconsequential as she had when she'd opened the gate at Uncle Roy's and the cows had pressed through before she'd been able to jump to one side, buffeting her in their eagerness to get to the paddock. She'd have liked a ride on her father's shoulders, but Shona was already in place looking goofy with her paper flag and her bottle teat clenched between her teeth. Maura tugged at her mother's hand but knew she was too heavy and that her mother couldn't lift her, not now with the baby inside. Mum looked down and said don't fuss poppet and hang on tight because there's such a crowd. Maura needed no instruction. Around her the huge bodies pressed and she took sticky hold of her mother's skirt. The crowd noise was like static which tuned in snatches into God Save the Queen and cheering. (The Mayor's wife was presenting Her Majesty with a white begonia in a silver casket, Mrs Barnett told them next morning, and the Mayor was giving the Prince a photo of the Begonia House to hang on the wall at Buckingham Palace.) Then the roar built like rain drumming and Mum stood tiptoe saying, 'Oh she's coming! Maura, you must see her properly, this is a Once-in-a-Lifetime Opportunity!' And before Maura could protest she had scooped her up, and was tapping a man's shoulder and asking, 'Could my daughter get down to the front please? She can't see.' Handing her over like a parcel, passed from person to person till she stood at the very edge of the crowd where there was no coach and no horses but an ordinary man and woman walking along the road past the baths, talking sometimes to the crowd or waving, and the woman's face was a bit like the Queen's but not peaches and cream and topped with an ordinary hat, not a crown. People were calling hurrah hurrah and the pipe band shrilled so Maura waved her flag uncertainly as the man and woman passed by and in a very ordinary way, exactly as anyone might, climbed up the stairs onto the train, turned and waved, and the train chugged (whooshaaah whooshaaah) away down the track.

Then the crowd broke. Maura stood with her paper flag but no hand came down out of the press of bodies and no voice said, 'Ah, there you are Maura,' lifting her up to safety... She was pushed and prodded, spun and stepped about until she found herself up against a floral arch and beyond it lay a smooth and empty lawn, so she went there, and once she was there she remembered the parrot and then Peter Pan and then the Begonia House where you could pick up fuchsias from the floor and wear them for earrings, and that was how she found the baby.

It was like finding the kittens mewing blind and wriggling in the long grass by the sand pit, except that the baby's eyes were open and it waved its hands sticky and streaked with cream but perfect just the same with proper nails. Maura took her hankie and spat on it as her mother did for a lick and a promise and wiped at the baby's dirty cheek. The baby turned instantly to her finger, opened its pink toothless mouth and sucked. Maura was entranced. She gathered the baby up as she had gathered the kittens, tucked firmly inside the dirty cardigan, and carried her discovery out into the sun.

PEG AND MARTY ARE GRANTED UNDERSTANDING

They stood by the gate, frantic, pale. 'Bloody irresponsible,' Marty was saying. 'Sending a child her age off on her own in a crowd like this.' He hadn't realised till this minute how much Peg's impulsive optimism, which he loved, also infuriated him and how much he longed to attack and destroy it. Predictably she was refusing to recognise how appalling this situation was. He knew. He'd seen the worst happen. He'd seen a man step on a patch of desert dust and his legs sever, the trunk falling after in a torn and heavy arc. He went to Mass, but knew it was useless, that this was simply habit, and that you could pray as Donovan prayed on the truck coming out at Sidi Rezegh and die mouthing Hail Mary in bubbles of blood. He voted Labour, argued with Jansen in the tea room who said that the unions were full of bloody commies and they'd been dead right to send in the troops in '51, but knew that this faith too was illusion, that there was no common cause, that the reality was each man alone, bleating, as the blow fell. And here was Peg with a daft bright desperate smile saying the swings, she'll have gone to play on the swings. And Peg is avoiding Marty's eye but knowing him there beside her, the heavy dark weight of him and his despair which she can't touch, ever, or relieve. She can make him laugh, she can love him, but when they lie together a bleak and faceless nothing sprawls between them grasping at her throat so she wakes, heart beating, night after night. She fights against it in Marty, suppressing panic as she does now, refusing to share his vision (Maura face down on the duckpond, dragged into the water lilies by the swans, hand in hand with some enticing nameless terror . . .). But at this moment she knows suddenly that she won't be able to struggle for ever, that her optimism is a frail thing and that in time she will have to choose: leave or give up the fight, let the blackness take her. Love and survival are in opposition. It's appalling. Too big a truth to face all at once. Better encountered bit by bit. But look, there is Maura now, safe and sound after all ('You see?'), her blue nylon dress stained and carrying a grubby bundle. And 'Mum,' Maura is saying, 'I've found us a baby.'

They take the baby along the street to Dr Orbell's surgery and as they pass people draw back on either side like waves parting and quiet for a second with curiosity. But when the family with its grubby bundle has passed, an extraordinary thing happens. People turn to one another and in a sudden rush, earnest and eager, they confess those things that have most oppressed them. They tell one another truths, pleasant and unpleasant. So McLean, most prominent of the prominent citizens, tells Davis the Town Clerk that he bought land on the northern river flats six months before development on a tip-off from a cousin on the Council. Jameson, junior partner in Lowe, Stout and Jameson, seeks out Lowe and tells him he has invested £5,000 of clients' money in a salmon hatchery which appears certain now to fail. Partner reveals that he has swindled partner, parent has coerced child, friend has failed friend. So the day of the Queen's visit ends for some in scuffling and recrimination, for others in forgiveness and pity. We make what we can of the truth.

WHAT HAPPENED TO LOUIE

When it grew dark Louie walked along the shingle to the river's mouth. Her legs still ran with blood and her breasts tingled so that she had to lie face down on the cold river sand to soothe their swelling. She followed the bank inland through dank grass willow and blackberry feeling her body lighten, her feet finding their accustomed rhythm and visible again across the sack of her vacated belly. That night she ate a pie she found in a safe hanging from a tree. Yellow pastry, gravy, meat. On the third night she ate only a handful of leaves so that her mouth ran with a green cud. The nor'-wester blew down the valley, burning the grass to brown crackle and a butter-moon slid across the sky. The river was loud with the sound of stones being dragged to sea. She came to a hall, brightly lit within its ring of cars, and climbed the smooth shoulder of the hill behind. Scraps of music, thump of dancing, laughter, the rattle of sheep running off into tussock and matagouri. Louie stands alone on the crest looking out over the valley. The power lines loop from hill to hill and Louie reaches out to swing down and away with them. Like in the movies. Like Tarzan.

She dazzles in a moment and rises splendid into the night sky.

THE YOUNG FARMERS' CLUB EXPERIENCES A BLACKOUT

In the valley the Young Farmers' Club summer dance is interrupted by a blackout halfway through the Military Two. Couples stand arm in arm in the dark while Mort Coker tries the switches and the fuse box in the kitchen. Someone has a look outside and shouts that the whole place is black, it must be bird strike or a line down up the valley. In the darkness body blunders against body, giggling. Then Ethne Moran finds a torch and the beam of it squiggles over faces caught wide-eyed like rabbits on a road. Someone brings in a tilly lamp. The band attempts a few bars, deee dum dee dum who'syerladyfren, but stops because no one seems interested. They stand about instead talking, and a few couples are edging away to the dimly lit corners. Then Ethne, who has organised the supper, claps her hands and jumps up onto the stage. 'Come on,' she says, lit by the tilly lamp and holding in her outstretched hands a strawberry cream sponge. 'No point in letting good food go to waste! Give us a hand, Margie.' Margie Pringle brings out the sausage rolls and finds a bread knife and Ethne kneels by the lamp to cut the cake into triangles, cream spurting beneath the blade. Side on her white dress is transparent and Ross Meikle watching thinks she's a cracker. Big breasts, curving stomach, long in the leg, and good teeth nice and even, with that little gap at the front. Ethne looks up. She hands him a piece of cake, then leans towards him and bites his ear lobe very gently leaving her uneven imprint in soft flesh. 'You do something to me,' she sings in a buzzing whisper, 'that electrifies me.' So they go outside into the warm night where it turns out that she isn't that struck on Bevan Waters after all, that she'd fancied Ross all along. On the back seat of the Holden she proves moreover to be astonishingly inventive, so that together they execute with ease a whole series of manoeuvres which Ross had previously discounted as possibly risky, definitely foreign and perilously close to deviance. Ross thinks as a result that it might be worth dropping Margie Pringle who was getting on his nerves anyway with her lisping sweetness and that he'd be better off with Ethne who was bossy god knows but had a few clues.

Meanwhile, within the hall, Warren Baty is confessing that it was his ram that had got in among the Coopers' Corriedale-Romney flock last winter and Jim Cooper, a whole season lost, is saying, never mind, no lasting harm done. And Alasdair McLeod is telling the Paterson brothers that it was him who nicked their chain-saw; he'd come over one afternoon when they were out and borrowed it and he'd meant to give it back but they'd made such a fuss calling the police and all that he hadn't felt he could face it and he'd be around next day just to get the bloody thing off his conscience. Miria Love is telling Joan Shaw that she doesn't like the way she conducts Women's Division meetings and Pie Fowler is telling anyone who'll listen that she can't stick the valley, they're a bunch of snobs who've never let her forget for one minute that she's a townie and she'll be off back to the city just as soon as she can settle things with Bill.

Around the walls hang the valley teams since 1919, lined up for the photographer, thighs spread, fists clenched, unamused by the extraordinary goings-on in the darkened hall: under the influence of the night, sausage roll in one hand, beer in the other, the young farmers appear to have been overwhelmed by truth. The room is buzzing with honesty and for some the accompaniment is love and forgiveness, for others bitter recrimination. There seems to have been a sudden rise in the temperature. 'Remember the morning after,' the valley teams counsel, stonily. 'In the morning will come the accounting.'

A Power Board gang went up to check the lines next day. They found nothing out of place and the power had come back on, of its own accord, at dawn. There was a pair of footprints burned deep in a rock by the pylon; about a size five, they reckoned. That was all.

So, that's the story of how Skinny Louie, daughter of Lilleas Symonds popularly known as Shanghai Lill, gave birth, and walked up the valley and vanished in splendour.

Her baby was taken in care by Marty and Peg Conlan. She'll be grown by now, ready to come into her territory. Any day we could hear of her, storming in from the desert, swooping down from the eye of the sun, casting truth about her like a bright shadow.

And won't we scatter.

Notes on Contributors

BARBARA ANDERSON (b. 1926) lives in Wellington and began her writing career in her late fifties. Her books include a collection of short stories *I Think We Should Go Into the Jungle* (1989) and a novel *Girls High* (1990) composed of linked short stories.

JAMES COURAGE (1905–63) grew up on his father's Canterbury sheep station, but lived in England from the age of twenty, except for a short period back in New Zealand. He published eight novels (the best known is *The Young Have Secrets*, 1954) and a volume of his stories *Such Separate Creatures* was published in 1973.

JOY COWLEY (b. 1936) has published five novels including *The Growing Season* (1974) and a collection of short stories *Heart Attack and Other Stories* (1985). She is also well-known for her writing for children.

JOHN CRANNA (b. 1954) grew up in the Waikato and now lives in Auckland. His first book of stories *Visitors* (1989) won the first book section of the Commonwealth Writers' Prize and he has just completed his first novel, *Arena*.

DAN DAVIN (1913–90) grew up in an Irish-Catholic family in Invercargill. He went to Oxford as a Rhodes scholar and after war service, joined the Clarendon Press there. He published poems, novels, criticism and memoirs, and his *Selected Stories* appeared in 1981.

YVONNE DU FRESNE (b. 1929) grew up in a Danish–French Huguenot community in the Manawatu, and now lives in Wellington. She has published two novels and three books of short stories: *Farvel and Other Stories* (1980), *The Growing of Astrid Westergaard and Other Stories* (1985) and *The Bear from the North: Tales of a New Zealand Childhood* (1987).

MAURICE DUGGAN (1922–74) was born in Auckland into an Irish-Catholic family. He wrote and published stories only, and his *Collected Stories* appeared in 1981.

RODERICK FINLAYSON (b. 1904) lives near Auckland. He spent his childhood summers in the Bay of Plenty, among the people he was to write of. His stories of Maori life are collected in *Brown Man's Burden and Later Stories* (1973) which also includes details of his other published work.

JANET FRAME (b. 1924) has published poetry but is well-known worldwide for her fiction, both stories and novels, the most recently released being *The Carpathians* (1988), her eleventh novel. A selection of stories *You Are Now Entering the Human Heart* appeared in 1983. She has also published volumes of autobiography.

A. P. GASKELL (b. 1913) lives in Hamilton. A volume of his collected stories *All Part of the Game* was published in 1978.

MAURICE GEE (b. 1931) lives in Wellington and is the author of nine novels (including the prize-winning *Plumb*) as well as several books for children. His *Collected Stories* (1986) reprints and expands his 1975 volume *A Glorious Morning, Comrade*.

MICHAEL GIFKINS (b. 1945) lives in Auckland. He has published three volumes of short stories: *After the Revolution and Other Stories* (1982), *Summer Is the Cote d'Azur* (1987) and *The Amphibians* (1989).

PATRICIA GRACE (b. 1937) lives near Wellington. She is of Ngati Raukawa, Ngati Toa and Te Ati Awa descent and is affiliated to Ngati Porou by marriage. She has published two novels, and three collections of stories: *Waiariki* (1975), *The Dream Sleepers* (1980) and *Electric City* (1987). Her *Selected Stories* appeared in 1991.

RUSSELL HALEY (b. 1934) grew up in Leeds and emigrated to New Zealand (via Australia) in 1966. He now lives in Auckland. He has published two volumes of poetry, two novels, and three books of short stories: *The Sauna Bath Mysteries and Other Stories* (1978), *Real Illusions* (1984) and *The Transfer Station* (1989).

KERI HULME (b. 1947) has Kai Tahu, Orkney Island and English ancestry. She lives in Okarito on the West Coast. Her prize-winning novel *The Bone People* appeared in 1983, and she has also published a novella *Lost Possessions* (1985) and a collection of short stories *Te Kaihau: The Windeater* (1986).

WITI IHIMAERA (b. 1944) belongs to Te Whanau a Kai, sub-tribe of Rongowhakaata, and now lives in Auckland. His first volume of short stories *Pounamu, Pounamu* (1972) deals with rural Maori, his second *The New Net Goes Fishing* with Maori in an urban environment, while his third *Dear Miss Mansfield: A Tribute to Kathleen Mansfield Beauchamp* (1989) plays with some of Mansfield's characters and situations. He has also published four novels.

ANNE KENNEDY (b. 1950) now lives in Sydney. She has not yet published a collection of stories but her novella *100 Traditional Smiles* appeared in 1988.

JOHN A. LEE (1891–1982) is best known as a socialist politician. Something of his life can be learned from his novels which are closely based on his own experiences. The best known is *Children of the Poor* (1934). More adventures of the Shiner can be found in *Shining with the Shiner* (1944) and *Shiner Slattery* (1964).

KATHERINE MANSFIELD (1888–1923) was born and grew up in Wellington. At fourteen she was sent to school in London, and after an unhappy return to New Zealand two years later, she went back to Europe in 1908 and wrote the stories which have made her internationally famous, many of which draw on her memories of a New Zealand childhood.

OWEN MARSHALL (b. 1941) lives in Timaru. He has published four individual volumes of short stories: *Supper Waltz Wilson* (1979), *The Master of Big Jingles* (1982), *The Day Hemingway Died* (1984) and *The Lynx Hunter* (1987). *The Divided World: Selected Stories* appeared in 1989.

O. E. MIDDLETON (b. 1925) lives in Dunedin. He has published several volumes of stories: *Short Stories* (1953), *The Stone and Other Stories* (1959), *A Walk on the Beach* (1964), *The Loners* (1972) and *Confessions of an Ocelot and Not for a Seagull* (1979). A *Selected Stories* appeared in 1976.

VINCENT O'SULLIVAN (b. 1937) lives in Wellington. He has published four books of short stories: *The Boy, The Bridge, The River* (1978), *Dandy Edison for Lunch and Other Stories* (1981), *Survivals* (1985) and *The Snow in Spain* (1990), as well as ten books of poetry and *Miracle: A Romance* (1976). He is also a playwright, critic and editor.

FIONA FARRELL POOLE (b. 1947) lives in Palmerston North. She has published a book of poetry *Cutting Out* (1987) and a collection of stories *The Rock Garden* (1989). She has also written several plays.

FRANK SARGESON (1903–82) is held by some to be more important even than Mansfield in the history of the New Zealand short story – largely for the way in which he sought to recreate the rhythms and idioms of New Zealand speech. A collection entitled *The Stories of Frank Sargeson* appeared in 1973 and he also published several novels and a three-volume autobiography.

C. K. STEAD (b. 1932) is poet, novelist, short-story writer, critic and editor. He has published four novels, several books of literary criticism, and a book of short stories *Five for the Symbol* (1981). He lives in Auckland.

IAN WEDDE (b. 1946) lives in Wellington and is probably best known for his poetry. He has published three novels, including *Symmes Hole* (1986), and a book of stories *The Shirt Factory and Other Stories* appeared in 1981.

Glossary of Maori Words and Phrases

Proper names are not included.

ae   yes (also used as an exclamation)
ana   look here
aue   alas, exclamation of distress or astonishment
e   Oh
ehoa   (loosely) my friend
haka   a vigorous chorus of voice and action performed by rows of men to express defiance or welcome; war dance
hoha   nuisance
kapai   good, fine
kauri   a tree
kete   kit, basket made of strips of flax
kuia   old woman
manuka   shrub or tree, so-called tea-tree
matagouri   a shrub
matai   a tree
me he manurere aue   If I were a bird (first line of a song)
mokopuna   grandchild
Pakeha   New Zealander of European descent
paua   large, edible shellfish
pounamu   greenstone
rangatira   chief
rangiora   a shrub
rimu   a tree
taiaha   a long, hard wood weapon
tama   son, child, man (*E tama* – form of address)
tangi   a wake, a ceremonial of mourning and farewell before burial
tapu   sacred and forbidden
te moananui a Kiwa   the Pacific Ocean
teka   liar
tiko bum   shitty bum
tohunga   learned man, priest, expert
torori   home-grown tobacco
totara   a tree
whanau   family
whare   house, often of only one or two rooms

Acknowledgements

For permission to reproduce copyright passages grateful acknowledgement is made to the publishers and copyright holders of the following:

Barbara Anderson, *I Think We Should Go Into the Jungle* (VUP, 1989). James Courage, *Such Separate Creatures* (Caxton Press, 1973). Joy Cowley, *Heart Attack and Other Stories* (Hodder & Stoughton, 1985). John Cranna, *Visitors* (Heinemann Reed, 1989). Dan Davin, *Selected Stories* (Hale, London and VUP/Price Milburn, 1981). Yvonne du Fresne, *Farvel and Other Stories* (VUP/Price Milburn, 1980). Maurice Duggan, *Collected Stories* (AUP/OUP, 1981). Roderick Finlayson, *Brown Man's Burden and Later Stories* (AUP/OUP, 1973). Janet Frame, *You Are Now Entering the Human Heart* (VUP, 1983); permission granted by Curtis Brown (Aust.) Pty Ltd Sydney. A. P. Gaskell, *All Part of the Game* (AUP/OUP, 1978). Maurice Gee, *A Glorious Morning, Comrade* (AUP/OUP, 1975). Michael Gifkins, *After the Revolution and Other Stories* (Longman Paul, 1982). Patricia Grace, *The Dream Sleepers* (Longman Paul, 1980). Russell Haley, *The Sauna Bath Mysteries and Other Stories* (The Mandrake Root, 1978). Keri Hulme, *Te Kaihau: The Windeater* (VUP, 1986). Witi Ihimaera, *Pounamu, Pounamu* (Heinemann, 1972). Anne Kennedy, *Landfall 172* (December 1989). John A. Lee, *Shining with the Shiner* (May Fair Books, 1963). Owen Marshall, *Landfall 142* (June 1982). O. E. Middleton, *Selected Stories* (John McIndoe, 1976). Vincent O'Sullivan, *The Boy, The Bridge, The River* (John McIndoe and A. H. & A. W. Reed, 1978). Fiona Farrell Poole, *NZ Listener* (28 May 1990). Frank Sargeson, *The Stories of Frank Sargeson* (Penguin, 1982). C. K. Stead, *Five for the Symbol* (Longman Paul, 1981). Ian Wedde, *The Shirt Factory and Other Stories* (VUP/Price Milburn, 1981).